Globalization: Debunking the Myths

Second Edition

Lui Hebron

California Maritime Academy
California State University

John F. Stack, Jr.

Florida International University

Longman

Boston Columbus Indianapolis New York San Francisco Upper Saddle River
Amsterdam Cape Town Dubai London Madrid Milan Munich Paris Montreal Toronto
Delhi Mexico City São Paulo Sydney Hong Kong Seoul Singapore Taipei Tokyo

Acquisitions Editor: Vikram Mukhija
Editorial Assistant: Toni Magyar
Marketing Manager: Lindsey Phrudhomme
Production Manager: Wanda Rockwell
Project Management: Integra
Creative Director: Jayne Conte
Cover Designer: Bruce Kenselaar/Mary Steiner
Cover Illustration/Photo: Corbis
Printer and Binder: Courier Companies, Inc.

Library of Congress Cataloging-in-Publication Data

Hebron, Lui.
  Globalization : debunking the myths / Lui Hebron, John F. Stack.—2nd ed.
    p. cm.
  Includes bibliographical references and index.
  ISBN-13: 978-0-205-77970-3 (alk. paper)
  ISBN-10: 0-205-77970-0 (alk. paper)
1. Globalization.   I. Stack, John F.   II. Title.
JZ1318.H427 2011
303.48'2—dc22

2010001415

1 2 3 4 5 6 7 8 9 10—CRS—13 12 11 10

Longman
is an imprint of

PEARSON

www.pearsonhighered.com

ISBN-13: 978-0-205-77970-3
ISBN-10:   0-205-77970-0

BRIEF CONTENTS

CONTENTS

CHAPTER 3
Market Integration   32

CHAPTER 4
Growth and Development   47

CHAPTER 5
Democratization   65

CHAPTER 6
Sovereignty   82

CHAPTER 7
Culture   99

PREFACE

Nine months from the publication of *Globalization*, the bottom fell out of the global economy. Countries across the globe scrambled to rescue financial institutions, bail out equity firms, provide stimulus packages, and above all stabilize integrated financial markets that teetered on the brink of collapse. The ramifications of the crash continue to reverberate across the globe. Mortgage foreclosures, massive layoffs, and bankruptcies and the closure of factories affected workers and governments from Wall Street to Dubai to Nairobi to Hong Kong. National governments and intergovernmental organizations frantically searched for ways to slow the downward slide of hemorrhaging integrated markets around the world. Political elites from the emerging market countries in Southeast Asia, Latin America, and Eastern Europe to the industrialized states in Western Europe, North America, and East Asia found themselves in the midst of an unprecedented, and for most, unpredictable economic free-fall. Indeed, the 2008–2009 global financial crisis has become second only to the Great Depression of 1929 as the single most destructive economic state of affairs in world history. Both the turmoil and the suffering have been global in scale.

The unpredicted and unexpected magnitude of the 2008 crash underscored for us the fundamental importance of globalization as a part of world politics—a perspective that our students need now more than ever. If an understanding of the nature of globalization was important before the economic meltdown of the past year, it is utterly crucial in 2010. Thus, with the guidance of our extraordinary editor Vik Mukhija at Pearson Longman, we decided to bring out a second edition as a way to better contextualize the unsettling events of the past year. In particular, we understand that globalization, now more than at any previous time, is subject to searching analyses and unrelenting critiques. Indeed, globalization is often viewed as an unrelenting force that relentlessly places material interests and values above sustainable human needs. Globalization is seen as a process threatening long-term political stability and democratic governance. Globalization, many warn, directly threatens the world's most distinctive cultural inheritances while rapaciously advancing seductive Western, and, in particular, American forms of mass-marketed culture. A more integrated world constitutes to many a fundamental threat to individuality, diversity, and distinct cultural inheritances. From this lens, the world of the twenty-first century will likely confront even more far-reaching changes than those of the nineteenth and twentieth centuries. Political disempowerment and uneven economic development, therefore, are hugely looming negative consequences of globalization.

Our goal throughout the two editions has been to use an approach generally supportive of globalization as a way to take another look at a phenomenon now defining so much scholarship, interest, and debate and so emblematic of the challenges facing the twenty-first century. The study of globalization is controversial for many of our colleagues and disfavored by some, but we believe that it is important for us to provide our students with a framework that considers globalization in light of politics, culture, economics, and the environment—a perspective that emphasized both its multidimensionality and its salience. One may find globalization threatening and distasteful, but it remains a fundamental part of integrated global economy in both positive and negative ways, and for some, globalization holds out the promise for a better, if not brighter, future for most of the inhabitants of the planet, although not all.

NEW TO THIS EDITION

To reflect the ongoing dynamics and new developments within the globalization debate, as well as to make this text even more user-friendly, we made the following revisions for the second edition:

- A brief history of globalization has been added to Chapter 1 in order to place the phenomenon in historical context. Many of our students approach globalization as an entirely new phenomenon. We illustrate how globalization in the form of technological innovations, the movement of peoples, and the spread of diseases throughout history has had major impacts on the development of politics, economics, and culture across the planet.
- Non-Western views of globalization—from the quotations at the start of each chapter to the conclusions at the end—are now integrated throughout.
- The statistical data have also been updated to provide the most accurate framework of the developments (affects/effects) of the globalization process.
- For each chapter, there is now included a boxed section entitled "Debating Globalization," in which we take a point–counterpoint position on a particular topic of globalization. Our goal is to demonstrate the reach of the globalization debate and to demonstrate to students how key aspects of the process can be discussed with civility despite basic disagreements on key concepts and applications to the real world. We have written the debates with an eye to both accessibility and analysis. We encourage our colleagues to employ the debate format as a teaching tool when using the text in class.
- At the end of each chapter, lists of key terms, discussion questions, and suggested readings are added to help with classroom participation and analysis.
- At the end of the book, we added a glossary to highlight and define key concepts that students need to learn in the study of globalization.

Our hope is that the second edition of *Globalization* will assist our colleagues and our students in a better understanding of one of the most dynamic forces of our time.

FEATURES

For this edition of *Globalization*, we retained several features of the first edition:

- *Approach*: This book continues to examine the ongoing debates framing contemporary assessments of globalization. But this is more than just a study of what scholars and commentators think about globalization. Central to the study is the belief that there is no single way to understand globalization in the twenty-first century. Because globalization is so contested, we examine a variety of perspectives along a sliding scale—a continuum of failures, accomplishments, expectations, beliefs, and aspirations. Our focus is on a number of political, economic, environmental, and cultural approaches to and consequences of globalization. Our analysis highlights the different ways that globalization is approached as a means of untangling various strands in the debate. We strive to avoid the oversimplification.

- *Organization*: Like the first edition, each theme chapter is organized around four main themes: (1) an **Introduction** of the main theoretical orientation of the issue area being examined; (2) a **Reality Check** providing empirical and/or anecdotal support and/or refutation of the theoretical concepts; (3) a **Debunking the Myths** that provides analysis; and (4) a **Conclusion** that presents future direction.

- *Pedagogy*: In our examination of the globalization phenomena, we strive to offer multilayered approaches that provide color, shape, impact, and depth to the study of one of the central phenomena of our time. Often students tend to think about globalization as an entirely new process. We emphasize throughout that globalization needs to be considered in the context of history driven by the diffusion of science, knowledge, and technological applications and innovations over time. The exchange of goods; the development of trade routes; migration of peoples; and the spread of information, ideas, and values are all part and parcel of the historical development of globalization. The Internet, instantaneous 24-hour news broadcasts, interconnected financial markets, the spread of communications and transportation systems, the unprecedented integration of economic activities, and the rise of increasingly important nonstate, transnational actors underscore that globalization is a process that reaches back to millennia.

- *Coverage*: This book addresses a number of consequences likely to ensue when the promise and perils, as well as the rhetoric and realities, of globalization collide. Specifically, this study examines six projections—three by globalists and three by antiglobalists—of the perceived benefits and dangers resulting from the globalization process. It also analyzes the arguments both for and against globalization by examining the effect of globalization in four central areas of the debate: economic (in terms of both greater integration and the worldwide increase in wealth and income); political (the loss of sovereignty and the collapse of states); sociocultural (the erosion of local cultural identities); and environmental (the ecological destruction of the planet).

Globalization begins with Chapter 1, "Globalization in the Twenty-First Century," which isolates and highlights the contending positions of the globalist and antiglobalist camps. Included in this examination of globalization's advocates and detractors are their respective conceptualization and assessment (attraction/abhorrence) of the phenomenon's effect in the economic, political, cultural, and environmental realms. Since globalization's meaning, development, and impact puzzle many, Chapter 2 then endeavors to provide a more organic working definition of the term, taking into account some of the process's political and cultural aspects, as well as a number of economic components.

Chapter 3 takes to task globalists' expectation that the liberalization and integration of markets is inevitable or unstoppable via the explosive increases in trade and investments. The effect of globalization on the distribution of incomes, both intra- and internationally in the developing countries, is the focus of Chapter 4. Specifically, we probe the globalists' contention that the process benefits everyone by bringing about greater wealth and well-being on a global scale.

Chapter 5 examines whether greater understanding, tolerance, and harmony will evolve as greater levels of globalization emerge. The contention that globalization has resulted in the loss of sovereignty is analyzed in Chapter 6. Here we address such issues as the increasing role, influence, and power of the globalizing economy as it affects the sovereignty of states and its impact on people's lives.

Chapter 7 critically examines the notion that globalization will result in the destruction of national cultures—specifically, that globalization results in the cultural (Americanization) homogenization of the globe.

The effect of globalization on the earth's environment is addressed in Chapter 8. Specifically, has globalization brought about a race to the bottom in terms of global environmental standards?

Finally, Chapter 9 puts into perspective our findings that indicate that both the perceived benefits and the dangers of globalization have been greatly exaggerated. The effects of globalization will continue to be felt worldwide, with both benefits and costs.

SUPPLEMENTS

Pearson Longman is pleased to offer several resources to qualified adopters of *Globalization* and their students that will make teaching and learning from this book even more effective and enjoyable.

For Instructors

MYPOLISCIKIT VIDEO CASE STUDIES   Featuring video from major news sources and providing reporting and insight on recent world affairs, this DVD series helps instructors integrate current events into their courses by letting them use the clips as lecture launchers or discussion starters.

For Students

LONGMAN ATLAS OF WORLD ISSUES (0-321-22456-5)   Introduced and selected by Robert J. Art of Brandeis University and excerpted from the acclaimed Penguin Atlas Series, the *Longman Atlas of World Issues* is designed to help students understand the geography and major issues facing the world today, such as terrorism, debt, and HIV/AIDS. These thematic, full-color maps examine forces shaping politics today at a global level. Explanatory information accompanies each map to help students better grasp the concepts being shown and how they affect our world today. Available at no additional charge when packaged with this book.

RESEARCH AND WRITING IN INTERNATIONAL RELATIONS (0-321-27766-X)   Written by Laura Roselle and Sharon Spray of Elon University, this brief and affordable guide provides the basic step-by-step process and essential resources that are needed to write political science papers that go beyond simple description and into more systematic and sophisticated inquiry. This text focuses on the key areas in which students need the most help: finding a topic, developing a question, reviewing literature, designing research, analyzing findings, and last, actually writing the paper. Available at a discount when packaged with this book.

ACKNOWLEDGMENTS

Our study benefited substantially from the generous assistance of many individuals and institutions. Our thanks to Mark B. Salter, Matt Davies, Astrid Ellie, and David Blaney for thoughtful comments and suggestions on earlier drafts and conference papers. We also owe a large debt of gratitude to the following reviewers for incisive comments, criticisms, and recommendations to improve the book: Michael Burayidi, University of Wisconsin-Osh Kosh; Peter Doesrshler, Bloomsburg University; Yogesh Grover, Winona State University; Alistair Howard, Temple University; and Pamela Martin, Coastal Carolina University. Its shortcomings, however, are ours alone.

We acknowledge with gratitude the work, support, and patience of Vikram Mukhija, Acquisitions Editor, Toni Magyar, Editorial Assistant, and Wanda Rockwell, Project Manager, both of Pearson Longman as well as Shiji Sashi, Project Manager of Integra Software Services Pvt. Ltd.

Lui Hebron is also grateful to President William Eisenhardt, Interim Provost Herman Lujan, Dean Paul Jackson and Director Donna Nincic of the California Maritime Academy as well as to the late Jeffers Chertok, former Dean of the College of Social and Behavioral Sciences (CSBS) at Eastern Washington University, and John F. Stack, Jr., Director of the Jack D. Gordon Institute for Public Policy and Citizenship Studies at Florida International University, for their support and encouragement of this project. The generous financial support provided by Cal Maritime, CSBS, and the Gordon Institute allowed me the opportunity to refine the ideas presented in this book at various conferences in North America, Europe, and Asia. I would also like to thank my colleagues Graham Benton, Julianne Chisholm, and Christopher Frick for their excellent suggestions and comments, my student assistants Jamie Whitman and Nicholas R. Marr for their work in collecting some of the empirical materials used in the text, and the students in my Globalization class for their helpful feedback on making the book more accessible. I am grateful to Charlyce Jones-Owen for her unwavering belief in the project. Finally, I wish to acknowledge my children, Christian, Danielle, and Skyler, for their patience and understanding of my academic pursuits, which frequently infringed on family time, and my wife, Maristel, for her support and encouragement, and for consistently demonstrating extraordinary patience and grace despite the pressures this project entailed. Lastly, I thank my parents Norberto H. Hebron (who impressed upon me the desire to make a difference) and Fe Pambid Hebron (who instilled in me the dedication, discipline, and determination to achieve my goals). It is with great personal satisfaction that I dedicate this book to them.

John Stack acknowledges the ongoing support of Florida International University and a number of colleagues and friends. Mark B. Rosenberg, who assumed the Presidency of Florida International University in summer 2009, has been a friend and colleague for more than three decades. His passion for the study of Latin America from the vantage point of international relations and comparative politics has helped to define better my understanding of the dynamics of globalization. Professors Thomas Breslin and Ralph Clem supported the development of this work wholeheartedly when I served as Director of the Jack D. Gordon Institution for Public Policy and Citizenship Studies. I am also grateful Dean Kenneth Furton for his support and ecouragement. Thanks, as well, to a number of colleagues at FIU or their support of efforts to teach and write as Director of the new School of International and Public Affairs: Nicol Rae, Robert Callahan, Pedro Botta, Sebastian Arcos, Steve Heine, Ed Glab, Myriam Rios, and Karla Maria. Finally, I am grateful to Tommie and Mal Kushner, Jeanne Kates, Patrick James, Steven Lamy, Sheila Croacher, James Piscatori, Richard B. Finnegan, Anthony Maingot, John Stuart, Eduardo Gamarra, Thomas Baker, Scott Norberg, Jose Gabalindo, and Marg Volcansek for their continuing support.

I dedicate this book to the loving memory of my Mother, Margaret J. Stack, for her enduring contributions to my life and to my sisters Pamela M. Stack and Nancy Savoie for their loving support.

Lui Hebron
John F. Stack, Jr.

Globalization in the Twenty-First Century

> . . . globalization has become a major issue that no longer interests only pundits and academics. It's entered the mainstream of popular concern.
>
> *—Jeffrey Garten, former Dean of the School of Management, Yale University*[1]

> We live in a world of transformations, affecting almost every aspect of what we do. For better or worse, we are being propelled into a global order that no one fully understands, but which is making its effects felt upon all of us.
>
> *—Anthony Giddens, former Director of the London School of Economics*[2]

> The difference in views are so great that one wonders, are the protestors and the policy makers talking about the same phenomena? Are they looking at the same data?
>
> *—Joseph Stiglitz, Nobel Prize Winner in Economics and former International Monetary Fund Chief Economist*[3]

GLOBALISTS AND ANTIGLOBALISTS

This book is a study about the unfolding processes known as **globalization**. We examine a number of critical dimensions of the ongoing debates framing assessments of globalization. Our goal is to provide both assessments and critiques capturing the divergent views of proponents and opponents, as well as the conceptual frameworks, expectations, and methodologies accompanying the debates. This is far more than just a study of what scholars think about globalization. Central to the text is the belief that there is no single way to understand globalization in the twenty-first century. Because globalization is so contested, we examine a variety of perspectives along a sliding scale, a continuum of failures, accomplishments, expectations, beliefs, and aspirations touching on fundamental political, economic, sociological, and cultural values. As such, our analysis highlights differences as a way to more clearly understand the dynamics of globalization.

In attempting to untangle various strands in the debate, we strive to avoid the oversimplification often characterizing perspectives supporting or opposing globalization. We approach globalization as a multilayered process. It involves more than one or two dimensions of "say" economics or culture. It is also an historical process driven by the diffusion of science, knowledge, and technological applications and innovations over time. The exchange of goods, the development of trade routes, migration of peoples, and the spread of information are all part and parcel of the historical process of globalization. The Internet, instantaneous 24-hour news stations, interconnected financial markets, the spread of communications and transportation systems, unprecedented **integration** of economic activities, and the rise of increasingly important nonstate, **transnational** actors are all examples of the process of globalization.

Authors Robert Keohane and Joseph Nye observe that globalization is not a unilinear process, suggesting, rather, that just as globalization moves forward linking many processes together, it can also stop and result in **deglobalization**—a process defined by a decrease in levels of globalization.[4] It remains to be seen whether the global economic meltdown of Autumn 2008 and Winter 2009 illustrates processes of globalization or deglobalization. It does suggest that globalization results in heightened levels of integration that can affect countries, international financial institutions, and billions of people across the globe in fundamental ways.

Globalization, therefore, is a process that has ancient roots. Globalization may appear new and threatening because of the uncertainty that accompanies many changes throughout the global system. But globalization is the further development of the processes initiated over many centuries, reflected in the trade expansion, exploration, conquest, migration, colonization, evangelization, and so on that have taken place throughout world history. The silk trade is an example of an early form of globalization because its impact was felt across continents and had a powerful economic effect stimulating trade and building strong trade-dependent city-states such as Venice and Naples. The Silk Road was also a venue for technological innovation. Marco Polo himself encountered asbestos and gunpowder in China. He also described innovations in trade, noting that paper currency was used for the purchase of goods. The expansion of trade routes and the movement of peoples from Mongolia illustrate the transforming by-products of globalization in European history—the introduction of bubonic plague, for example. Pandemics have accompanied the movement of people throughout history. The effects of the plague were far reaching, transforming the economic, cultural, and sociological structures of Medieval Europe. The Age of Discovery in the fifteenth century was followed by the establishment of European empires across the world. One of the by-products of globalization was the creation of pandemics, resulting in the deaths of millions of indigenous peoples in the Americas, Africa, and Asia. The death of millions reinforced and solidified European colonial rule throughout the world. Global pandemics throughout history are a fundamental manifestation of globalization in history. During the worldwide outbreak of the so-called "Spanish" flu, it was brought to the United States by soldiers returning from World War I, resulting in the deaths of tens of millions of people around the world. Evangelization too has been a crucial dimension of globalization, as seen in the expansion of the Ottoman Empire into Europe in Spain and Central Europe during the twelfth and thirteenth centuries. The current spread of Islam in Africa and Asia is but the latest version of globalization assisted by twenty-first-century transportation, travel, and media networks.

As global ties "thicken" and become more "dense" over time, globalization becomes an even more formidable global force. In this sense, globalization refers to "the shrinkage of distance on a large scale"[5] but also encompasses the weight and influence of the contacts among societies. The "heavier" the contacts—in other words, the more the capacity to transform transcontinental interactions—the more we speak of globalization. As such, globalization is based on the weight and ultimately power of the levels of **interdependence** and transnational connections across the globe.[6]

The middle decades of the nineteenth century looked upon a world that was experiencing rapid **globalism** in the form of speed: the development of steamship travel and the laying of the transatlantic telegraph cable. Over time, there was a dramatic decrease in cost and an increase in speed of the movement of goods and travel as well as communications, making for more interconnections in communications, financial markets, and economic systems among others across the globe. As the Asian financial crisis of the late 1990s intensified, its unexpected and devastating impacts were felt around the world.[7] Keohane and Nye point to three dimensions of globalization that help us to envision a multidimensional process: the density of networks, institutional velocity, and the level of transnational participation. The concept of density of networks is illustrated by the development of the Internet. As more people use a service or product, its value increases. Increased usage, that is, density, may spill over into other areas. "There are more interconnections. Intensive economic interdependence effects social and environmental interdependence; awareness of these connections in turn effects economic relationships."[8] The impact of globalized transportation, communications, and technology networks has been both exhilarating and unnerving.

Institutional velocity is a second important dimension of globalization: "it has made possible the transnational organization of work and the expansion of markets, thereby facilitating a new transnational division of labor."[9] Technological innovations such as the development of steamships and the transatlantic telegraph were major innovations, but they affected a relatively small elite stratum of the population.[10] In the twenty-first century, computer access and the Internet have transformed the effects of transnational networks, allowing global markets and financial systems to respond to events immediately. These networks have become more interdependent. "National" economies have undergone increasing transnational integration due to the dramatic and continuing increases in the cross-border flows of trade in both goods and services, investment and financial capital, technology and information, and people.

Transnational participation is a third dimension of globalization. It means that global issues are increasingly shaped by nonstate actors; states no longer determine interactions between people and organizations across state lines. This results in much greater levels of participation by individuals; business enterprises (multinational corporations [MNCs]); and private special interest organizations such as scientific, technological, and advocacy organizations with concerns ranging from those about the environment to human rights. The growth of nongovernmental organizations is also marked by the rise of myriad intergovernmental and supranational organizations during the twentieth century.

Viewed from the time of the collapse of the Soviet empire in 1989, it appeared as though **world politics** was in the midst of a "sea change," a transformation so fundamental as to render the force of globalization unstoppable. For both its detractors and its advocates, globalization constitutes one of the potentially great forces of human transformation in the new century and beyond because it appears to be restructuring (in a most consequential manner) the ways in which we work, play, communicate, consume, produce, and exchange—in short, how we live. The process can at once bolster the potential for universal human development or bring about conditions that would result in the unprecedented impoverishment of humankind on a global scale.

It is important at the outset to underscore three perspectives that orient our analysis. First, we believe the globalization process is not a new phenomenon. It is a process routed in the outward expansion of human societies. What makes globalization appear "different" is its unpredictability, as a number of networks are connected in unexpected ways. As Keohane and Nye suggest, the unpredictability of globalization makes it a process that raises fears and concerns.[11]

Second, globalization is not a unilinear, unstoppable process. There are many historical examples where globalization has stopped or retrenched, most obviously, in the period between World War I and World War II. The economic instability of the 1920s gave rise to the Great Depression in 1929, accompanied by the political instability in Europe, the Soviet Union, and Asia, which ultimately resulted in global warfare. The bipolar conflict between the United States and the Soviet Union massively slowed globalization in Central and East Europe and in Asia.

Finally, globalization, as Keohane and Nye perceptively point out, "does not imply universality."[12] As a multidimensional process, globalization may stitch new economic networks together in unexpected ways, while energizing cultural, ethnic, and religious conflicts. The very success of Al-Jazeera illustrates how globalization serves as a catalyst for religious and regional separatism.

DEBATING GLOBALIZATION

In its most dichotomous form, proponents and critics of globalization conceptualize it as either a blessing that must be expanded to benefit all of humankind or a curse that must be exorcized from the globe. For the former, globalization is a positive development for people around the world for it holds out the promise of increased economic well-being by opening up the world's markets, enhanced cultural understanding via free-flowing information, and far greater levels of political empowerment and personal freedom. Globalization will, thus, initiate new and comprehensive changes geared toward improving people's lives.

Those contesting globalization envision it as a perverse process accelerating the erosion of cultural identities; the ecological and environmental destruction of the planet; the subjugation of women and minorities at the hand of ruthless economic systems; a growing gap between North and South; and the consolidation of power in the hands of big, unaccountable transnational corporations and financial elites. Such a vision spells a declining quality of life for humanity in general, and the vast majority of the world's people living in the Southern Hemisphere in particular.

Globalization's principal battlefield is the poor, underdeveloped countries.[13] Particularly for those states struggling to overcome poverty and subsistence-living conditions, globalization holds out the prospect of a world order aligning itself ever more closely with remote and unaccountable power centers programmed toward the relentless homogenization of cultures based on capitalist greed. Progressive levels of globalization deprive developing countries of achieving authentic political, cultural, and economic institutions. This feeling of despair was best captured by Anthony Giddens when he observed, "A pessimistic view of globalization would consider it largely an affair of the industrial North, in which the developing societies of the South play little or no active part. It would see it as destroying local cultures, widening world inequalities and worsening the lot of the impoverished."[14]

In contrast, proponents[15] foresee the political, economic, social, and cultural transformations resulting in greater affluence, self-fulfillment, and creativity for individuals and their societies throughout the world. Globalization represents the possibility of realizing democratic values and individual achievements, heretofore simply unattainable for the world's poor. Wars, economic stagnation, and political instability will become the scourges of the nonglobalizing world. From this perspective, globalization offers the promise of solutions to age-old problems rooted in parochial institutions that limit human growth and potential. Said Theo-Ben Gurirab, the former Foreign Minister of Namibia and the 1999–2000 UN General Assembly President,

"Globalization is seen by some as a force for social change, that it will help to close the gap between the rich and the poor, the industrialized north and the developing south."[16]

What is most significant about this debate is not the contending perspectives and/or expectations but rather the total lack of dialogue between the two viewpoints. Our view as stated earlier in the chapter and throughout the book is that globalization is much more complex and nuanced. In a word, it is multidimensional. Focusing on the extremes of the globalization debate only reinforces simplistic assumptions that are impossible to reconcile on their own terms. Instead of assessments of the key economic, political, transnational, social, and cultural dimensions of globalization, the debate has become so contentious and the positions so rigid that both sides usually talk past each other—without listening to the counterarguments.

Champions of the process condemn globalization's antagonists as parochial nationalists who are unable to grasp the principles of economic liberalism and the complexities of integrated markets. Perhaps the most well-known advocate of globalization is *New York Times* columnist Thomas L. Friedman, who unabashedly and unapologetically contends that globalization is helping to bring about a more prosperous and a safer world. Globalization's detractors, on the other hand, fault globalists' narrow, technocratic perspective and lack of a basic understanding of how the real world works among the least powerful countries and societies. Two of the most visible crusaders against globalization are the Canadian political journalist and anticorporate activist Naomi Klein[17] and the French cheese farmer and McDonald's basher Jose Bove.[18] For both Klein and Bove, globalization is the personification of economic evil and as such will settle for nothing less than its eventual destruction. As a consequence of this polemic, there has been too much opponent bashing— and too little understanding—from either side. The overarching objective of this book is to make a more thoughtful and even-handed assessment of globalization's supposed virtues and vices, as well as its benefits and costs. In so doing, we hope to help demystify some of the rhetoric attached to the debate.

WHITHER GLOBALIZATION?

How to define and evaluate the impacts of globalization has itself become a topic of heated debate among policymakers, scholars, intellectuals, and citizens because the era of the fax machine, airplane, and the Internet appears to bring unanticipated changes of a fundamental nature.[19] In this study, globalization is conceptualized in a broad manner: as the development of a unified global economic culture and a new stage in world politics that merges and melds smaller units into larger embracing global processes. At the same time, globalization can also be viewed as a battle about how far countries are willing to accept constraints on domestic policy in sensitive areas such as economic, financial, political, social, and cultural sovereignty for the sake of economic growth and development.

GLOBALIZATION AS A NEW WORLD SHANGRI-LA

Champions of globalization argue that it provides the potential to raise living standards via global production and consumerism; to bolster fundamental freedoms via the spread of democratic norms and institutions; and to decrease social strife via the development of global cosmopolitan communities based on the acceptance of common, unifying cultural norms and values.[20]

The boosters of globally integrated markets envision a network leading to far more efficient international divisions of production among societies because capital and labor can be easily shifted to whichever country offers the most favorable opportunities. This allows low-wage countries to specialize in labor-intensive tasks, while high-wage countries can concentrate on capital- and technological-intensive enterprises. This becomes the promise of global capitalism—the creation of economies of scale responsive to producers and consumers, where both production and pricing are most effectively regulated by the market. It makes no sense for the United States to produce sugarcane when it leads the world in the development of computer technology. Similarly, countries producing primary agricultural products such as coffee, cocoa, and bananas can effectively hone production and labor costs to maximize advantages in the global marketplace.

Even before the global economic boom in the late 1990s, the globalizing process has worked remarkably well. In a span of just ten years, Asia's abject poverty has not only declined precipitously but has been replaced with phenomenal income growth and economic development. As more countries have become integrated into the global economy, the quality of life has improved for developing and developed states alike. "The reason is that, as poor countries prosper, they buy more of rich countries' advanced exports (from computers to commercial jets) that [in turn] support high-paying jobs,"[21] as well as increased investments in research and development, including human capital. The resulting technological gains benefit all sectors in the global system as the increased knowledge base provided by the Internet attest. The peoples of the world are given the means to prosper unlike any development in human history. In sum, globalization is a symbiotic experience for all participants because it has not only increased the prosperity of the advanced industrial states, but has given the emerging economies of many developing countries a role and a place in an internationalized economy that would otherwise not exist.

Globalization also entails the continued democratization of the world's political-economic institutions and systems. Empirical analyses show a correlation between democratic systems and peace and stability in an expanding global system.[22] A number of scholars dismiss the belief that the sovereignty of states is under attack by the globalization process.[23] Rather than usurping sovereignty, higher levels of globalization offer greater opportunities for involvement in the democratic process. Mass communications give people greater knowledge. Politicians are made more accountable. The isolation that characterizes the gulf separating the individual from her/his national government has evaporated. Global chauvinism and parochialism are similarly placed on the defensive as understanding about different states proliferates.

As with the proliferation of knowledge, greater understanding and higher levels of tolerance toward other cultures are now occurring. Since the fall of the Berlin Wall in 1989, the face of Europe has been transformed, as manifested by the greater levels of political, social, legal, and economic integration of societies. Perhaps the most obvious expression of this trend is the eastward expansions of the North Atlantic Treaty Organization (NATO) and the European Union (EU). Spurred on by the success of the EU and the North American Free Trade Agreement (NAFTA), more and more states in Africa, Asia, Eastern Europe, and South America are building regional economic institutions to stimulate greater cooperation in commerce, politics, and security affairs.

The result of rising levels of income, heightening currents of democratization, and an increase in cooperation among states, societies, and individuals is the emergence of an evolving "global village." Given these benefits and positive trends, defenders contend that continuing indifference and/or hostility to globalization can be blamed on a lack of understanding and appreciation of its eventual benefits because it is a long and arduous process. Robert K. Schaeffer perhaps captured these sentiments when he observed, "As proof that 'everyone' wants globalization, or would want it if they knew what it really was and were in a position to 'choose' it, proponents note that people now clamor for foreign investment, rush to purchase imported goods, line up for jobs in export-processing zones, embrace new technologies, and vote for greater democracy." He further notes that "[w]here people are denied an opportunity to choose, they migrate or flee to places where these goods and opportunities are available. . . ."[24]

Advocates of globalization argue that the real question is not whether increased world integration is worth pursuing, but rather how to accelerate the process. For globalists, a return to the parochialism, conflict, and upheaval of the twentieth century is no longer an option.

GLOBALIZATION AND A BRAVE NEW WORLD REPRISED

Critics of globalization envision a much darker process of global command and control of resources, reduced human achievement, and an increasing gulf between rich elites and exploited masses throughout the world.[25] The erosion of state sovereignty is a central concern as omnipotent international organizations increasingly dictate the rules and relationships of the new global economy, in which unelected intergovernmental organizations, such as the World Bank, the International Monetary Fund (IMF), and the World Trade Organization (WTO), and transnational/multinational corporations, reign supreme. They reduce democratic participation to a thinly disguised symbolic level whereby political publics are increasingly becoming marginalized, if not disenfranchised. Far from bringing greater equality, globalization will likely mean larger gulfs

DEBATING GLOBALIZATION

Lui Hebron: Globalization Is Good for the World

John, as I think about globalization even amid the global economic turbulence and slowdown of the past year, I want you to consider the following: Thanks primarily to globalization, the world has experienced significant reductions in both global poverty and international inequality. Since the late 1980s, the global economy has been raising living standards, not only in the rich world but among the poor too, and hence closing the gap between developed and developing worlds. From Southeast Asia to Latin America to even Sub-Saharan Africa and the Middle East, global inequality has been decreasing appreciably with large segments of the earth's population successfully escaping from their poverty-stricken existence as a result of their government's decision to open their economies to international trade and foreign capital. In contrast, countries that have not integrated into the world economy, through either lack of opportunity or by choice, have not fared as well.

Accompanying this more encompassing growth in economic development has been the notable expansion of political and civil freedoms. Studies have repeatedly shown that globalized states tend to enjoy greater levels of civil liberties and political rights than those countries that are not politically engaged with the global community. Furthermore, these same internationally engaged states are also often less corrupt. This correlation indicates a strong relationship between globalization and clean government, one in which increased integration facilitates the implementation of higher international standards for transparency and oversight that, in turn, acts as a deterrent against corruption and thereby increasing government accountability.

Without question, globalization is a phenomenon that has alleviated much human misery: Numerous studies have repeatedly found that most globalized nation-states are also those that have achieved the highest degree of economic equality; attained the most inclusive political system; enacted the strongest policies for environmental protection; provided the largest opportunities for cultural experiences; as well as are places where residents enjoy the longest, healthiest, and most fulfilling lives. Indeed, if one were to look at what globalization has achieved over the past 20 years alone and take into account the overwhelming grassroots support for the continuation of the process, the fact that its beneficial effects and legitimacy as a positive force for humankind continues to be so hotly debated is rather surprising, if not down-right illogical.—Lui

John Stack: Globalization Is an Unrealistic Hope

Lui, as you are well aware, I recognize globalization as a fact of life and one that must be dealt with. It is certainly correct that millions of members of the planet have benefitted from increasing levels of globalization. But the growing ranks of the affluent should also alert us to the other side of the story—the increasing economic, social, and political gulfs among societies, affecting millions of people across the globe living in close proximity to one another *and, thanks to globalization, who are* increasingly aware that they are receiving the short end of the globalization stick. The swelling ranks of the world's dispossessed underscore the realization that the global economic uplift–in good times–and the creation greater levels of misery in bad times, raise fundamental issues of political stability, economic growth and socioeconomic welfare across the entire spectrum of societies throughout the world.

I am far more cautious than you in accepting that the process of globalization contains the seeds of democratic governance now sprouting across the planet. While I recognize that the fall of the Soviet Union in 1989 is largely seen as a harbinger of globalization's and democracy's coming of age, I remain skeptical of the assumption that free trade is the necessary and sufficient catalyst in building democratic societies. The fall of the worn-out Soviet empire released new economic forces within Russia, the Russian Federation, and the independent states once comprising the Soviet Union, but their economic uplift and liberalization do not translate into democratic governance, as ethnic, linguistic, religious, and cultural conflicts in Central Europe, the Caucuses, and Asia suggest. The power of globalization elsewhere, for example, in Latin America, and in China by no means foreshadows the forward triumphs of democracy linked to the process of globalization, as the push to the left in Venezuela, Nicaragua, and Bolivia suggest.

Globalization is a powerful, perhaps transforming, force in world affairs, but its ability to both sustain increased economic growth and foster greater levels of democratic participation across the globe is unproven at best. It remains to be seen how a 20-year rollout of prosperity and equality will fare in the current global economic crisis that now confronts the globalized world.—John   ■

between rich and developing societies. Control of the media and communications networks will weaken distinctive national and subnational identities. The three days of riots and civil disturbances in Seattle, Washington, during the 1999 meeting of the WTO, and the subsequent worldwide antiglobal protests illustrate the public's concern about the unbridled influences of global institutions, such as the IMF and the Organization of the Petroleum Exporting Countries (OPEC), and other transnational corporations that challenge the sovereignty of states.

On the political front, critics claim that globalization has "infiltrated" the sanctity of state sovereignty. They observe that the pressure to conform to the globalizing processes' dictates has eroded the efficacy of governments to determine their own political, economic, and social policies. The state's vulnerabilities to the global economy's power include "economic interdependence without international political influence; open markets without political stability or legal-regulatory infrastructure; economic transitions without social safety nets";[26] and the jettisoning of human rights values in favor of shareholder prerogatives and privileges. Finally, critics note that in several instances globalization has helped to influence a country's political leadership: The 1997–1998 Asian financial crisis triggered the ouster of the 32-year rule of President Suharto in Indonesia; Russia's inability to integrate the Russian economy is viewed as a key factor behind Boris Yeltsin's withdrawal from the presidency; and Japan's 14-year effort to correct its economic ship of state via a succession of prime ministers.

The supposed unqualified economic benefits of globalization have also increasingly come under fire. While globalization has created enormous prosperity for some countries, it has also accelerated the widening of the economic gulf between people in a number of societies around the world. As more developing nations become integrated into the global economy, many analysts foresee a world flooded with chronic overproduction that initiates periods of boom and bust, similar to the instability characterizing late-nineteenth-century and early-twentieth-century monopolistic capitalism in the United States. The globalization process is just the latest mechanism designed to keep poor countries in a perpetual state of **underdevelopment**. For the enormous populations around the world not sharing in the bounty of globalization, the integration of the world economy conforms to long-established patterns of center–periphery development, but with a twist. Elite domination is presently a worldwide phenomenon. The European model of outward expansion/intrusion into the western hemisphere and into long-established colonies in Asia, Africa, and the Middle East is no longer needed. Multinational corporations and other transnational entities are unencumbered by the constraints of territorially based states in their expansion of capitalism beyond the European continent.

Worldwide interdependence, from this perspective, will trigger a "race to the bottom" as firms in economically developed states reduce wages down toward the same level as those of the poorest developing countries. Thus, labor is held in check, making inhuman treatment routine, and environmental controls are weakened or reversed in order to remain competitive. Global and globalized transnational elites search relentlessly for the means of management, the technological breakthroughs, and the resources to conduct business on a worldwide scale. Thomas L. Friedman captures the misgivings of many workers confronting globalization as companies move from state to state: " . . . in search of those who will work for the lowest wages and lowest standards. To some, the Nike swoosh is now as scary as the hammer and sickle."[27] Echoing these feelings, Tom Plate writes,

> This is not globalization's kinder, gentler wealth-producing, raising-all-boats image, of course, but the icy cold face of a relentless modernity that the environmentalists, union activists, human rights lobbyists, anti-multi nationalists and crank opportunists causing chaos outside Seattle's five-star hotels want in plain view.[28]

As Benjamin Barber notes, "Markets give us the goods but not the lives we want; they provide prosperity for some but lead to despair for many and dignity for none."[29]

In the area of culture, antiglobalists are disturbed by two trends, dare we say requirements, that come with the globalizing process. First, critics charge that the establishment of the two most important components of globalization (free markets and democracy) requires the acceptance of a liberal political-economic culture. Unfortunately, for most underdeveloped, developing, and even some developed countries, entrenched ethnic (linguistic, religious, and/or racial) estrangements still permeate due to the colonial nation-building framework of the state. That is, the state was established before the nation had the opportunity to develop a common, unifying culture. Consequently, marketization and democratization, rather than complementing and reinforcing one another toward the betterment of the human condition, have the opposite effect of greater instability by fostering ethnic competition and dissension: "Markets often reinforce the economic dominance of certain ethnic minorities," while " . . . democracy characteristically pits a politically powerful but impoverished 'indigenous' majority against an economically dominant ethnic minority."[30] As ethnicity rises to the forefront in establishing people's identity, intolerance, if not outright hostility, toward other cultures also increases, leading critics of globalization to predict more, not less, conflict in the future.

Second, critics also fear globalization's potential to indiscriminately overwhelm and invade the indigenous cultures and, in the process, reengineer them into one homogenized global monolith. Lost among the tear-gas-filled demonstrations in Seattle, Washington, and Prague, the Czech Republic, was one of the most vociferous voices: critics who viewed the homogenizing process of globalization as destroying cultures because the process leads inexorably to the triumph of American popular culture.[31] This widespread fear underscores the fact that globalization's impact can no longer be narrowly focused on only economic processes and reverberations. The events in Seattle and Prague brought globalization's political, social, cultural, and economic consequences into focus. The reason is not just that together they form parts of an embracing system, but that relations ranging among the various aspects of globalization are themselves changing and being transnationalized.

It should be further noted that opponents of globalization are emanating from the full spectrum of humanity. It is under attack from both the North (Canada and France) and the South (Iran and India), as well as from various groups—labor unions, farmers, environmentalists, and even consumer advocates. Both Iran and France now appear to have been locked in a decades-long battle with the seductive forces of globalization. Indeed, *the Economist* reported, "[the] French believe this so strongly that they have repeatedly threatened to scuttle trade talks unless 'cultural' goods are exempted."[32] The core concern is that globalization advances the interests of multinational corporations at the expense of sustainable economic development, jobs, and the environment, while irrevocably changing countries and their societies for the worst. With increasingly more vociferous calls for deglobalization in the wake of the global financial crisis, the debate over globalization's future direction and its impact on a state's economy, international relations, and cultural affairs will only intensify. If there has ever been a need to better understand globalization, that time is now.

PLAN OF THE BOOK

The book addresses a number of perspectives resulting from the ongoing globalization debate in four areas: economics, politics, culture, and the environment.

Chapter 2 addresses the meaning, development, and impact of globalization. It strives to place globalization within a broader context by addressing the contested conceptual perspectives. Globalization's impact is assessed in the political and cultural arenas.[33] Key questions addressed in this chapter include the following: What precisely is meant by globalization, and what are its causes and dynamics? What are the principal assumptions that frame the debate? How does globalization affect and is influenced by world politics?

Chapter 3 examines the globalist's expectation that the liberalization and integration of markets are inevitable and/or unstoppable. The following are the key questions addressed in this chapter: To what extent has the global economy become unified? What needs to be done to accelerate the integration process?

Chapter 4 provides an assessment of the effect of globalization on the distribution of income, both within states and among states in the developing world. The chapter challenges the neoliberal proposition that globalization is a positive force for income growth and poverty reduction. Key questions addressed are as follows: Does engagement in the world economy add to the wealth of nations so that the resultant rising tide lifts all boats? What are the consequences of globalization for the distribution of income, both among and within nations?

Chapter 5 examines the political struggles likely to occur within states under conditions of globalization. The following are the key questions addressed in this chapter: Has globalization ushered in a new era of greater peace among the world's peoples? Has globalization made a state's political, economic, and social decision-making process more inclusive? Will states, especially small economically fragile countries, survive the onslaught of globalization? Is globalization a force promoting stability and growth or the degradation of the world's diverse peoples and cultures?

Chapter 6 examines the crucial dimension of the sovereignty of the state, looking at the increasing role, influence, and power of an integrated global economy. Key questions addressed in this chapter are the following: Are individuals, particularly those in developing countries, better off when states cede some of their power and policymaking to the global marketplace? How far is globalization eroding and undermining the sovereignty of states and national institutions and reducing their autonomy in policymaking?

Does the integration of national economies constitute a serious threat to the power of the nation-state?

Chapter 7 addresses the widespread belief that globalization will result in the wholesale unraveling of distinctive "national" and local cultures around the globe. We address the contention that globalization is leading to the homogenization/Americanization of the world's cultural inheritances. Questions addressed in this chapter are as follows: Is globalization compatible with cultural sovereignty? Can economic globalization continue to integrate the world economy without destroying the social fabric or local community? Can local culture resist global processes? Is globalization really a threat to local cultures? How far is globalization an economically, socially, and culturally homogenizing force?

Chapter 8 examines the effect of globalization on the earth's environment. The following are the key questions addressed in this chapter: What are the environmental consequences of economic globalization? What scope exists for local, national, and international solutions to global environmental problems? Is globalization driving a "race to the bottom" with regard to environmental protection and the sustainability of planet earth?

Chapter 9 puts into perspective our contention that both the perceived benefits and the dangers of globalization have been exaggerated. Moreover, we argue that the benefits of globalization outweigh its costs. The key question then for economists and policymakers is this: How to reap the economic, political, and cultural benefits of the globalization process, while minimizing its detrimental effects on society, the state, and the environment?

KEY TERMS

deglobalization 2	integration 2	underdevelopment 11
globalism 3	interdependence 3	world politics 4
globalization 1	transnational 2	

FIVE QUESTIONS TO CONSIDER

1. How does globalization affect your life? List five dimensions of globalization in order of importance that directly affect your life. How would you define globalization as a force in your community?
2. How would you characterize globalization in terms of your political values? Is it a conservative or a liberal phenomenon? How would you locate globalization on your own political spectrum? Does globalization veer to the conservative, middle of the road, or liberal (left) side of your political compass?
3. To what extent is globalization rooted in economics?
4. To what extent can you describe globalization in a political context? How about a sociological context or a cultural one? When you think about globalization in the context of academic disciplines, do you conceptualize globalization differently?
5. Is globalization more or less a positive or a negative force in world politics? To what extent is it a positive or a negative force in your life? If globalization does not matter to you, why is it irrelevant?

FURTHER READINGS

Roger C. Altman, "Globalization in Retreat," *Foreign Affairs*, 88 (4) (July/August 2009): 2–8.

Altman argues that the era of free-market capitalism and deregulation has come to an end. China's economic influence is growing as the acceptance of the U.S. economic model is in decline. To put U.S. economic interests in the foreground, President Obama must use his unique position in the world to support open markets and free trade.

Jagdish Bhagwati, *In Defense of Globalization*. New York: Oxford University Press, 2004.

Bhagwati, argues that globalization is the most powerful force for social good in the world when governed properly. Drawing on international and development economics, Bhagwati sees in globalization the central dynamics to structure solutions to global poverty through the diffusion of technology and the generation of wealth.

Economist, "Turning Their Backs on the World," February 19, 2009, electronic version.

The global economic meltdown raises the possibility of deglobalization. The speed and scale of the global recession raise doubts about the continuing integration of global markets and the inability to provide economic benefits that globalization promises. This most directly impacts the world's poor.

Gideon Rachman, "When Globalisation Goes into Reverse," *Financial Times*, February 2, 2009, electronic version.

Rachman analyzes the increasing pressure on banks and financial institutions to retreat from international business and embrace protectionism in domestic markets. Political leaders endorse open markets, free trade, and global investment flows while attempting to respond to constituents who are angry, frightened and demanding protection.

Joseph E. Stiglitz, *Globalization and Its Discontents*. New York: W.W. Norton and Company, Inc., 2003.

Stiglitz won the Nobel Prize and served as chief economist at the World Bank. He offers a penetrating critique of how the International Monetary Fund and other economic institutions put the interests of Wall Street ahead of the poorer nations. He explains the rationale of antiglobalization movements across the globe.

NOTES

1. Cited from Steven Greenhouse, "After Seattle, Unions Point to Sustained Fight on Trade," *New York Times*, December 6, 1999, electronic version.
2. Anthony Giddens, *Runaway World*. New York: Routledge, 2003: 6–7.
3. Joseph Stiglitz, *Globalization and Its Discontents*. New York: W.W. Norton and Company, 2003.
4. Robert O. Keohane and Joseph S. Nye, "Globalization: What's New? What's Not? (And So What?)," *Foreign Policy* 118 (Spring 2000): 104–119. For a detailed assessment of globalization and globalism, see also Robert O. Keohane and Joseph Nye, *Power and Interdependence*, 3rd ed. New York: Longman, 2001: part 5, 213–264.
5. Ibid.
6. Ibid., 105–109.
7. Ibid., 108–118.
8. Ibid., 109.

9. Ibid.

10. Ibid.

11. Ibid., 112.

12. Ibid., 106.

13. Skeptics and critics are a diverse lot. They include human rights and labor advocates; religious, feminist, and consumer groups; and environmental and public policy research organizations.

14. Giddens, *Runaway World*, 15.

15. Globalists count among their ranks most economists and many in the policy community, as well the three intergovernmental organizations charged with "managing" the global economy—the World Bank, the International Monetary Fund, and the World Trade Organization.

16. Quoted from Barbara Crossette, "Globalization Tops 3-Day U.N. Agenda for World Leaders," *New York Times*, September 3, 2000, electronic version.

17. Naomi Klein, *No Logos: No Space, No Choice, No Jobs*. New York: Picador, 2002.

18. Jose Bove and Francoise Dufour, *The World Is Not for Sale: Farmers Against Junk Foods*, Anna de Casparis (trans.). New York: Verso, 2001.

19. Thomas L. Friedman, *The Lexus and the Olive Tree*. New York: Farrar, Straus & Giroux, 1999; John Gray, *False Dawn: The Delusions of Global Capitalism*. New York: The New Press, 1999; Benjamin R. Barber, "Democracy at Risk: American Culture in a Global Culture," *World Policy Journal* 15(2) (1998): 29–41; Peter L. Berger, "Four Faces of Global Culture," *The National Interest* 49 (1997): 23–29; William Greider, *One World, Ready or Not: The Manic Logic of Global Capitalism*. New York: Simon & Schuster, 1997; Samuel Huntington, *The Clash of Civilizations and the Remaking of World Order*. New York: Simon & Schuster, 1996.

20. Jagdish Bhagwati, *In Defence of Globalisation*. Oxford, UK: Oxford University Press, 2004; John Micklethwait and Alan Wooldridge, *A Future Perfect: The Challenge and Promise of Globalization*. New York: Random House, 2002; Robert Gilpin, *The Challenge of Global Capitalism: The World Economy in the 21st Century*. Princeton: Princeton University Press, 2000; David Held, Anthony McGrew, David Goldblatt, and Jonathan Perraton, *Global Transformations: Politics, Economics and Culture*. Oxford: Polity, 2000; Jan Aarte Scholte, *Globalization: A Critical Introduction*. New York: Palgrave, 2000; Herman M. Schwartz, *States Versus Markets: The Emergence of a Global Economy*, 2nd ed. New York: St. Martin's Press, 2000; R.J. Barry Jones, *The World Turned Upside Down? Globalization and the Future of the State*. Manchester, UK: Manchester University Press, 2000; Richard Rosecrance, *The Rise of the Virtual State: Wealth and Power in the Coming Century*. New York: Basic Books, 1999; and Thomas L. Friedman, *The Lexus and the Olive Tree*. New York: Farrar, Straus & Giroux, 1999.

21. Robert J. Samuelson, "Globalization's Downside," *Washington Post*, December 17, 1997, electronic version.

22. Bruce Russett, "How Democracy, Interdependence and International Organizations Create a System for Peace," in Charles W. Kegley, Jr. and Eugene R. Wittkopf, eds., *The Global Agenda: Issues and Perspectives*. Boston: McGraw-Hill, 2000; John R. Oneal and Bruce Russett, "The Kantian Peace: The Pacific Benefits of Democracy, Interdependence and International Organizations, 1885–1992," *World Politics* 52 (1999): 1–37; Steve Chan, "Mirror, Mirror, on the Wall . . . Are the Freer Countries More Pacific?" *Journal of Conflict Resolution* 28 (1984): 617–664; William J. Dixon, "Democracy and the Management of International Conflict," *Journal of Conflict Resolution* 37 (1993): 42–68; David Lake, "Powerful Pacifists: Democratic

States and War," *American Political Science Review* 86 (1992): 24–37; Zeev Maoz and Nasrin Abdolali, "Regime Type and International Conflict, 1816–1976," *Journal of Conflict Resolution* 33 (1989): 3–35; Zeev Maoz and Bruce Russett, "Alliances, Wealth, Contiguity and Political Stability: Is the Lack of Conflict between Democracies a Statistical Artifact?" *International Interactions* 17 (1992): 245–267; T. Clifton Morgan and Valerie Schwebach, "Take Two Democracies and Call Me in the Morning: A Prescription for Peace?" *International Interactions* 17 (1992): 305–320; and Bruce Russett and William Antholis, "Do Democracies Rarely Fight Each Other? Evidence from the Peloponnesian War," *Journal of Peace Research* 29 (1992): 415–434.

23. James N. Rosenau, *Along the Domestic-Foreign Frontier: Exploring Governance in a Turbulent World*. Cambridge, UK: Cambridge University Press, 1997; Stephen D. Krasner, *Sovereignty: Organized Hypocrisy*. Princeton: Princeton University Press, 1999; and Stephen D. Krasner, "Sovereignty," *Foreign Policy* 122 (January/February 2001): 20–29.

24. Robert K. Schaeffer, *Understanding Globalization*. Lanham, MD: Rowman and Littlefield Publishers, Inc., 2003.

25. Naomi Klein, *No Logos: No Space, No Choice, No Jobs*. New York: Picador, 2002; James H. Mittelman, *The Globalization Syndrome: Transformation and Resistance*. Princeton: Princeton University Press, 2000; John Gray, *False Dawn: The Delusions of Global Capitalism*. New York: The New Press, 1999; Margaret E. Kock and Kathryn Sikkink, *Activists Beyond Borders*. Ithaca: Cornell University Press, 1998; Edward Luttwak, *Turbo Capitalism: Winners and Losers in the Global Economy*. London: Weidenfelf and Nicolson, 1998; Saskia Sassen and Kwame Anthony Appiah, *Globalization and Its Discontents*. New York: New Press, 1998; William Greider, *One World, Ready or Not: The Manic Logic of Global Capitalism*. New York: Simon & Schuster, 1997; Dani Rodrik, *Has Globalization Gone Too Far?* Washington, DC: Institute for International Economics, 1997.

26. Rosabeth M. Kanter, "Don't Give Up on Globalization," *Los Angeles Times*, November 18, 1998, electronic version.

27. Thomas L. Friedman, "The New Human Rights," *New York Times*, July 30, 1999, electronic version.

28. Tom Plate, "Globalization Isn't a One-Size-Fits-All Answer," *Los Angeles Times*, December 1, 1999, electronic version.

29. Barber, "Democracy at Risk".

30. Amy L. Chua, "Markets, Democracy, and Ethnicity: Toward a New Paradigm for Law and Development," *Yale Law Journal* 108 (1998): 1–107.

31. Paul Farhi and Megan Rosenfeld, "American Pop Penetrates Worldwide," *Washington Post*, October 25, 1998, electronic version; and Sharon Waxman, "Hollywood Tailors Its Movies to Sell In Foreign Markets," *Washington Post*, October 26, 1998, electronic version.

32. *Economist*, "Pokémania V Globophobia," November 20, 1999, electronic version.

33. Paul Lewis, "As Nations Shed Roles, Is Medieval the Future?" *New York Times*, January 2, 1999, electronic version; Edgar Morin, "The Agents of Double Globalization," *World Futures* 53(2) (1999): 149; and Stacy Takacs, "Alien-nation: Immigration, National Identity and Transnationalism," *Cultural Studies* 13(4) (1999): 591–621.

Conceptual Perspectives on Globalization

Globalization creates new markets and wealth, even as it causes widespread suffering, disorder, and unrest. It is both a source of repression and a catalyst for global movements of social justice and emancipation.

—Global Policy Forum[1]

. . . the quantitative change in each of globalization's components—economic, cultural, military, etc.—is so enormous that it creates a qualitative change. This alone has opened possibilities that are completely new—and also consequences that humanity has never seen before.

—Moisés Naím, Editor in Chief of Foreign Policy *magazine and former Minister of Trade and Industry for Venezuela*[2]

INTRODUCTION: UNTANGLING GLOBALIZATION

This chapter assesses a number of approaches to the study of globalization. These include how globalization is defined, the kinds of forces and processes that drive globalization, its dynamics, and the growing focus on globalization as a primary explanation for change in world politics. As we noted in Chapter 1, globalization is controversial because the concept stands for so many simultaneous, mutually exclusive, and contradictory meanings. These include those pertaining to adverse changes in politics, **culture**, and economics, which seemingly threaten the foundations of states, peoples, and regions throughout the world. Worse still, the process of globalizing and the results of globalization appear to be so far reaching that levels of predictability in politics, economics, culture, and **finance** seem to be thrust in the midst of ongoing, far-reaching, and unpredictable change. From our perspective, it is important to understand two key dimensions of globalization.

First, it is not a new phenomenon. It is part and parcel of the process of expansion across continents based on **trade**, exploration, conquest, colonization, military alliances and warfare, migration, and technological developments throughout world history. Contacts among peoples, societies, empires, and states from the Stone Age to the twenty-first century have knit the world together in patterns of interdependence that have intensified and attenuated over time. It is, therefore, critical to underscore that globalization is part of a historically driven process.

Second, the study of transnational relations offers a perspective that helps to contextualize arguments as to the novelty, uncertainty, and unpredictability of globalization, as the sustained work of Robert Keohane and Joseph Nye suggests.[3] The extent to which globalization is characterized as a unique product of the twenty-first century and as such an unpredictable destabilizing force in all circumstances needs to be analyzed carefully.

This chapter also examines the striking absence of a consensus on the definition, nature, and/or the significance of globalization as a point of departure for the study of world politics. We argue that the polarization of the globalization debate ultimately weakens efforts to analyze and assess the reach of globalization in world politics.

Our task is to try to make sense of dramatically conflicting perspectives by assessing the impact of globalization in a number of different contexts: political, economic, cultural, social, and environmental, among others. Because we look at globalization from an **international relations** perspective, it is important to underscore the different ways that globalization impacts countries, societies, nonstate or transnational actors, intergovernmental organizations, and people throughout the world. Globalization is a process that is complex. One size does not fit all countries, transnational organizations, cultures, and societies in the same manner. There are winners and losers. Our goal is to look at the globalization process from the perspectives of advocates and opponents as a way of describing world politics.

For one group of observers, globalization represents a relentless and unstoppable economic force, in which national **markets**, firms, labor, and financial services are being integrated globally on an unprecedented scale. This process is characterized by the increasingly massive and unrestricted flow of goods and services, technology, information, and **capital** to virtually every part of the world.[4]

A second group focuses on the extraordinary escalation of the free flow of ideas across state borders. Such transnational interactions linking individuals, groups, organizations, states, and cultures result in the emergence of global social and political movements. This, in turn, may result in greater levels of political engagement, as the extraordinary growth of private nongovernmental organizations (NGOs) suggests and as the increase in citizen activism concerning AIDS, economic development, the environment, or opposition to the World Trade Organization (WTO) or the war in Iraq attests.[5] It may also manifest itself in the increasing impact of ethnonationalist groups, drug and criminal cartels, and terrorist organizations across the globe.

Yet a third perspective conceptualizes globalization in terms such as the "entanglement of diverse cultures"[6] and "the spread of a universal language." Here, globalization focuses on the manner in which global exchanges of ideas, foods, fashion, lifestyles, and social structures are, in effect, changing the makeup, dynamics, and interaction of societies throughout the world.

In light of the complexity of these processes and actors, any definition of globalization should at a minimum be viewed not in terms of a single dimension, but as a multitiered, multidimensional, and multinational set of processes involving activities and consequences (both intended and unintended) affecting economic, political, and sociocultural aspects of life across the planet. Because globalization is so diffuse culturally, socially, economically, and politically, our assessment works toward an understanding of the ideas, processes, and manifestations of globalization that follows throughout the book.

Globalization as a concept and a process has been likened mainly to economics. Our exploration begins with a brief assessment of the central economic aspects of globalization in terms of integration, trade, finance, and production. Next we turn our attention to globalization in political contexts, especially states, and the global system as well as its influence on state–society relationships. Our inquiry continues with an assessment of the cultural dynamics of globalization, both the diffusion and convergence of the globe's cultures. In the words of Keohane and Nye, "This division of globalism into separate dimensions is inevitably somewhat arbitrary. Nonetheless, it is useful for analysis, because changes in the various dimensions of globalization do not necessarily occur simultaneously."[7]

ECONOMIC GLOBALIZATION

In economic discourse, globalization refers to the progressive "networking" of national market economies into a single, tightly interconnected global political economy (via advances in communications technology and falling transportation costs) whose accumulation and distribution of resources are increasingly governed by neoliberal principles—emphasizing the role of the market while minimizing governmental involvement in economic matters.[8] This networking occurs through the transnational decentralization of production factors and services by which the markets of different countries are integrated into the global economy, enabling the farther, faster, cheaper, and more efficient flow of goods, services, capital, information, and people across national borders than ever before.[9] This process is fueled by augmenting methods and systems of international transportation, by conceiving revolutionary and innovative information technologies and ideas, and by onrushing economic and ecological forces that demand integration and uniformity, as well as by governmental policies of deregulation and liberalization.[10]

In the area of trade, globalization can be seen in the growing openness of markets for goods and services,[11] and an ever-increasing dependence on international commerce as a source of income and domestic prosperity.[12] According to James Mittelman, "Today all countries trade internationally and, with the odd exception like North Korea, they trade significant proportions of their national income." Indeed, "[t]rade has now reached unprecedented level, both absolutely and proportionate to world output."[13] The *Economist* reported a 16-fold increase in the value of world trade between 1950 and 1995, and the doubling of the ratio of world exports to world gross domestic product over the same period.[14] Wayne Ellwood projects that the continued expansion of trade will lead to an increase in global income to $500 billion early in the twenty-first century.[15]

In the realm of finance, globalization is manifested in a rising level of capital flow and in an unprecedented integration of international financial markets, that is, ever-higher volumes of foreign (private) lending and investment across national frontiers, and an increase in the number of joint ventures. According to Jeffrey Sachs, "The growth and spread of investment, capital, money, and financial services are counted by virtually all scholars as an important feature of globalization."[16] Along with the flow of information (electronic-commerce), these networked national markets enjoy an openness and "freedom" that allow them to operate beyond national governmental oversight. "In the new global electronic economy, fund managers, banks, corporations, as well as millions of individual investors, can transfer vast amounts of capital from one side of the world to another at the click of a mouse. As they do so, they can destablize what might have seemed rock-solid economies—as happened in the events in Asia," cautioned Anthony Giddens.[17]

The most notable feature of this process involves the changing nature of global production: the increasing consolidation of global production and trade under the direction and supervision of a few hundred transnational corporations and a handful of intergovernmental institutions like the WTO, the IMF, and the World Bank.[18] Hence, many of the traditional instruments of economic policy (i.e., exchange rates, interest rates, and research and development financing) increasingly are no longer under the jurisdiction of national governments.

It should be noted that not all countries have profited equally—or at all—from globalization,[19] although the broad experience has been economic growth, which in turn promotes general welfare. Indeed, the proliferation of short-term capital in the global financial market presents the potential for economic and social instability. The 1997 Asian financial crisis, for example, not only put the economies of Thailand, Indonesia, Malaysia, and South Korea into a tailspin, but the social disruption that accompanied the economic crisis also brought forth much suffering, dislocation, marginalization, and ethnic conflict.

Economic globalization, therefore, has many facets: from the explosion in worldwide commerce to the surging flows of transnational capital, the continued dismantling of national markets (via the proliferation of new high-technology innovation in conjunction with plummeting communication and transportation costs), as well as the march toward the establishment of a truly global marketplace. Despite these mainly positive effects, globalization gives rise to profound misgivings about the consequences of these processes, bringing out more fully globalized economies. The very processes of globalization create anxieties about where those processes may lead. The shift from national or state-centered economic priorities brings with it the specter of a loss of control. Thus embedded in the concepts and processes of economic globalization is a normative perspective, indeed a fear, that the process will forever alter the structure and dynamics of international political economic relations. The power of these fears, real or imagined, understated or exaggerated, forms part and parcel of how globalization is defined and how it is viewed as a process of economic change.

POLITICAL GLOBALIZATION

Much of the discourse about political globalization centers on two areas of inquiry: the globalizing process' impact on (1) the state and (2) the **state system** at regional and global levels. We examine each one in turn.

Overwhelmingly, the globalization debate revolves around how the process is reframing the nature, role, and function of states as manifested by "the stretching of political relations across space and time; [and] the extension of political power and political activity across the boundaries of the modern nation-state."[20] This divergence in perspective is fragmented between two poles: one claiming that globalization has, in essence, made the nation-state irrelevant, and the other vociferously defending the nation-state's continued primacy, if not preeminence, in global politics.

The first camp sees globalization as a relentless process resulting in the diminished capacity of states. It cites primarily the declining authority of states and their inability to determine their own fate. The power of states to make independent and unfettered decisions is at stake. Thus, for Ian Clark, "it is **sovereignty** which is most at risk from globalization."[21] As Linda Weiss cautions, because "changes in the international political economy have radically restricted policy choice and forced policy shifts that play to the preferences of global investors and mobile corporations, rather than to the needs of the domestic political economy and its citizenry."[22] As a result, governments have not only "lost the authority over national societies and economies they used to have" according to Susan Strange,[23] but Anthony Giddens argues that they have also "lost their capability to influence events."[24] Indeed, Kenichi Ohmae argues that the transition to a "borderless economy" is rendering the nation-state increasingly irrelevant and impotent.[25] Predicted Nicholas Negroponte, "Like a mothball, which goes from solid to gas directly, I expect the nation-state to evaporate."[26]

Quite naturally, those in the **statecentric** camp vigorously contend that "[s]tates still are at the center of the international system."[27] Indeed, the continuation of a statecentric world order was the product of geopolitics, economic expansion, and post–Cold War policy decisions by the world's most powerful states.[28] States are simply adapting to a political and economic structure put in place following the end of World War II. The creation of the General Agreement of Tariff and Trade in 1944 has become the WTO reflecting U.S. economic and geopolitical policies. For James Rosenau, this means that "[s]tates are changing, but they are not disappearing. State sovereignty has been eroded, but it is still vigorously asserted. Governments are weaker, but they can still throw their weight around."[29] In like manner, Stephen Krasner views these developments as just part of the continued evolution of the state system whereby "[t]he reach of the state has increased in some areas but contracted in others."[30] And for former UN secretary general Kofi Annan, "the sovereign State remains a highly relevant and necessary institution; indeed, the very linchpin of human security."[31] While it is difficult to imagine the collapse of states entirely, differences in power capabilities at the state, regional, and global levels certainly provide some states with more leverage and others with far less. Yet, even among the most fragile, barely functioning "shadow" states in Africa, the element of statehood—international recognition and territorial control over a defined population—continues to matter in profound-enough ways that warfare is always on the agenda. There is never a shortage of factions, armies, ethnic and national groups, criminal cartels, and terrorist organizations contriving to control states. If anything, scholars and policymakers alike view competent, well-organized states as more, not less, indispensable as threats to sovereignty become ever more global.

The continued resilience of states is accompanied by the reconfiguration of regional and international systems, characterized by the rise in number and significance of international and regional intergovernmental organizations and nonstate transnational actors.[32] As Jessica T. Mathew notes, states are increasingly "sharing powers—including political, social, and security roles at the core of sovereignty—with other authorities."[33] Gabriela Kutting describes this trend as "a move from statecentric or institutional IR to a more pluralistic, or globalist, *Weltanschauung*."[34] Gabriela Kutting's emphasis on a changing *Weltanschauung* or worldview underscores the key role and, indeed, the decisive presence of globalization as a process worldwide.

The implications of this trend, in turn, demand a reexamination of international relations based on the power of both actors and processes in terms of global governance. Observing that, increasingly, states are bound up in complex institutionalized interdependencies, much of the debate on political globalization shows an attempt to move away from the existing state-centered paradigms of international relations theory,[35] arguing that the transnational networks of intergovernmental and nongovernmental organizations that play political roles arguably represent a structural change in the international system and therefore constitute a new form of global governance.[36]

CULTURAL GLOBALIZATION

The economic and political dynamics of globalization, however, reveal only part of the story because globalization is not merely an economic and/or political process. The power and influence of globalization must be examined as more than either the onrushing, explosive exchanges in goods, services, capital, and people or the reconfiguration/evolution of the state and state system. The cultural sphere is a central dimension of a globalizing world where people confront major shifts in the basic conditions of social relations that are both simple and profound. The world is becoming a "single place" due to what Roland Robertson describes as the "intensification of the consciousness of the world as a whole"[37] and what Anthony Giddens interprets as the compression of "worldwide social relations which link distant localities in such a way that local happenings are shaped by events occurring many miles away and vice-versa."[38] "It is also the first time in history that virtually every individual at every level of society can sense the impact of international changes," David Rothkopf notes. "They can see and hear it in their media, taste it in their food, and sense it in the products that they buy."[39] In this respect, globalization may be viewed as the overreaching international framework that shapes domestic politics, markets, and the foreign relations of virtually every country. Observes Anthony Giddens, "Globalization isn't only about what is 'out there,' remote and far away from the individual. It is an 'in here' phenomenon too, influencing intimate and personal aspects of our lives."[40]

The power of culture in the global milieu begins to come into focus as one of the most subtle yet far-reaching dimensions of the globalization process. Cultural globalization encompasses the transfers of popular culture in food, music, dance, and fashion, as well as business practices and procedural techniques in industries and cross-national social movements. The proliferation of ideas, based on political participation, gender, race, ethnicity, poverty, and affluence, as well as the spread of religious fundamentalism are all part and parcel of the process of globalization.[41]

On the positive end, this march toward a supposed universal homogenous culture in which all ethnic, linguistic, racial, and religious distinctions and discords are washed away provides the promise of a modernized, rationalized, and institutionalized global culture tied together by increases in communications, resulting in greater understanding. In such a worldwide social arrangement, one in which old divisions and hostilities are eliminated, the expectation is that humanity may finally move toward the realization of a genuine transnationalism that will help create a more tolerant and peaceful world order.[42]

A contrary perspective, one of several, views the global proliferation of norms, practices, symbols, and values of the predominant (Western and/or American) culture as a form of cultural imperialism—cultural equivalent of a global pandemic. Challenging basic group identities, globalization threatens the obliteration of authentic cultural communities through the power of an expanding interactive order of ideas, self-conceptions, values, norms, and identities spanning the globe. David Harvey summed up this group apprehension and fear when he wrote that globalization has caused "an intense phase of time-space compression that has had a disorienting and disruptive impact upon political-economic practices, and the balance of class power, as well as upon cultural and social life."[43] In this context, the threat posed to authentic cultural identity is as threatening as any political and economic transformation imaginable because it carries with it the very destruction of the individual and the group upon which political and socioeconomic systems rest.[44]

DEBATING GLOBALIZATION

Lui Hebron: Why Measuring Globalization Matters

John, a major fault line between globalists and antiglobalists traverses across one of the most basic issues—namely, the measurement and impact of the phenomenon. For both advocates and skeptics of globalization, the lack of a universally accepted matrix poses difficulty in determining not only the extent to which the world is really becoming more integrated, but even more basically, the beneficial and/or detrimental effects of the processes.

Though it is widely acknowledged that globalization encompasses a range of economic, political, and cultural issues (i.e., opportunities and constraints), a universally accepted matrix for measuring these main components of the globalizing process has not yet been definitively established. Nevertheless, an examination of the numerous studies that track globalization allows us to extrapolate the key proxy variables with which to measure the extent and impact of the process (A.T. Kearney, Inc. "Globalization Index," *Foreign Policy*, 2001, 2002, 2003, 2004, 2005, 2006, 2007; Randolph Kluver and Wayne Fu, "The Cultural Globalization Index," *Foreign Policy*, February 2004; Global Policy Forum, "Globalization," http://www.globalpolicy.org/globalization.html).

Economically, data on trade, foreign direct investment (FDI), and portfolio capital flows have been employed to measure the extent and impact of economic integration. In terms of commerce, trade agreements (the European Union and the North American Free Trade Agreement) have facilitated greater international trade. In like manner, the infusion of foreign capital (FDI and portfolio investments) into emerging economies has been instrumental in spurring their growth and development.

Politically, state membership in international organizations (the World Bank, the International Monetary Fund, the WTO, and the United Nations) and the ratification of international agreements (social justice and environmental treaties) as well as the emergence of worldwide civil society organizations (World Social Forum, Oxfam International, and Amnesty International) have been utilized to quantify the degree and effect of political engagement. These trends toward greater global political participation are all helping to bring about a more inclusive and accountable form of global governance.

Culturally, the movement of popular media is used as a proxy for measuring the level and magnitude of cultural globalization. These proxy signifiers include cinematic films, television programming, and print (books, newspapers, and magazines) publications. The free flow of information and greater interaction between societies via the Internet, satellite television, and international travel have been credited with breaking down cultural boundaries and bringing about a global culture characterized by greater shared values, an increased sense of community, and stronger social solidarity.—Lui

John Stack: Who Measures Globalization and Why

Lui, measurement is a necessary step in getting a handle on how globalization works. It is empirical in the sense that it is one of the ways we view reality. My concern is how we measure and what we measure—both matter in allowing us to conceptualize what globalization is and who benefits and who loses as a result of the global processes and networks. We need to be especially cognizant of the subtle dynamics of so-called free trade because rich industrial and postindustrial countries benefit more from the trade agreements that they have created. Free trade is supposed to level the playing field, but since the post–World War II reconstruction of the global economic system at Bretton Woods and with the establishment of the General Agreement on Tarriffs and Trade (GATT) as reincarnated into the WTO, industrialized countries have traditionally benefitted more in part because the rules of the game were structured by the strongest and largest national economies following the end of World War II. The elimination of protectionist policies is a fundamental goal of trade organizations. How protectionism is defined and who monitors trade agreements also illustrate sources of power and influence not immediately observable in the worlds of multilateral diplomacy and international governmental organizations (IGOs) and large multinational corporations.

My concern focuses on how trade agreements have traditionally privileged industrial and postindustrial societies. For those countries producing primary agricultural products, the terms of trade often hurt poor countries plunging them deeper into poverty amid falling prices and paltry domestic support. Capital investment flows in the form of FDI via corporations and portfolio investments frequently end up challenging environmental, health, and labor standards of countries as the trade off for foreign investments. Additionally, the inflow of international capital has also often increased instability and inequality in developing societies.

How increasing levels of global governance is measured and assessed is also very important. Increasingly, greater political engagement via membership in IGOs along with the proliferation and more aggressive tactics of global movements via nongovernmental organizations have intensified a loss of control within often fragile states because political activity increasingly takes place at the global level instead of within traditional, national political systems.

The task of cataloging the successes and the failures of globalization matters hugely. What is measured and how as indicators of the successes and/or failures of globalization require careful analysis. It is very important for us to consider precisely how globalization is measured within the context of both winners and losers across the globe.—John ∎

CONCLUSION: THE MULTIDIMENSIONALITY OF GLOBALIZATION

In light of the preceding discussion, globalization is without question a "multi-causal and multi-stranded process"[45] that directly or indirectly conditions and shapes the economic, political, and sociocultural dynamics and global relations of virtually every country. A comprehensive and more nuanced understanding of globalization, therefore, must take into account the simultaneous emergence of multiple dimensions of structural and relational reality, which includes a political, cultural, as well as an economic component: Economically, globalization is conceived as the development and progress toward a unified global marketplace in which economies "are not simply more connected; [but that] the distinctions between them are becoming less meaningful"[46] as more and more national economies follow market-oriented practices and policies. Politically, globalization can be viewed as a new stage in world politics that signals a convergence in political thinking and practice "whereby power is [increasingly] located in global social formations and expressed through global networks rather than through territorially-based states."[47] And culturally, globalization is understood as reflecting a "widespread perception that the world is rapidly being molded into a shared social space"[48] via the "process of increasing interconnectedness between societies."[49]

But before we embark on our examination of globalization and its assumed triumphs and failings, a human dimension needs to be placed in steady focus. As a process, globalization is powerful because it is so embracing in politics, economics, law, social structures, the mass media, and information technology. It appears to be a force and a process that is at once unstoppable and inevitable. It is, therefore, perhaps easy to lose sight of its impact on individuals and groups whose lives will be influenced and perhaps altered by its reach. As the dominant process of the early twenty-first century making claims about the global economic, political, and sociocultural dynamics currently in play, globalization will also be examined within the context of how far countries are willing to accept constraints on domestic policy in an array of vital areas such as economic, political, and sociocultural sovereignty for the sake of economic growth and development.

KEY TERMS

capital 19	international relations 19	statecentric 23
culture 19	markets 19	state system 22
finance 19	sovereignty 22	trade 19

FIVE QUESTIONS TO CONSIDER

1. Is globalization the product of technology more so than of international relations?
2. Describe three central features of economic globalization?
3. How does globalization manifest itself as a political phenomenon?

4. What is cultural globalization? How does it differ from political and economic forms of globalization? Of the three forms of globalization, which is the most important dimension to your life and career?
5. The authors describe globalization as a multidimensional process. How is it multi-dimensional? If you were to define globalization in terms of an individual, whom would you choose and why?

FURTHER READINGS

Jose Bova, "Globalization's Misguided Assumptions," *The OECD Observer*, September 2001.

Global markets are not self-regulating, and competition does not generate wealth for everyone. Bova also takes on the assumptions that world market prices are a relevant criterion for guiding output and the belief that free trade is the engine of economic development. He argues that there are other roads to prosperity.

Thomas L. Friedman, *The World Is Flat, 3.0*. New York: Picador, 2007.

Friedman writes about the power of information technology and accompanying empowerment, the lifting of millions out of poverty, and some of the drawbacks of globalization—environmental, social, and political. He also considers the role of political activists and social entrepreneurs and the problems posed to reputations and privacy.

Peter Marber, "Globalization and Its Contents," *World Policy Journal*, Winter 2004/2005.

Globalization has different meanings for different people, often depending on their political perspective. Marber assesses the positive and negative impacts of this process from a broad historical perspective. The author concludes that the evidence strongly suggests that human prosperity is improving as boundaries between people are lowered.

Moisés Naím, "The Five Wars of Globalization," *Foreign Policy*, November/December, 2002.

Illegal trade in drugs, arms, intellectual property, people, and money is booming. Governments will continue to lose these wars until they adopt new strategies. Naim advocates developing more flexible notions of sovereignty, strengthening multilateral institutions, devising new institutions, and moving from repression to regulation.

NOTES

1. http://www.globalpolicy.org/globalization.htm.
2. Moisés Naím, "Globalization," *Foreign Policy*, 171 (March/April 2009): 28–35.
3. Robert O. Keohane and Joseph S. Nye, "Globalization: What's New? What's Not? (And So What?)," *Foreign Policy* 118 (Spring 2000): 104–119; and Robert O. Keohane and Joseph S. Nye, *Power and Interdependence*, 3rd ed. New York: Longman, 2001.
4. John-ren Chen, Richard Hule, and Herbert Stocker, "Introduction," in John-ren Chen, ed., *Economic Effects of Globalization*. Aldershot, UK: Ashgate, 1998; and Thomas L. Friedman, *The Lexus and the Olive Tree*. New York: Farrar, Straus & Giroux, 1999.

5. John W. Meyer, John Boli, George M. Thomas, and Francisco O. Ramirez, "World Society and the Nation-State," *American Journal of Sociology* 103(1) (1997): 144–181.

6. Wayne Ellwood, *The No-Nonsense Guide to Globalization*. London: New Internationalist Publications Ltd., 2003.

7. Keohane and Nye, "Globalization."

8. Caroline Thomas and Melvyn Reader, "Development and Inequality," in Brian White, Richard Little, and Michael Smith, eds., *Issues in World Politics*, 2nd ed. New York: Palgrave, 2001; David Henderson, *The MAI Affair: A Story and Its Lessons*. London: Royal Institute of International Affairs, 1999; and Hans-Peter Martin and Harold Schumann, *The Global Trap: Globalization and the Assault on Prosperity and Democracy*. Patrick Camiller (trans.), Montreal: Black Rose Books, 1998.

9. Peter Katzenstein, Robert Keohane, and Stephen Krasner, "International Organization and the Study of World Politics," *International Organization* 52(4) (Autumn 1998): 669.

10. Robert T. Kurdle, "The Three Types of Globalization: Communication, Market and Direct," in Raimo Bayrynen, ed., *Globalization and Global Governance*. Lanham, MD: Roman and Littlefield, 1999: 3–23; C. P. Rao, ed., *Globalization, Privatization and Free Market Economy*. Westport, CT: Quorum Books, 1998; Lowell Bryan and Diana Farrell, *Market Unbound: Unleashing Global Capitalism*. New York: Wiley, 1996.

11. Jessica T. Mathews observed, "Today, a global marketplace is developing for retail sales as well as manufacturing," Law, advertising, business consulting, and financial and other services are also marketed internationally. Jessica T. Mathews, "Power Shift," *Foreign Affairs* 76(1) (January/February 1997): 56.

12. Jeffrey Sachs, "International Economics: Unlocking the Mysteries of Globalization," *Foreign Policy* 110 (Spring 1998): 97–111.

13. James Mittelman, *The Globalization Syndrome*. Princeton, NJ: Princeton University Press, 2000: 21.

14. *Economist*, "Trade Winds," November 8, 1997, electronic version.

15. Ellwood, *The No-Nonsense Guide to Globalization*.

16. Sachs, "International Economics," 97–111.

17. Anthony Giddens, *Runaway World: How Globalization is Reshaping Our Lives*. New York: Routledge, 2003: 9.

18. K. C. Abraham, "Globalization: a Gospel and Culture Perspective," *International Review of Mission* 85(36) (1996): 85–92; Benjamin R. Barber, "Democracy at Risk: American Culture in a Global Culture," *World Policy Journal* 15(2) (1998): 29–41; and David Rothkopf, "In Praise of Cultural Imperialism? (Effects of Globalization on Culture)," *Foreign Policy* 107 (1997): 38–53.

19. Abraham (1996) notes that "[i]t is rooted in the culture of capitalism, whose predominant logic of development is profit-making." Consequently, it can be inferred that "[t]he poor and the marginalized do not find protection and security under it."

20. UNCTAD, *World Investment Report 1997: Transnational Corporations, Market Structure and Competition Policy*. New York: United Nations, 1997: 49.

21. Ian Clark, *Globalization and International Relations Theory*. Oxford, UK: Oxford University Press, 1999: 71.

22. Linda Weiss, ed., "Introduction: Bringing the State Back In." In *States in the Global Economy*. Cambridge: Cambridge University Press, 2003: 3.

23. Susan Strange, *The Retreat of the State: The Diffusion of Power in the World Economy.* Cambridge: Cambridge University Press, 1996: 3.
24. Anthony Giddens, *Runaway World: How Globalization Is Reshaping Our Lives.* New York: Routledge, 2000: 26.
25. Kenichi Ohmae, *The End of the Nation State.* New York: Free Press, 1995; and Kenichi Ohmae, *The Borderless World.* New York: Harper Business, 1999.
26. Quoted in John Gray, *False Dawn: The Delusions of Global Capitalism.* London: Granta Books, 1998: 68.
27. Alexander Wendt, *Social Theory of International Politics.* Cambridge: Cambridge University Press, 1999: 9.
28. Ethan Kapstein, *Sharing the Wealth.* New York: W. W. Norton, 1999.
29. James N. Rosenau, *Along the Domestic–Foreign Frontier: Exploring Governance in a Turbulent World.* Cambridge, UK: Cambridge University Press, 1997: 4.
30. Stephen D. Krasner, "Sovereignty," *Foreign Policy* 122 (January/February 2001): 24.
31. Excerpted from Kofi Annan, "The Role of the State in the Age of Globalization," keynote address to Conference on Globalization and International Relations in the 21st Century, June 2002, cited from Lechner and Boli, 2004: 241.
32. Stanley Hoffman, "Clash of Globalization," *Foreign Affairs* 81 (July/August 2002): 104–115.
33. Mathews, "Power Shift," 50.
34. Gabriela Kutting, "Back to the Future: Time, IR and the Environment," *Global Society* 15(4) (2001): 345–360.
35. Clark, *Globalization and International Relations Theory.*; Linda Weiss, *The Myth of the Powerless State.* Ithaca, NY: Cornell University Press, 1998; Richard Falk, "State of Siege: Will Globalization Win Out?" *International Affairs* 73(1) (1997): 123–136; Strange, *The Retreat of the State*; and Philip Cerny, "Globalization and Other Stories: The Search for a New Paradigm in International Relations," *International Journal* 51(4) (1996): 617–637.
36. David M. Andrews, "Capital Mobility and State Autonomy: Toward a Structural Theory of International Monetary Relations," *International Studies Quarterly* 38(2) (1994): 193–218; and Philip Cerny, *The Changing Architecture of Politics: Structure, Agency and the Future of the State.* London: Sage, 1990.
37. Roland Robertson, *Globalization: Social Theory and Global Culture.* London: Sage, 1992: 8.
38. Anthony Giddens, *The Consequences of Modernity.* Stanford, CA: Stanford University Press, 1990.
39. Rothkopf, "In Praise of Cultural Imperialism?," 38.
40. Giddens, *Runaway World*, 2003: 12.
41. Peter L. Berger, "Four Faces of Global Culture," *The National Interest* 49 (1997): 23–29.
42. Richard Begam, "The Novel and the Globalization of Culture," *CLIO* 27(1) (1997): 109–119; and Berger, "Four Faces of Global Culture."
43. David Harvey, "Time-Space Compression and the Rise of Modernism as a Cultural Force," *The Conditions of Postmodernity.* Oxford: Blackwell, 1990.
44. Barber, "Democracy at Risk," 29–41.
45. Giddens, *The Consequences of Modernity.*
46. James Lee Ray and Juliet Kaarbo, *Global Politics*, 8th ed. Boston, MA: Houghton Mifflin, 2005: 487.

47. Caroline Thomas, "Globalization and the South," in Caroline Thomas and Peter Wilkin, eds., *Globalization and the South*. New York: St. Martin's Press, 1997: 6.
48. David Held, Anthony McGrew, David Goldblatt, and Jonathan Perraton, *Global Transformation: Politics, Economics and Culture*. Stanford, CA: Stanford University Press, 1999: 1.
49. John Baylis and Steve Smith, eds., *The Globalization of World Politics*, 2nd ed. Oxford: Oxford University Press, 2001: 7.

CHAPTER

3

Market Integration

The emergence of China, India, and the former
communist-bloc countries implies that the greater part of
the earth's population is now engaged, at least potentially,
in the global economy.

—Ben Bernanke, Federal Reserve Board Chairman[1]

I understand that globalization is supposedly a means by
which the so-called economic playing field is leveled all
over the world. The idea is to enable businesses in the
developing world, like the Philippines and Indonesia, to
compete freely with businesses in the developed world ...
What is happening is that the developed world is literally
dumping their excess goods into the markets of the
developing world so that instead of being developed, we
are being conditioned to accept our dependency for what
we eat, for what we wear, for what we need, indeed, for
what we think upon the developed world.

—Aquilino Pimentel, Philippine Senator[2]

INTRODUCTION: THE LOGIC OF GLOBAL ECONOMIC ENGAGEMENT

For advocates of globalization, its benefits are not only obvious but compelling—grounded in theory and tested by experience. Globalization is a
process, therefore, mandating the increasing linkage of national
economies through the following: (1) higher levels of international trade
of goods and services, (2) enhanced cross-border movements of the factors

of production—**foreign direct investments**, and (3) huge financial flows of capital throughout the globe.[3] Together, these three related, though mutually interdependent, processes are the driving force that makes globalization appear to be the inevitable, irreversible, and the overwhelmingly beneficial phenomenon of the twenty-first century.

First, developing countries avail themselves of the opportunities of the global economy by gaining access to investment capital needed to finance economic and social development. Increasing integration into the global economy is the engine of change providing financing for the development of infrastructure desperately needed to get an emerging economy off the ground. This includes not only more traditional types of infrastructure, such as air and sea ports, highways, railroads, and power plants, but also the crucial task of building the information technology infrastructures essential to global business activities in the twenty-first century, such as telecommunications, banking, e-commerce, and the Internet.[4] For economists and governments alike, a state's ability to attract investment capital is seen "as the global market's 'seal of approval' on a country's policies and prospects . . . ."[5]

Second, advocates contend that integration into the global economy is also the best avenue to attain managerial and technological knowledge at a discounted price. This so-called **"latecomer's advantage"** allows developing countries to import the technology they need instead of having to incur the cost of expensive, up-front research and development. Such an unprecedented transfer of technology (and skills) from abroad brings not only new production techniques and innovations, but also employee training that ought to bolster the host nation's stock of human capital. The most obvious effect is the creation of more economic opportunities for women throughout the world. As we argue throughout, globalization is a multidimensional process that has different effects on different groups in the economy.

Third, globalization also offers domestic producers the tools to "break out" from a limited and inequitable national market by providing access to larger and potentially more lucrative markets around the world. Globalization as a process and a fact of economic life promises increasing productivity and improved product quality, and offers the prospect of improving market performance as a means of achieving higher levels of global competitiveness and, thus, prosperity. Specifically, as inefficient jobs and shoddy goods that have been created behind protectionist walls are eliminated, and resources are forced to move from less-productive, labor-intensive manufacturers to more-productive and sophisticated kinds of production, a country's income is enhanced.[6]

Fourth, proponents of globalization believe that heightened levels of global and regional integration will force economically marginal states to overhaul economies and discontinue arcane regulations, protectionist policies, and tariff barriers that have long held back entrepreneurial activities. As the success of a number of Southeast Asian countries documents, protected and inefficient markets pull down the entire economy, retarding manufacturing and other sectors. Globalization offers emerging market economies the tools to liberalize markets through foreign competition that advances the development and growth of the economy.

Fifth, foreign investment is a powerful catalyst for economic change within countries. Globalization helps to force change through a host of domestic changes, including the elimination of bureaucratic inefficiency and unresponsiveness (red tape), nepotism, and corruption. It also helps to displace the economic dominance of hereditary elites, while opening up opportunities for historically disadvantaged groups with limited access to full participation in the economy.[7] In Jamaica, for example, global integration has afforded a substantial segment of its laborers the opportunity to become entrepreneurs in a system that had long been monopolized by a couple of dozen families who owned the majority of the country's wealth.[8]

Finally, globalists envision working with international organizations (such as the WTO, the IMF, and the **World Bank**) and a host of nongovernmental organizations as well as **transnational corporations** to facilitate greater cooperation, and expand access to capital, knowledge, technology, and managerial skills that are all essential to enhance global opportunities.

REALITY CHECK: INTEGRATION IN FINANCE AND TRADE

The end of World War II and the rise of the United States during the Cold War were necessary predicates for globalization in the twenty-first century. As noted earlier, a host of new **intergovernmental organizations** were created to stabilize the world economic system led by the United States. The 1980s and 1990s have seen an explosion in levels of economic liberalization and integration throughout the world: spreading from the economically advanced countries to most of the developing world, and to the transition economies of the former communist bloc.

In terms of commerce, from the conclusion of World War II through the 1970s, advanced industrialized countries, led by the United States—through the **General Agreement on Tariff and Trade (GATT)** established in 1945, which has emerged as the **World Trade Organization** (1994)—worked to systematically lower tariff barriers to trade. By 2010, WTO membership stood at just over 150, with another 30-plus states in the queue to join. In terms of trade, therefore, most countries by 1990 had a trading relationship with most of the other states in the world.[9] At the dawn of the new millennium, not a single economically significant state was still committed to an economic policy centered on autarky and protectionism.

International financial flows are powerful global forces that are fragmented by geography, by history, especially colonialism, and by circumstance. In the latter case, India's domestic economic reforms coincided with huge flows of foreign direct investments from U.S. Internet companies looking for overseas investment opportunities in the 1990s. India's higher education system and the use of English as a national language helped to make India a logical recipient.[10] Since the 1990s, international investors from American, European, and Asian investment companies have increasingly redirected their portfolio allocations toward emerging markets in Latin America, China, and India, as well as in the transition economies of the former communist bloc.[11]

Despite the tremendous increase in the size of transnational economic flows as an indication of the arrival of an integrated global economy, critics continue to insist that national economies are not really globally integrated at all, but comprised of regionally fragmented economies. From this perspective, globalization is not an inclusive, all-encompassing, universal development; it is instead a process that is partial and selectively bypasses large populations and continents, particularly people living in sub-Saharan Africa and parts of Latin America, and Southeast, Central, and Western Asia. Rather than constituting a rising tide lifting all boats toward greater affluence and self-fulfillment, globalization rewards and benefits a few countries, while it deepens and intensifies the economic, political, and cultural (ethnic, linguistic, racial, or religious) divides separating the world's poor from the world's affluent. This is a process, critics contend, that occurs even within prospering developing countries. The economic losers far outnumber the economic winners, who comprise a small part of the entire population. Globalization is thus a pernicious process that will deepen the divisions between the rich and the poor.

A closer examination of economic integration in terms of trade and financial flows reveals that the world is indeed not globalized, but is in fact much more concentrated among the economically advanced countries that make up the three major financial and trading blocs of North America, Western Europe, and East Asia.[12]

While the total stock of foreign direct investment may have increased dramatically (rising almost sevenfold from 1980 to 1997 and increasing from 4 to 12 percent of world GDP during that period),[13] very little has gone to the least developed countries. According to World Bank data, about 70 percent of investments goes from one developed bloc to another (North American, Western Europe, and East Asia), some 20 percent goes to a handful of emerging economies (e.g., Brazil, Mexico, China, and India), and the remainder is divided between the poorest states (much of Africa). These investment allocations and trends prompted Maurice Obstfeld and Alan M. Taylor to conclude that "capital transactions seem to be mostly a rich–rich affair, a process of 'diversification finance' rather than 'development finance.'"[14] The same holds true for trade, where the countries of the European Union, the Asia-Pacific, and North American blocs mostly trade among and between themselves. In other words, world trade is overwhelmingly comprised of goods and services being transported from one economically advanced country and/or region to another. Martin Wolf summed it up best when he stated, "The problem of the world's poorest countries, it appears, is not that they are exploited by multinationals, but rather that they are ignored by them."[15]

DEBATING GLOBALIZATION

Lui Hebron: Greater Economic Integration Is Beneficial

John, globalization has made countries more interconnected and interdependent than ever before. To be sure, the integration of the world's markets is not a new phenomenon. The global economic integration of markets for goods and capital has been an ongoing process for thousands of years. In the last two decades (since 1989), however, globalization has accelerated both the breadth and depth of economic integration. In terms of both trade and financial openness, never before have world markets been so integrated, and this interconnectedness is expected to become even stronger as the process moves forward.

Measured in terms of international capital flows and global trade volumes, the integration of states into the world economy clearly indicates an upward trajectory in the last 20 years. Since 1989, global trade as a share of world gross domestic product has risen from under 10 to over 20 percent, while the share of recipient countries soliciting international capital investments has increased from 25 to almost 40 percent. Within these trends, emerging countries are occupying an ever-larger profile in the global economy: By 2006, they accounted for over 50 percent of the world's annual energy consumption, held 70 percent of the international community's foreign-exchange reserves, and generated more than half of global GDP (measured at purchasing-power parity) (Economist, "Globalization Offspring" April 4, 2007).

Despite the fact that membership to the World Trade Organization, the institutional framework governing global trade, continues to expand (the WTO now has 153 members, while those that are not yet full participants are eagerly seeking to become so) and emerging economies have become more fully engaged (i.e., defining unified goals and coordinating tactics) than ever before, continued progress toward greater global economic integration should not be taken for granted. A case in point is the breakdown of the **Doha Round** of the World Trade Organization. Aimed at ushering in a new era of greater and more inclusive free trade, the talks collapsed when China and India refused to support the latest compromise proposal. The current failure of the Doha Round to reach an accord indicates not only that emerging states have now gained much greater economic power at the bargaining table than in the past (and in turn that the industrialized countries can no longer unilaterally dictate the terms of the agreement), but that a truly integrated system is being established.—Lui

John Stack: Global Economic Integration Is Illusory

Lui, the continuing global economic turmoil (the Great Recession of 2008–2009) is enough to convince many that increasingly integrated global economic structures may not be a particularly appealing prospect when financial markets crash like neatly stacked dominos. Globalization is not necessarily a linear process nor is it inclusive. It divides more effortlessly than it builds affluence and opportunity.

But, just as markets integrate, they also shatter, attenuate, and decouple. The history of globalization has been defined by periods of integration followed by periods of fragmentation and/or decoupling based on war, pandemics, economic upheaval, and natural disasters among other factors. The promise of wealth creating global economic and financial markets needs to be approached with a good deal of skepticism. The Asian economic crisis of the 1990s followed a similar pattern and took nearly a decade to return to 1990s levels. The promise of globally integrated markets is also accompanied by a steep downside—instability and unpredictability. The danger is magnified by a nonstop 24-hour financial system. The 2008 crash amply demonstrates just how swiftly economic dislocations can engulf the world.

International financial flows are powerful economic forces that are fragmented by geography, history, culture, and circumstance. Investment decisions follow global economic trends as reflected in the policy preferences of international financial organizations like the **International Monetary Fund** and the World Bank, and the investment strategies of large institutional investors to be sure. But decisions based on when to invest and where to invest are also guided by hunches, cultural queues, and personal networks. In the 1990s, American, European, and Asian investment houses saw not only strong investment potential in the emerging markets of China and India but also market opportunities in the countries of the former Soviet block as they transitioned to capitalism. In Latin America, the 1990s also ushered in a period of democratic reform and a rising tide of neoliberalism, which were expressed in both politics and economics that valued privatizing public sectors of the economy.

Far from epitomizing the triumph of globally integrated markets, globalization is a partial and selective process bypassing large populations and countries, especially in Africa, Latin America, and Southeast, Central, and Western Asia. Far from lifting all boats, globalization rewards a few countries while intensifying the socioeconomic, linguistic, cultural, and religious divides separating the world's poor from the more privileged emerging economies of the twenty-first century.—John ■

DEBUNKING THE MYTHS: EXCLUSION FROM THE CLUB

Although globalization has increased the size of transnational economic flows, the breadth of international economic integration remains limited. For while the economically advanced countries are more open than ever before, the benefits of greater investment and trade integration continue to elude the economically developing countries of the South. The persistence of the South's lack of integration into the global economy begs the question, "Why does the performance of these emerging economies continue to fall far short of globalists' projections?" Critics of globalization place the failure of developing states to integrate themselves into the global economic system squarely on the shoulders of Western countries that manipulate globalization's institutions (i.e., IMF, WTO, and World Bank) by shaping the globalization agenda to advance their own interests at the expense of the developing world.[16]

In the area of commerce, though the G8 member states (i.e., Canada, France, Germany, Italy, Japan, Russia, the United Kingdom, and the United States) and other rich countries claim to embrace the virtues of free trade, they persist in employing various means—high tariffs, export subsidies, and nontariff measures (including safeguards, standards, and antidumping regulations)—to shelter their own agricultural and labor-intensive industries from global competition. By continuing to maintain significant restrictions on the imports in these basic product areas, in which developing countries enjoy a huge comparative advantage, industrialized states have for all practical purposes blocked developing countries from gaining a greater share in those markets.[17] In so doing, not only are the potential benefits derived from greater economic integration being squandered, but, more disturbingly, the continuation of these practices by the economically advanced states perpetuates considerable damage and destruction to developing countries' economies.

One of the most repugnant practices employed by the advanced economies of the West is the use of "**tariff escalation**," in which the tariff rate increases as value is added through the processing of a product. The World Bank and Oxfam report that while average tariffs on all manufactured imports into developed states are only 3 percent, tariffs on labor-intensive manufactured imports from developing countries are 8 percent.[18] While "tariff escalation" may preserve the manufacturing jobs of the developed states, the practice means that emerging economies are being dissuaded from producing more-advanced, higher value products and moving up the development ladder. Such tariff treatment not only undermines efforts to diversify and expand their product line and export base, but it also prevents developing countries from taking the next step to increase their income and wealth generated from exports.

But the most shameless Western practice, say critics, is the perpetual granting of **agricultural subsidies** by developed countries that not only bestows unmerited benefits to their own farmers, but also weakens prices and diminishes markets for the products of developing states. Even though agriculture for advanced industrialized states is of inconsequential economic importance in terms of the amount of GDP, employment, and trade generated, the scale of subsidies given to farmers and agribusiness is quite staggering. According to data complied by the Organization for Economic Cooperation and Development, the total amount of subsidies given to farmers in industrialized states in 2001 was $311 billion, approximately six times as much as all development assistance, and more than the GDP for all of sub-Saharan Africa, home to the majority of developing countries.[19] This practice becomes a double whammy for developing countries as it not only often destroys local markets when food surpluses are dumped but also undermines their food independence because local growers who cannot compete are driven out of the market.

In a rebuke to the West, Nicholas Stern, chief economist of the World Bank, stated quite bluntly, "This kind of protectionism as practiced by the wealthiest industrialized countries is simply indefensible."[20] If the West is serious about sharing the benefits of globalization, then these protectionist practices must cease, for they hurt not only the development and growth of these emerging economies but also the industrialized states themselves. The elimination of these barriers to trade by the developed North would give the developing South benefits equal to "more than three times the level of official development assistance" rich countries give their poorer neighbors.[21] In other words, these protectionist policies are actually perpetuating the need for the West to continue with developmental aid.

Unfortunately for the developing world and globalization's drive for greater openness and integration, the current round of trade negotiations under the WTO is in tatters. Billed as the "development round," the Doha Round of trade liberalization talks was supposed to make a quantum leap to boost growth and ease poverty in the lesser developed world by lowering barriers to trade in textiles and agricultural products. Launched shortly after the tragic and traumatic events of 9/11 (November 2001), it was hoped that a successfully negotiated treaty, by creating and encouraging opportunities for wealth and alleviating human suffering, would protect the developed states from future attacks. After five years of negotiations, however, the talks collapsed in July 2006. The "official" reason given for the breakdown in negotiations was a stalemate over agricultural subsidies and market access for farm products. In actuality, both sides are equally culpable, with the advanced industrial states' inability to expose their politically powerful farmers to competition and the developing countries' reluctance to lower their own trade barriers to manufactured goods and services as well as agricultural products from the West. Hopefully, some progress can be made toward breaking the deadlock at the latest (November 30–December 2, 2009) meeting in Geneva.

While Doha's collapse is unlikely to lead to either a contraction in global commerce or a breakdown in the trading system, the Round's failure could lead to a "fracturing of the multilateral trading system"[22] or worst yet "introduce a higher level of tension into the global economy."[23] In acknowledging the systemic and domestic hurdles limiting poor countries' integration into the global economy, India's transformation illustrates how both indigenous domestic factors and favorable external conditions can result in a success.

India provides a clear-cut example of successful market-oriented policies. Beginning in the 1980s (and especially in 1991), India undertook reforms designed to reduce government control, free the economy, and open its economy to foreign trade and investment. The result has been higher rates of economic growth and a substantial reduction in poverty.

As perhaps the best example of globalization's ability to spread the wealth, India during the 1990s has created an $8 billion computer software industry, employing 2.8 million people virtually from scratch. India now exports software to 91 countries, including the United States. Observed Thomas L. Friedman, "the broad globalization strategy that India opted for in the early 1990's has succeeded in unlocking the country's incredible brainpower and stimulating sustained growth, which is the best antipoverty program."[24]

In the coming years, the industry is expected to generate 800,000 new jobs and $17 billion for India, according to the consultant McKinsey & Company.[25] In so doing, it could spread the wealth of India's technology revolution beyond the pockets of prosperity that exist today in Bangalore, Hyderabad, and a few other hubs of high technology. Indeed, in the last two years, India has installed reliable high-capacity telephone lines in most of its major cities. That makes it possible for people in this country to communicate with customers throughout the world, by phone or over the Internet.

Even more impressive is the explosive growth in information technology businesses. Since opening its economy to foreign investment and deregulating its domestic industry in 1991, a genuine entrepreneurial spirit has arisen. As a result, not only have millions of jobs been created in private industry, but the corporations that have been established—including Infosys, Tata Consultancy Services, Wipro Spectramind, and Cognizant—are among the world's best. In 2003, the industry reported sales of $16 billion, three-quarters of which came from abroad.[26] According to the *Economist*, "NASSCOM, the Indian IT-industry lobby, has high hopes for these young export industries. By 2008, it thinks they will employ over 4m Indians, generating up to $80 billion-worth of sales."[27]

Previously, India had watched helplessly as its best and brightest graduates had no other alternative but to emigrate abroad in search of jobs in the high-technology sectors, which simply were not available at home. With the take-off of India's nascent high-tech industry, however, a small but growing segment of these highly trained (and prized) computer engineers, programmers, and scientists are choosing to stay home to launch their careers, instead of hustling to the United States or Europe. As a result, India's brain drain is beginning to taper off. "In the 1970s and 1980s there were more opportunities in the U.S., but that's changed now. There are a lot of multinationals here, and they pay very well," said Lalit Malhotra, a professor of physics at the New Delhi campus of the Indian Institute of Technology. "There was a time here when the whole of the computer class would disappear from India after their studies. Now it is more like 50–50."[28]

Moreover, as India's high-tech industry has matured, dozens of expatriates trained in the United States have returned to set up their own firms, offering bright students another attractive alternative at home. And a growing number of big-name American firms[29]—led by Microsoft, which opened a research and development center in Hyderabad in 1998[30]—are taking advantage of newly liberalized Indian laws that allow more foreign investment and joint ventures.

A central concern of this book is that globalization is multidimensional, crossing political, social, cultural, technological, and economic boundaries. As such, it is important to recognize the huge diversity of underdeveloped countries expressed in natural resources; ethnic, racial, and linguistic pluralism; governance structures; and history. Developing countries, therefore, are far from monolithic. Globalization's impact shows huge variation across continents, within regions, and among political systems. Globalization is not a process in which one size fits all.

CONCLUSION: INCOMPLETE INTEGRATION

For many elites and "nonelites" in both the advanced and developing/emerging economies, there seems to be a willingness to accept that most of the time economic integration into the global economy through international flows of trade, finance, and liberal (promarket) economic policies represents the best course of action in order to stimulate economic development and growth. And though globalists concede the unequal distribution of globalization's benefits, they nevertheless insist that the process's deficiencies will eventually correct themselves. This assumption is an inaccurate assessment of previous historical experience—for global economic integration is not a natural process. Rather, it is the product of an ad hoc, decentralized, bottom-up process. And since globalization (and all its benefits) is not destined, it is neither inevitable nor unstoppable. Rather it is a choice: a decision by government to engage in the global economic system to enhance its economic well-being.

As Kofi Annan said, "Globalization is real. It is highly beneficial to some. It is potentially beneficial to all, but only if states work together to put its benefits within reach of all their people."[31] Given the fact that globalization's benefits are not being universally distributed and shared, however, reform of the current system is imperative.

As indicated by the discussion above, advanced industrialized states without question must bear some responsibility for the inferior performance of the developing countries. And to a certain extent they have. In principle, developed countries have acknowledged that they need to open their markets to the goods that many developing states have a comparative advantage to produce, namely agricultural products and textiles. Beyond opening up their markets and acknowledging the unfair structure currently in place, the advanced economies of the North can demonstrate their commitment to genuinely aid the developing world by greatly reducing, if not eliminating, their farm subsidies and pushing for greater liberalization on textiles and services at the Doha Round of multilateral trade negotiations.

For developing states, the problem is institutional and not economic. As former Colombian diplomat Oswaldo De Rivera pointed out: "It has become increasingly evident that merely liberalising, deregulating and privatising does not guarantee the formation of a critical mass of investment capable of modernising technologically the primary, backward economies."[32] This entails the creation and wide-ranging modernization of the institutions needed to underpin their markets.

First, developing nations must eliminate corruption and strengthen democratic institutions by instituting policies and practices that make their governments accountable and transparent. As the World Bank notes, countries deemed to have good investment climates—as characterized by "rule of law, quality of the regulatory regime, government effectiveness, and political stability"[33]—are the same ones that tended to attract and receive an increasing share of foreign direct investment during the 1990s.

Second, international economic integration and prosperity also require economic freedom. According to the Fraser Institute's Economic Freedom of the World Report,[34] "Countries with the greatest economic freedom saw much higher growth rates, between 1990 and 2000, than their less free peers."[35]

Third, governments in developing countries must also be willing to enact friendlier economic policies and practices for domestic businesses. A 2004 report by the World Bank places the blame on poor states' inability to develop on the "thicket of regulation" currently required in most developing countries. A World Bank report noted how the act of simplifying governmental regulations increased new businesses. It pointed to Ethiopia, where the numbers of new businesses increased by nearly 50 percent after reducing red tape.[36]

International financial arrangements are not, however, set in stone, as the decision by the G8 states (at their 2005 annual summit meeting in Gleneagles, Scotland) to forgive the debt of some African countries shows.[37] Tony Blair, former UK prime minister, understood the importance of addressing poverty and AIDS in Africa, especially in light of the United Kingdom's support for the war in Iraq. In so doing, he tapped into powerful humanitarian sentiments that, in fact, reflected the activism of a host of NGOs advocating for "structural changes" that will benefit desperately poor countries.[38] As Martin Wolf observed, "Yet none of these difficulties, real though they are, is sufficient reason for giving up on the aim of greater net capital flows to poorer countries. These should be treated as constraints to be lifted, not one to be accepted. For if they are treated as binding and reinforced with capital controls, the world's poorest people will find it still more difficult to escape their plight."[39]

The challenges in bringing about greater cooperation between the North and the South are formidable, given the distrust on both sides. Nevertheless, if the promises of globalization are to be fulfilled, reform of the system must be undertaken. Joseph Stiglitz advocates undertaking these reforms to ensure the creation of a better, safer, and more equitable world.[40] The alternative could possibly be the breakdown of the system, if not worse.

KEY TERMS

agricultural subsidies 38
Doha Round 36
Foreign Direct
   Investments (FDI) 33
General Agreement on
   Tariff and Trade
   (GATT) 34

Intergovernmental
   Organizations
   (IGOs) 34
International Monetary
   Fund (IMF) 37
latecomer's advantage 33
tariff escalation 38

Transnational
   Corporations
   (TNCs) 34
World Bank 34
World Trade Organization
   (WTO) 34

FIVE QUESTIONS TO CONSIDER

1. What is meant by the logic of global economic engagement? Provide three examples of how it affects key participants in the global economy?
2. Why are international financial flows important? To what extent do they represent a constructive dimension of globalization? How important is economic trade as a key dimension of globalization?
3. To what extent should globalization be used to aid the poorest segments of the world economy? Is poverty a necessary consequence of globalization?
4. How should a country best prepare itself for entry into the global economy? What are the "fundamentals" that supporters of globalization envision as a way to promote economic growth among developing countries?
5. Why do some countries and some regions seem to benefit more from globalization?

FURTHER READINGS

Aaditya Mattoo, Arvind Subramanian, "From Doha to the Next Bretton Woods: A New Multilateral Trade Agenda," *Foreign Affairs* 88(1) (January/February 2009): 15–26.

> World leaders may be tempted to revive the failed Doha Round of international trade talks. But Doha does not address the world's urgent economic problems, first and foremost, the current financial crisis. A global conversation must occur—a Bretton Woods II—capable of addressing the concerns of traditional and emerging powers alike.

Joshua Cooper Ramo, "The Beijing Consensus," The Foreign Policy Center Spring 2004, http://fpc.org.uk/fsblob/244.pdf.

> A new Beijing Consensus is emerging with new perspectives on politics, development, and the global balance of power. It is driven by a ruthless willingness to innovate, a strong belief in sovereignty and multilateralism, and a desire to accumulate the tools of "asymmetric power projection" to limit U.S. political and military action in its region.

Peter D. Sutherland, "Transforming Nations; How the WTO Boosts Economies and Opens Societies," *Foreign Affairs* 87(2) (March/April 2008).

> The power of the WTO to aid national transformation is a reality. Many developing countries measure their success in the WTO's Doha Round of trade negotiations by the extent to which they avoid obligations to open up their economies. But WTO's ability to encourage radical market, institutional, and regulatory reform is politically incorrect.

John Williamson, "The Washington Consensus as Policy Prescription for Development." A lecture in the series "Practitioners of Development" delivered at the World Bank on January 13, 2004 Institute for International Economics.

> Williamson, the British economist who originally coined the term "Washington Consensus," discusses the ongoing debate regarding the term's impact on economic development and the globalization process. In so doing, Williamson responds to the concept's critics as well as the misinterpretation and misapplication of the term's key policy components.

Martin Wolf, *The Making of a Mess: Who Broke Global Finance, and Who Should Pay for It? Fixing Global Finance.* Johns Hopkins University Press, 2008.

Global imbalances cause financial crises. Wolf outlines the steps for ending this destructive cycle. He reveals the links between the microeconomics of finance and the macroeconomics of the balance of payments, demonstrating how the subprime lending crisis in the United States fits into an established pattern resulting in economic crises.

NOTES

1. Quoted from Speech Delivered at Federal Reserve Bank of Kansas City's Thirtieth Annual Economic Symposium, Jackson Hole, Wyoming August 25, 2006, electronic version.
2. Quoted from "Globalization: Gobbling up the Developing World," Speech Delivered at the Symposium on Globalization. Quezon City, The Philippines, February 18, 2002, electronic version.
3. Jagdish Bhagwati, *In Defence of Globalisation*. Oxford, UK: Oxford University Press, 2004; Philippe Legrain, *Open World: The Truth about Globalization*. London: Abacus, 2002; Brink Lindsey, *Against the Dead Hand: The Uncertain Struggle for Global Capitalism*. New York: Wiley, 2002; John Micklethwait and Alan Wooldridge, *A Future Perfect: The Challenge and Promise of Globalization*. New York: Random House, 2002; Richard Langhorne, *The Coming of Globalization: Its Evolution and Contemporary Consequences*. New York: Palgrave, 2001; Johan Norberg, *In Defense of Global Capitalism*. Stockholm: Timbro, 2001; Mary Kaldor, " 'Civilising' Globalization? The Implications of the 'Battle in Seattle'," *Millennium* 29(1) (2000): 105–115; Peter Schwatz, Peter Leyden, and Joel Hyatt, *The Long Boom*. Reading, MA: Perseus Books, 2000; Robert Gilpin, *The Challenge of Global Capitalism: The World Economy in the 21st Century*. Princeton: Princeton University Press, 2000; David Held, Anthony McGrew, David Goldblatt, and Jonathan Perraton, *Global Transformations: Politics, Economics and Culture*. Stanford, CA: Stanford University Press, 1999; Jan Aarte Scholte, *Globalization: A Critical Introduction*. New York: Palgrave, 2000; Herman M. Schwartz, *States Versus Markets: The Emergence of a Global Economy*, 2nd ed. New York: St. Martin's Press, 2000; David Held and Anthony McGrew, eds., *The Globalization Reader*. Oxford: Polity, 2000; Richard A. Higgot and Anthony Payne, eds., *The New Political Economy of Globalization: Vols. 1 & 2*. London: Elgar, 2000; R. J. Barry Jones, *The World Turned Upside Down? Globalization and the Future of the State*. Manchester, UK: Manchester University Press, 2000; Clare Cutler, Viginia Hauf, and Tony Porter, eds., *Private Authority and International Affairs*. Albany: State University of New York Press, 1999; Richard Rosecrance, *The Rise of the Virtual State: Wealth and Power in the Coming Century*. New York: Basic Books, 1999; David A. Smith, Dorothy J. Solinger, and Steven C. Topik, eds., *States and Sovereignty in the Global Economy*. London: Routledge, 1999; and Thomas L. Friedman, *The Lexus and the Olive Tree*. New York: Farrar, Straus & Giroux, 1999.
4. Daniel T. Griswold, "The Blessings and Challenges of Globalization," *World and I* 15(9) (September 2000): 266–281.
5. *Economist*, "The Cutting Edge," February 22, 2001, electronic version.
6. Bruce R. Scott, "The Great Divide in the Global Village," *Foreign Affairs* 80 (1) (January 2001): 160–177.
7. Amy L. Chua, "Markets, Democracy, and Ethnicity: Toward a New Paradigm for Law and Development," *Yale Law Journal*, 108 (October 1998): 1–107.
8. E. M. Brown, "Learning to Love the I.M.F.," *New York Times*, April 18, 2000, electronic version.

9. T. Nierop, *Systems and Regions in Global Politics: An Empirical Study of Diplomacy, International Organization and Trade, 1950–1991*. New York: Wiley, 1994.

10. Thomas L. Friedman, *The World Is Flat: A Brief History of the Twenty-first Century*, New York: Farrar, Straus & Giroux, 2005.

11. Nierop, *Systems and Regions in Global Politics*.

12. Paul Hirst and Graham Thompson, *Globalization in Question: The International Economy and the Possibilities of Governance*, 2nd ed. Cambridge: Polity Press, 1999; and David Held, Anthony McGrew, David Goldblatt, and Jonathan Perraton, *Global Transformation: Politics, Economics and Culture*. Stanford, CA: Stanford University Press, 1999.

13. Scott, "The Great Divide in the Global Village."

14. Maurice Obstfeld and Alan M. Taylor, "Globalization and Capital Markets," National Bureau of Economic Research Working Paper 8846 (March 2002): 59.

15. Martin Wolf, *Why Globalization Works*. New Haven: Yale Nota Bene, 2005: 115.

16. Joseph P. Stiglitz, *Globalization and Its Discontents*. New York: W. W. Norton, 2003; and John J. Mearsheimer, *The Tragedy of Great Power Politics*. New York: W. W. Norton, 2001.

17. According to World Bank figures, tariffs on imports of agricultural commodities from developing countries hovers around 14 percent. World Bank, *Global Economic Prospects and the Developing Countries 2002: Making Trade Work for the World's Poor*. Washington, DC: World Bank, 2002.

18. World Bank, *Global Economic Prospects and the Developing Countries 2002: Making Trade Work for the World's Poor*. Washington, DC, 2002; and Oxfam, *Rigged Rules and Double Standards: Trade, Globalization and the Fight Against Poverty*. Oxford: Oxfam International, 2002.

19. United Nations Development Programme Human Development Report 2003, *Millennium Development Goals: A Compact Among Nations to End Human Poverty*. New York: Oxford University Press, 2003.

20. Quoted from William Drozdiak, "Poor Nations May Not Buy Trade Talks," *Washington Post*, May 15, 2001: E01.

21. Mike Moore, "How to Lift the Barriers to Growth," *Financial Times*, May 13, 2001, electronic version.

22. Paul Blustein, "Trade Deal Looks More Like a Distant Dream," *Washington Post*, July 4, 2006: D01.

23. Tom Wright and Steven R. Weisman, "Trade Talks Fail Over an Impasse on Farm Tariffs," *New York Times*, July 25, 2006, electronic version.

24. Thomas L. Friedman, "Making India Shine," *New York Times*, May 20, 2004, electronic version.

25. Cited in Mark Landler, "Hi, I'm in Bangalore (But I Dare Not Tell)," *New York Times*, March 21, 2001, electronic version.

26. *Economist*, "The Place to Be," November 11, 2004, electronic version.

27. *Economist*, "Men and Machines," November 11, 2004, electronic version.

28. Cited from Pamela Constable, "For Best and Brightest, Staying Home Rivals a High-Tech Job in U.S.," *Washington Post*, September 14, 2000: A23.

29. General Electric, American Express, Intel.

30. The Microsoft Corporation announced that it was significantly expanding its software development operations in India as it opened a new campus near Hyderabad, its second-largest campus after its headquarters in Redmond, Washington. Saritha Rai, "Microsoft Expands Operations in India," *New York Times*, November 16, 2004, electronic version.

31. Kofi A. Annan, address before the UN 2000 Millennium Summit, quoted from the *International Herald Tribune*, September 5, 2000, electronic version.

32. Oswaldo De Rivera, *The Myth of Development*. London: Zed Books, 2003: 91.

33. World Bank, *Global Economic Prospects and the Developing Countries 2003: Investing to Unlock Global Opportunities*. Washington, DC: World Bank, 2003: 68.

34. The Fraser Institute's Economic Freedom of the World Report is an annual publication based on detailed assessments of 37 variables (low taxes, protection of property rights, ability to trade freely, etc.) to measure economic freedom. *Economist*, "The Prosperity League," June 20, 2002.

35. Cited from the *Economist*, "The Prosperity League," June 20, 2002, electronic version.

36. Editorial, "Red Tape Stifles Third World," *New York Times*, September 13, 2004, electronic version.

37. John Daniszewski, "Activists Plan 'Final Push' to Pressure G-8," *Los Angeles Times*, July 6, 2005, electronic version.

38. *Economist*, "Helping Africa," June 14, 2005, electronic version; and *Economist*, "To Give or Forgive," June 16, 2005, electronic version.

39. Wolf, *Why Globalization Works*, 85.

40. Joseph Stiglitz, "We Have to Make Globalization Work for All," *Yale Global*, October 17, 2003, electronic version.

Growth and Development

Globalisation used to mean, by and large, that business expanded from developed to emerging economies. Now it flows in both directions, and increasingly also from one developing economy to another.

—*The Economist*[1]

Chile has the greatest gap between the rich and the poor after Brazil. The advocates of globalization as we know it emphasize economic growth. But growth itself is no guarantee that people also benefit from that growth.

—*Sara Larraín, Coordinator of the Chilean Ecological Action Network (RENACE)*[2]

INTRODUCTION: THE NEOLIBERAL PROMISE AND HOPE

Neoliberal economic theory is premised on the belief that globalization benefits everyone by bringing about greater wealth and well-being on a global scale.[3] This proposition suggests that integration into the global economy based on trade in goods, services, and capital, combined with the adoption of promarket economic policies, results in economic development, in turn, leading to increasing economic capacity and the reduction of poverty.[4] According to Robert Gilpin, "[t]he most successful economies among the less developed countries are precisely those that have put their houses in order and [have] participate[d] most aggressively in the world economy."[5] On the other hand, those countries that have spurned globalization have stood still or regressed. As Joseph Nye observed, "Although free trade is not alone sufficient, it is difficult to find any countries that have prospered while closing themselves off from globalization."[6]

The proposition that integration into the global economy is the best way to bootstrap economic opportunities and raise standards of living for people in the developing world is based on three sets of long-standing assumptions. First, by exploiting international opportunities, integration into the global economy provides for a more efficient allocation of resources.[7] Developing economies can take full advantage of their tremendous **comparative advantage**—huge reserves of cheap labor. Second, **human capital** development, which is an indispensable precursor to growth in developing economies, can occur. In other words, integration into the global economy not only brings new employment opportunities—jobs and wages—but also bolsters employee training and development of skills that frequently spill over into other areas. Thus, the receiving country strengthens its stock of human capital and builds more economic opportunities for its workers, including women. Lastly, globalization facilitates the spread of a more stable macroeconomic environment. Central to this assumption is the belief that secure property rights help to restrain nationalist and protectionist governmental policies, resulting in a political and economic climate conducive to attracting private investment and, thus, leading to further economic growth. Cumulatively greater levels of global economic engagement, it is argued, leads to the unprecedented transfer of capital from rich to poor states, thus allowing millions of people in developing countries to experience substantial increases in economic standards of living.[8]

REALITY CHECK: DEVELOPMENT, GROWTH, AND POVERTY REDUCTION

How has globalization fared in terms of expected economic development, income growth, and poverty reduction in developing countries? Several systematic studies conducted lend support to the neoliberal view that free-market policies and integration into the global economy do indeed result in economic growth and higher incomes for the poor.

Jeffrey Sachs and Andrew Warner in their 1995 study of 117 countries found that those countries that maintained open economies grew much faster than those that remained closed. Specifically, developing countries with open economies throughout the 1970s and 1980s grew at an average annual rate of 4.5 percent, compared with an average growth rate of 0.7 percent for closed economies.[9] A 1998 study by the Organization for Economic Cooperation and Development (OECD) also concluded that open-trading states grew on average twice as fast as those relatively closed to trade.[10]

Jeffrey Frankel and David Romer came to similar conclusions, finding that trade exerts "a qualitatively large and robust positive effect on income." In a study of 150 countries, Frankel and Romer found that increasing the ratio of trade to GDP by 1 percentage point raises income per person by between 0.5 and 2 percent.[11]

Reinforcing these positive trends is a 2001 World Bank study on the performance of developing economies during the 1990s, which cites the importance of trade as a measure of globalization.[12] According to that report, the most important indicator was a country's ratio of international trade to overall national income, thus indicating the significance of foreign trade in terms of the state's whole economy. In the case of the two-dozen developing nations (that are home to 3 billion people) for which trade was most significant, there was an average increase in per capita GNP of nearly 5 percent a year—striking better than the 2 percent increase registered by the developed nations.[13] It was also dramatically better than the rest of the developing world where trade was far less significant, and GNP actually declined by 1 percent a year over the same period—a devastating blow to already economically disadvantaged states.[14]

Perhaps the strongest indication of linkage between openness and economic growth is a study conducted by two economists of the World Bank's Development Research Group. David Dollar and Aart Kraay found that over the last 40 years, those less developed countries that have embraced globalization have undergone significant progress in their development—specifically, an acceleration in per capita income growth:[15] "The aggregate annual per capita growth rate of the globalizing group accelerated steadily from one percent in the 1960s to three percent in the 1970s, four percent in the 1980s, and five percent in the 1990s."[16] More heartening is the revelation that gaps between upper- and lower-income people stayed reasonably steady in globalizing countries, an indication that the poor were not falling even further behind. According to Martin Wolf, "manufactures rose from less than a quarter of developing country exports in 1980 to more than 80 per cent by 1998 [while] the countries that strongly increased their participation in the world economy have doubled their ratios of trade to income."[17] Throughout the 1980s and 1990s, the quantity of exports from developing states expanded more rapidly than those from developed countries, meaning that an increasing share of world trade had shifted to these emerging economies.[18]

Finally, during the 1990s, the economies of the globalizers have grown more than twice as fast as the advanced industrialized countries, the world's most affluent states. These trends have continued into the new millennium. The *Economist* reports that in 2005, the combined GDP for emerging economies "grew in current dollar terms by $1.6 trillion, more than the $1.4 trillion increase of developed economies. And there is more to this than just China and India: these two countries together accounted for only one-fifth of the total increase in emerging economies' GDP" in 2005.[19] Furthermore, the IMF projects growth for the developing world to be 6.9 percent in 2006—more than double the 3 percent growth rate of the developed states.[20] The nonglobalizers, by way of contrast, have grown only half as fast.[21] Indeed, the nonglobalizing group saw growth decline from "3.3 percent per year in the 1970s to 0.8 percent in the 1980s, recovering to only 1.4 percent in the 1990s."[22]

How has globalization fared with regard to poverty reduction and enhancing human welfare? Over the past two decades, countries that have successfully integrated their economies with the global market have reduced poverty and global inequality. A major study addressing how globalization has affected 34 developing and developed countries concluded that "1.4 billion people escaped absolute poverty as a result of economic growth associated with globalization."[23]

Recent studies independently conducted by Xavier Sala-i-Martin and Surjit Bhalla provide further evidence of reductions in global poverty and substantial decline in inequality between 1970 and 1998.[24] By 2003, "only 23 percent of the global population lives on less than $1 a day, compared with 30 percent in 1990."[25] Supporters of globalization frequently cite these accomplishments as further proof that economic globalization reduces, rather than increases, poverty.

It is important for us to note that these tremendous breakthroughs in the reduction of poverty have not been universally realized, but are region specific. World Bank data indicate that while some regions of the developing world have indeed achieved levels of growth high enough to dramatically reduce absolute poverty in recent decades, other regions have not fared nearly so well. For East and South Asia, the proportion in extreme poverty fell sharply, from 28 percent in 1978 to 9 percent in 1998 and from 51 percent in 1977–1978 to 26 percent in 1999–2000, respectively.[26] Since 2003, poverty in Latin America has declined "by 13 million people to 213 million, or 41 percent of the population," according to a 2005 UN study.[27] In contrast, for Africa, poverty has actually increased. Despite repeated pledges by the industrialized world of poverty alleviation for Africa made over the last two decades, the proportion of the continent's population living on $1 per day or less has increased from 46.7 percent in 1981 to 46.9 percent in 1990 to 49.3 percent by 2001.[28] Perhaps most disturbing is the fact that "[t]his occurred at the same time that total world income increased by an average of 2.5 percent annually."[29]

Of the "globalizing" group of countries experiencing rapid development and income growth over the last two decades, the stunning economic progress accomplished by China[30] and India stand out. John Micklethwait and Alan Wooldridge report that China's and India's economies in 2004 were growing by 8.8 percent and 6 percent, respectively.[31] More importantly, by liberalizing their economies and opening up their borders to foreign trade and investment, India and China have liberated millions of people from poverty. Indeed, virtually all the poverty reduction in the developing world during the 1990s occurred in just two nations, India and China. The *Economist* concluded that "[s]uch globalisation has already narrowed the overall gap between North and South."[32]

A survey of the world today confirms that countries that have integrated themselves into the global economy tend to be more prosperous than states less economically open and engaged. The wealthiest states and regions of the world—Western Europe, North America (the United States and Canada), and East Asia (Japan, Hong Kong, Taiwan, South Korea, and Singapore)—are all firmly engaged in the process of globalization. Many of the countries of the world that have failed to generate sustained growth, such as North Korea, Cuba, and the states of sub-Saharan Africa, have either turned their backs on global integration or have not fully taken advantage of the opportunities presented by globalization as in the case of the African countries—overwhelmed by social and economic problems such as AIDS/HIV, punishing terms of trade, and unstable governmental systems, to name but a few.

DEBATING GLOBALIZATION

Lui Hebron: Globalization Promotes Development

John, since the turn of the twenty-first century, the economic performance of emerging markets has far exceeded projections. By 2005, emerging states' share of global GDP at purchasing-power-parity (PPP) accounted for greater than 50 percent of the world economy for the first time. The enormous and rapid growth rates of emerging economies provide a clear indication that the benefits of globalization are now clearly a two-way street, as well as signaling the beginning of a shift in the balance of power between the developing and developed worlds.

A major reason why emerging countries have become a force in the global economy can be attributed to the ability of their homegrown multinational companies to successfully challenge the dominant position of transnational corporations from the developed world. The rise of multinational companies from emerging economies has two implications for development and growth. First, firms from Brazil, China, India, Mexico, Russia, and other developing states in industries from cement to consumer electronics, from steel to telecommunications, and from accounting to aircraft and automobile manufacture, have marched onto the global stage to successfully compete against their industrialized state counterparts.

Second, with multinational companies from emerging states now either acquiring or merging with businesses in developed countries, the developing world is no longer viewed as merely a destination, but increasingly a source of capital and investment. In 2007, Indian firms bought over 30 foreign companies in excess of $10 billion combined, while Russian corporations spent over $11 billion in its acquisitions abroad (Economist, "Globalization's Offspring" April 4, 2007). To be sure, Global South investments remain relatively small in comparison to investments from the Global North. Nevertheless, emerging market investments are growing at a much faster pace than those coming from most other regions. Based on current trends, emerging market companies are projected to account for one-third of the world's biggest firms by 2020.

In sum, globalization has not only expanded the consumer base by opening new markets for transnational corporations, but the process has also been instrumental in promoting the rise of dynamic and aggressive multinational companies emerging from the developing world. And with two-thirds of global economic growth originating from emerging states in recent years, economists and policy makers increasingly view the Global South as an economic force to be reckoned with.—Lui

John Stack: Globalization Destabilizes Economies

Lui, on a fundamental level we agree. Change is occurring in the global system. The rise of developing economies led by China, India, Brazil, Mexico, and other countries is a signal development in world economics and politics. Few could have imagined such a transformation just 20 years ago following the collapse of the Soviet Union in 1989. But the Achilles' heel of the unprecedented economic expansion of the global economy and the rise of developing economies was the absence of structures that could constrain financial markets and assure long-term economic stability. The price to be paid for a more stable global economic structure was less breathtaking rates of growth and a regulatory framework to be sure. Is it a price worth paying? I vote in the affirmative! The remarkable growth rates you cite, therefore, came at the price of a global economic collapse—the worst since the Great Depression in 1929. In the wake of the collapse, there was untold human suffering across the planet.

As Fareed Zakaria explains in the new preface to the paperback edition of *The Post-American World*, published (Norton) in 2009, the past 20 years were accompanied by general conditions of political stability and extraordinary technological innovation. The global economy grew from $31 trillion in 1999 to $62 trillion in 2008, spreading wealth across the planet. The post–World War II international economic system provided an overall structure in the form of the General Agreement on Tariffs and Trade (GATT)—now the World Trade Organization, the International Monetary Fund, and the World Bank. The emerging economies entered this existing global framework and prospered.

What was missing from this overall governance structure were institutions charged with regulating financial markets. In other words, the missing piece of the framework was a regulatory structure capable of constraining the greed of global financial markets originating in the United States and Europe and that were exported globally with lightening speed. The economic potential of the emerging economies is extraordinary. But laissez faire economics in the form of deregulated, and underregulated, financial markets pose a threat to future economic growth and political stability.—John ■

DEBUNKING THE MYTHS: WHY THE NEOLIBERAL MODEL FAILS POOR STATES

Given the overwhelmingly positive effects of globalization, why has not every country embraced it as the most powerful force for positive economic change, income growth, and the reduction of poverty? Why have the world's most powerful international organizations, both public and private, not moved to implement globalizing strategies? The answer points to the uneven results, anticipated and unanticipated consequences, and anxieties raised by globalization as a process and as conceptualized in neoliberal economic thought. For while some states have been able to reap spectacular benefits from engaging in the global economy, most developing countries have been excluded from the economic benefits of globalization.[33] And for many developing countries that have harnessed the economic benefits of globalization, successful economic development has come because local decision makers chose to follow indigenous paths to globalization, in effect, implementing a modified, if you will, an "Asianized" version of neoliberal theory and practice.[34]

The "success stories" of global emersion and the impressive rates of economic development and income growth have not been universally achieved. As David Landes notes, developing countries, since decolonization, have attained a broad variance of results: "These have ranged from the spectacular successes of East Asia," and South and Southeast Asia, to modest and "mixed results in Latin America" to unconditional "regression in much of Africa" and continued abject failures and misery in much of the Middle East, Central Asia, and Russia.[35] Empirical evidence seems to support this position. Let us examine each of these regions in turn.

For Robert Gilpin, "[t]he poster children for successful economic development are, of course, the so-called **East Asian 'tigers'** or newly industrializing countries (NICs)."[36] East Asian development policies, according to Gilpin, "have worked with the market and not against it. They have demonstrated that the liberals are quite correct in their emphasis on the benefits of the price mechanism in the efficient allocation of resources."[37]

By embracing international trade as an engine of economic growth, some historically poor countries of East Asia have by Joseph Nye's estimate "used networks of globalization to greatly increase their wealth and status. . . ."[38] In so doing, the so-called "tiger" economies of East Asia have entered the ranks of industrialized, economically developed countries in an amazingly short period of time that would have been undreamed of a few decades ago. Taking South Korea as a specific case study, Joseph Stiglitz notes that in 30 years ". . . countries like Korea saw their per capita incomes increase eight-fold. Poverty was almost eliminated, literacy had become universal, health standards had been improved, life expectancy had increased—all these gains were based on globalization."[39] As a result, East Asia is the only developing region where incomes of the less developed countries are converging toward those of the economically developed countries.[40]

Unfortunately, East Asia's model of development by creating growth has proven to be very much the exception rather than the rule. In Latin America, while Chile has experienced nearly two decades of sustained economic growth,[41] unrivaled elsewhere in the region (and Mexico and Brazil have also enjoyed tremendous growth in recent years), the rest of the continent has remained stuck in the cycle of poverty and unequal distribution of income and wealth—hurt by a combination of poor infrastructure, human skills, and capital formation along with misguided governmental policies.

Likewise, sub-Saharan Africa, where civil war, political instability, the failure of the public sector, autocratic rule, and corrupt regimes are a fact of life, has not benefited much from the globalization process: "per capita incomes today are lower than they were in 1970"[42] and the region has also witnessed "their market share decline."[43] As George Monbiot noted, "[o]ver the past twenty years the forty-nine poorest countries in the world have seen their share of world trade fall by about half."[44]

Promoting Inequality and Poverty

Though acknowledging that some gains have been realized—that a few nations have made considerable progress in generating wealth and opportunity for their peoples in the last decade—critics charge that whatever the claims of globalization's advocates, a substantial segment of the world has not fared well—that there remains unequal access and benefits to the rewards promoted to developing and underdeveloped countries for engaging in the globalizing economy. The repercussions are an expansion of global inequality and a concentration of abject poverty in the states that either have failed to board on the globalization express or have joined the globalizing world order but have not been able to benefit fully from it.[45]

Antiglobalists have offered solid evidence that global economic gaps actually widened despite any trends in greater economic globalization, and some argue if anything, globalization is the prime force responsible for developing governments' inability to satisfy even citizens' most fundamental needs.[46] The World Development Report of the United Nations Development Program documents that for many countries, the 1990s—far from being a period of economic growth and opportunities—were in reality years of despair. The United Nations Development Report (UNDP) statistics show that the share of world income going to the globe's poorest states slipped from 2.4 percent in 1960 to 1.1 percent in 1994.[47]

Critics further document how globalization, accompanied by the creation of a global market and the international division of labor and production, has resulted in a sharp rise in inequality between the world's richest and poorest countries, even though it connects more people than ever before. According to United Nations Development Program 2002 data, in 1960, a fifth of the world's people who live in the richest countries had 30 times more income than the fifth living in the poorest countries. By 1997, this income gap had more than doubled to 74 to 1. In like manner, one-fifth of the world's people live in the high-income countries that have 86 percent of the world's gross domestic product (GDP), whereas the poorest fifth received only 1 percent.[48] World Bank 2002 data report that the average income in the richest 20 countries is 37 times that in the poorest 20—a ratio that has doubled in the past 40 years.[49] Finally, Ignacio Ramonet, Director del mensual Le Monde diplomatique, Paris, reported, "The richest fifth of the world's population owns 80 percent of the world's resources, while the poorest fifth owns barely .5 percent."[50]

Examining these trends in regional terms, one finds that even as North America, Western Europe, and East and South Asia experience unprecedented prosperity, much of Africa slips further into poverty. As reported by Jeff Madrick, presently "fifty-four countries are poorer, as measured by per capita G.D.P." Of this group, "Sub-Saharan Africa is worst off, with per-capita G.D.P. falling in 20 nations."[51] Indeed, in some African countries, living conditions have fallen not just in relative terms but in absolute ones too during the 1980s and 1990s. Many African states actually endured a depreciation in living standards as measured by per capita gross national product, and in some cases to below pre-independence (1930–1950) levels.[52] Finally, it should be pointed out that even for those countries that have made significant progress in alleviating poverty, there remains large zones of deprivation, especially in less accessible regions and in isolated rural areas. By all accounts, it would appear that "[e]conomic liberalization has increased the wealth of a minority without a corresponding gain for the majority."[53]

If globalization's efforts in combating income inequality have been less than stellar, its efforts to reduce poverty rates are even worse. Despite increasing globalization, the number of persons subsisting in absolute poverty—living on less than $1 per day—continues to hover at around 1.2 billion people—a fifth of the world population—while an additional 2.8 billion live on less than $2 per day according to the World Bank.[54] The most prominent setbacks in poverty reduction have been in Africa, "where 29 of the 34 lowest-ranked countries are located" and "where dozens of countries are worse off than 20 years ago"[55] as government debts continue to soar, conflicts are never-ending, levels of political legitimacy decline, the HIV/AIDS epidemic propagates, and development ventures fail.

The persistence, if not increase, of economic marginalization and inequality among, between, and within countries has had the consequence of condemning the African continent to a perpetual state of abject poverty and hopelessness.

Additionally, the rate of hunger has increased in 21 nations, while about 840 million people in the world are malnourished.[56] The proportion of children who die under the age of 5 has risen in 14 nations.[57] Furthermore, over 1 billion people do not have adequate access to safe water, and an additional 2 billion lack adequate sanitation.[58] These figures, combined with the fact that "about 2 billion do not have adequate access to essential medicines,"[59] have more or less subjugated these people to an existence of "disease and premature death."[60] In surveying the process of globalization, Ignacio Ramonet observed, "Poverty, illiteracy, violence, and illness are on the rise. That, it seems, is the brave new world of globalization."[61]

The development index itself, which almost always rises over time, fell in 11 nations—Congo, Lestho, Zimbabwe, Kenya, Tanzania, Ivory Cost, Zambia, Malawi, Central African Republic, Guinea-Bissau, and Burkina Faso.[62]

So even if globalization's proponents are correct, the process's objective to bring about a little less inequality and modest poverty reduction via greater trade and investments has not been very effective in a world where, if current trends persist, 2.8 billion people living on 2 dollars or less per day (about half of the world's population) is simply an unacceptable level of global poverty. Is it any wonder that Joseph Stiglitz pointedly quipped, "[i]f trade agreements [and we may add foreign investments] were bringing prosperity to developing countries, they did not seem to know it."[63]

States, Development, and Globalization

If we were to judge the globalization process in terms of results, the verdict would, at best, be mixed, if not a devastating indictment of its impact on the world's poorest countries and peoples. Indeed, the globalists' bold proclamation of globalization's "promise" to bring about economic development, income growth, and poverty reduction to the world's developing countries has not lived up to its potential.

The toughest question that must be addressed by proponents of globalization is this: Why have so few countries been able to exploit all the economic benefits that globalization appears to offer? As noted earlier, East Asia accounts for many of the gains in development achieved by countries through the 1990s, with huge advances for India and China in the first years of the twenty-first century. The Asian example has been held up as an indication of how countries can become engaged in the globalization process and reap enormous benefits, including economic development, income growth, and the reduction of poverty.

The problem with this conclusion is that the highly touted Asian Tiger economies did not reach their phenomenal levels of economic growth simply by following the free-market prescriptions of the "**Washington Consensus**." Rather, the "secret of their success" lies with their ability to effectively implement what has come to be known as the "developmental state model" of economic growth. As its name would indicate, the developmental state considers the state rather than the market as the essential institution that enables developing countries to achieve successful economic development.[64] Rather than just limiting its exercise of power over the economy to regulatory oversight, the state is an actively engaged participant—orchestrating (some scholars would go so far as to say manipulating) market forces so as to achieve national economic goals.

The recent experience of both India and China reinforces the developmental state model of economic growth. India worked to harness and capitalize on the opportunities offered by developing Internet connectivity and gaining knowledge in appropriate software programs, thereby allowing for the development of much less costly "workforce platforms" among an English-speaking and highly skilled knowledgeable workforce.[65] China's admission to the World Trade Organization in 2001 provided a huge boost to "off sourcing," the establishment of entire factories and manufacturing plants in China, with enough guarantees of control by offshore companies and greater standardization in business practices to fuel the move to China, and thus, realizing spectacular economic growth.[66] In each instance, globalization worked not in a cookie-cutter fashion but based on local, indigenous changes in how these states chose to implement development.[67]

A close examination of the development policies of these countries indicates that they were employing strategies that embraced market forces[68] as well as state-based development strategies. As a result, these countries defined the direction of economic development within the context of a complex global economic process in such a way as to produce rapid growth and modernization.[69] The 1993 World Bank study, noted earlier, confirmed that in most of the Tiger economies, "the government intervened—systematically and through multiple channels—to foster development. . . ."[70] These markets, therefore, cannot be regarded as models of free-market economic development and growth.

The Problem of Failed and Failing States

If indigenous economic development strategies work hand in hand with successful globalization, dozens of states lacking adequate infrastructure and legitimacy will remain outside of the process of economic growth that globalization seemingly promises. Two dimensions are especially important to the problem of failed and failing states. The first addresses the ability of states to adequately function as a sovereign entity. This means the ability of the government to exercise political control and draw support from its people in order to provide the infrastructure necessary to govern: the distribution of resources and stable avenues of political participation. The second has to do, as noted throughout this chapter, with the ability of states to take control of their own "economic" destiny to such an extent that globalization is tailored and channeled to the economic needs and strengths of individual participants in the global economy. As Joseph Stiglitz notes, "One attribute of the success cases is that they are 'homegrown,' designed by people within each country sensitive to the needs and concerns of their country."[71]

If globalization is to work for all, if we have any hope of tapping the process's full potential of economic integration and reaping its benefits—of liberating the globe's impoverished from their prison of abject poverty, debilitating illiteracy, and deplorable health conditions—globalist policy makers and practitioners must first address the critical challenge of developing countries' need to acquire the kinds of institutions that will allow them to prosper under globalization. As Joseph Tulchin and Gary Bland note, "Generally, countries with an effective institutional base appear to do better in the globalized world than countries where the rule of law is weak, corruption is rampant, property rights are unprotected, and civil society is not able to force accountability from government."[72]

For globalists, the key to spreading the benefits of globalization, therefore, is about getting one's fundamentals right—specifically, good governance and rule of law. Governments of failed and failing states are often unresponsive and/or ineffective agents for their country in the globalizing process because they have corrupt or incompetent governments. A case in point is Nigeria: Since the country's independence in 1960, Nigeria's anticorruption commission reports that approximately $375 billion in Western assistance has disappeared or has been misappropriated during the past 40 years, far more dollars than provided to Western Europe during the Marshall Plan. "Because of the mass theft, two-thirds of Nigeria's 130 million people live in abject poverty, one-third are illiterate and 40% have no safe water supply."[73] Indeed, it should come as no surprise that many of the world's poorest nations, in Africa,[74] Latin America,[75] and Southeast Asia,[76] are the same ones that have not been able to take advantage of the opportunities and benefits of globalization. As Jean-Claude Shanda Tonme, a consultant on international law and a columnist for *Le Messager*, a Cameroonian daily, lamented, ". . . fighting poverty is fruitless if dictatorships remain in place. Africa's real problem is the lack of freedom of expression, the usurpation of power, the brutal oppression. . . ."[77] Though Mr. Tonme was speaking specifically of Africa, his description of the problems plaguing the ability of these states to effectively govern themselves and provide for their citizens is applicable to all **failed states**. The sad fact of the matter is that the political houses of these failed states are too busy trying to escape from corrupt, predatory, brutal, and/or incompetent governments, never mind trying to tap into the globalizing process. Consequently, the wretched and/or uncertain political and economic conditions of these failed states have left them being unattractive to foreign investors and, in so doing, have banished them to an area outside of the globalizing economy. For as noted in Chapter 3, investments will not flow to states that lack stable governments and at least a basic infrastructure.

The elimination of corrupt, predatory, and/or brutal governments, however, must also be complemented by policy makers' acceptance of the establishment for greater state involvement in the economy. James Cypher, in evaluating the Chilean "miracle," concluded, "Despite the claims of free marke-teers, . . . its successes owe more to state intervention than to the invisible hand of the free market. In fact, it would be hard to find any major sector of the economy that did not owe much of its existence to state intervention . . ."[78]

In sum, globalists argue that globalization can still fulfill its promise of bringing about the most good to the majority of the world's people if only these developing countries can muster the will to implement a political reform revolution to complement its economic one. As noted earlier, this is a very difficult challenge.

CONCLUSION: MAKING GLOBALIZATION WORK FOR ALL

In an assessment of globalization's objectives of increasing growth and reducing poverty, two points stand out: First, globalization has not benefited everyone by bringing about greater wealth and well-being universally. Second, the policy prescription of the Washington Consensus has worked in a very limited political, economic, and cultural ambit.

Yet, defenders of globalization continue to believe that globalization remains the most viable avenue/method/approach with which to improve the economic fortunes of the globe's people—particularly those living in the poorer states, who have thus far been left behind. Though globalization has thus far fallen short of fulfilling its promise and its beneficial results have been both limited and uneven, the fact remains that a significant group of countries in East, South, and Southeast Asia (as well as parts of Latin America) have achieved a certain degree of economic development and growth via the globalization process. As Jagdish Bhagwati, observed, "So when we have moved away from the anti-globalization rhetoric and looked at the fears, even convictions, dispassionately with the available empirical evidence, we can conclude that globalization (in the shape of trade and investment) helps, not harms, the cause of poverty reduction in the poor countries."[79] One of the key issues confronting the process of globalization is whether the impressive economic successes of these countries can be replicated elsewhere in the developing world. Ultimately, the success of globalization as a "model" for economic development will rest on just how successful the process becomes elsewhere.

Throughout this book we have illustrated how globalization as a concept, process, value system, and an end is neither black nor white, good nor bad. "The backlash to globalization that has emerged over the past few years is centered on a single concept globalization right, in the sense of making the benefits more available and making them more equitable between countries and within countries," as Joseph Tulchin and Gary Bland have written.[80] In this regard, engagement in the globalizing process has shown itself, if placed in the proper setting, to be an effective strategy for economic growth and poverty reduction in some countries. It remains to be seen if globalization can work to save economically nonviable and politically failed states.

KEY TERMS

comparative advantage 48	failed states 58	Neoliberal 47
East Asian "tigers" 53	human capital 48	Washington Consensus 56

FIVE QUESTIONS TO CONSIDER

1. Why is the study of globalization so sharply divided by those supporting globalization and those opposed to it?
2. Construct a political scale or a continuum from conservative to liberal viewpoints? Where would you place supports of globalization and critics of globalization?
3. Define neoliberalism. How does it differ from liberalism? Why do neoliberals generally support globalization?
4. How do processes of globalization promote inequality and poverty?
5. What difficulties do failed and failing states pose to economic investment under conditions of globalization?

FURTHER READINGS

David Dollar and Aart Kraay, "Spreading the Wealth," *Foreign Affairs*, January/February 2002.

Antiglobalization activists are convinced that economic integration has been widening the gap between rich and poor. The best evidence, however, proves them wrong. Thanks to higher growth driven by greater openness to trade and investment, global inequality has narrowed and global poverty has been reduced.

Dani Rodrik, *One Economics, Many Recipes: Globalization, Institutions, and Economic Growth*. Princeton University Press, 2007.

Neither globalizers nor antiglobalizers have got it right. While economic globalization can be a boon for countries that are trying to dig out of poverty, success usually requires following policies that are tailored to local economic and political realities rather than obeying the dictates of the international globalization establishment.

Jeffery D. Sachs, "Can Extreme Poverty be Eliminated?" *Scientific American*, September 2005.

Market economics and globalization are lifting much of humanity out of extreme poverty, but special measures are needed to help the poorest of the poor. One out of six inhabitants of this planet still struggles daily to meet some or all of such critical requirements as adequate nutrition, potable drinking water, safe shelter, sanitation, and basic health care.

David M. Smick, *The World Is Curved: Hidden Dangers to the Global Economy*. Portfolio, 2008.

Smick reveals how today's risky environment came to be—and why the mortgage mess is a symptom of potentially far more devastating trouble. He wrestles with the two questions on everyone's mind: How bad could things really get in today's volatile economy? And what can we do about it.

Joseph E. Stiglitz, "Globalism's Discontents," *The American Prospectus*, 13(1) (January 1–14, 2002).

Integration with the global economy works just fine when sovereign countries define the terms. It works disastrously when terms are dictated. Stiglitz examines the proper and improper management of globalization.

NOTES

1. Quoted from *Economist*, "A Bigger World," September 18, 2008, electronic version.
2. Quoted from "What Latin America Thinks About Globalization," December 14, 2006 http://www.globalization101.org/index.php?file=news1&id=78#
3. This so-called Washington Consensus draws from the writings of "neoclassical" economic philosophies of Milton Friedman and Friedreich von Hayek and converges around a faith in free markets and minimal governmental involvement in the economy. It is advocated by most mainstream economists, public policy research institutes, and government policy makers in North America, Western Europe, and Japan, and promoted by the World Bank, the IMF, the WTO, and the World Economic Forum.
4. According to a study done by Dollar and Kraay (2002: 121), "... a strong correlation links increased participation in international trade and investment on the one hand and faster growth on the other." David Dollar and Aart Kraay, "Spreading the Wealth," *Foreign Affairs* 91(1) (January/February 2002): 120–133. Jagdish Bhagwati

takes the proposition further: "The scientific analysis of the effect of trade on poverty is even more compelling. It has centered on a two-step argument: that trade enhances growth, and that growth reduces poverty . . . Hence, growth reduces poverty." Jagdish Bhagwati, *In Defense of Globalization*. Oxford: Oxford University Press, 2004: 53, 64.

5. Robert Gilpin, *The Political Economy of International Relations*. Princeton: Princeton University Press, 1987: 268.

6. Joseph S. Nye, "Globalization Can Turn Back Terror," *Boston Globe*, November 18, 2001, electronic version.

7. Anne Krueger, *Trade and Employment in Developing Countries: Synthesis and Conclusions*. Chicago: University of Chicago Press, 1982.

8. It should be noted that if developing economies benefit from globalization, so too do industrialized states and societies. Increasingly, those states with maturing (saturated) markets need the growth potential of developing economies, for both investments and customers, to sustain economic levels. This group includes the United States, where about 30 percent of economic growth since 1993 is generated from overseas markets (Rosabeth M. Kanter, "Don't Give Up on Globalization," *Los Angeles Times*, November 18, 1998, electronic version).

9. Jeffrey Sachs and Andrew Warner, "Economic Reform and the Process of Global Integration," *Brookings Papers on Economic Activity* 1 (1995): 1–118.

10. Organization for Economic Cooperation and Development, *Open Markets Matter: The Benefits of Trade and Investment Liberalization*. Paris: Organization for Economic Cooperation and Development, 1998: 10.

11. Jeffrey Frankel and David Romer, "Does Trade Cause Growth?" *American Economic Review*, American Economic Association 89(3) (June 1999): 379–399.

12. Cited from *Economist*, "Going Global: Globalization and Prosperity," December 8, 2001: 67.

13. Ibid.

14. Ibid.

15. The authors look at data on growth, incomes, and a variety of other variables for a sample of 80 countries extending over four decades. The study divided the developing countries into two groups—those that embraced globalization during the 1980s and 1990s, and those that resisted it. The "globalizers" were defined as countries that had increased their imports and exports as a share of their gross domestic product and those that had reduced their average tariffs the most, while the "nonglobalizers" were countries where trade as a percentage of GDP had declined and tariffs had been reduced less. Dollar and Kraay, "Spreading the Wealth," 120–133.

16. Dollar and Kraay, "Spreading the Wealth," 127.

17. Martin Wolf, "A Stepping Stone from Poverty," *Financial Times*, December 18, 2001, electronic version.

18. Greg Buckman, *Globalization: Tame It or Scrap It?* New York: Zed Books, 2004: 83.

19. *Economist*, "Climbing Back," January 19, 2006, electronic version.

20. Cited from Tom Petruno, "Emerging Nations Powering Global Economic Boom," *Los Angeles Times*, May 14, 2006, electronic version.

21. Dollar and Kraay, "Spreading the Wealth,"128.

22. Paul Blustein, "Cause, Effect and the Wealth of Nations," *Washington Post*, November 4, 2001, electronic version.

23. Cited in Thomas L. Friedman, "Parsing the Protests," *New York Times*, April 14, 2000, electronic version.

24. Xavier Sala-i-Martin, "The World Distribution of Income Estimated from Individual Country Distributions," National Bureau of Economic Research Working Paper No. 8933, Cambridge, MA, May 2002; and Surjit Bhalla, *Imagine There's No Country: Poverty, Inequality and Growth in the Era of Globalization.* Washington, DC: Institute for International Economics, 2002.

25. Jeff Madrick, "Grim Facts on Global Poverty," *New York Times*, August 7, 2003, electronic version.

26. Bhagwati, *In Defense of Globalization*, 65.

27. Cited from Chris Kraul, "Soaring Export Prices Lift Hope for Latin America," *Los Angles Times*, December 8, 2005, electronic version.

28. Cited from Shaohua Chen and Martin Ravallion, "How Have the World's Poorest Fared since the Early 1980s?" *World Bank Research Observer* 19(2) (Fall 2004): 141–170.

29. Stiglitz, *Globalization and Its Discontents*, 5.

30. Dollar and Kraay (2002: 132) report that between 1992 and 1998, China's per capita GDP grew 9.9 percent, while its poverty reduction rate was 8.4 percent. In so doing, China has experienced the most spectacular reduction of poverty in world history.

31. John Micklethwait and Alan Wooldridge, "The Silent Disaster of World Poverty," *Los Angeles Times*, January 10, 2005, electronic version.

32. *Economist*, "Sustaining the Poor's Development," August 29, 2002, electronic version.

33. Kevin Watkins, et al., *Rigged Rules and Double Standards: Trade, Globalization and the Fight Against Poverty.* Washington, DC: Oxfam International, 2002.

34. Alice Amsden, *Asia's Next Generation: South Korea and Late Industrialization.* New York: Oxford University Press, 1989; World Bank, *The East Asian Miracle: Economic Growth and Public Policy.* New York: Oxford University Press, 1993; Peter Evans, *Embedded Autonomy: States and Industrial Transformation.* Princeton, NJ: Princeton University Press, 1995; and Masahiko Aoki, Hyung-Ki Kim, and Masahiro Okuno-Fujiwara, eds., *The Role of Government in East Asian Economic Development.* Oxford: Clarendon Press, 1997.

35. David Landes, *The Wealth and Poverty of Nations: Why Some Nations Are So Rich and Some Are So Poor.* New York: W.W. Norton, 1998: 433.

36. They are the so-called Gang of Four: Hong Kong, Singapore, South Korea, and Taiwan. Gilpin, *The Political Economy of International Relations*, 268.

37. Gilpin, *The Political Economy of International Relations*, 302.

38. Nye, "Globalization Can Turn Back Terror."

39. Stiglitz, "We Have to Make Globalization Work for All."

40. Martin Dickson, "Increasing Gap between Rich and Poor," *Financial Times*, September 20, 2000, electronic version.

41. Daniel Yergin and Joseph Stanislaw, *The Commanding Heights: The Battle between Government and the Marketplace That Is Remaking the Modern World.* New York: Simon & Schuster, 1998.

42. Dickson, "Increasing Gap between Rich and Poor."

43. Watkins, et al., *Rigged Rules and Double Standards*, 69.

44. George Monbiot, *The Age of Consent: A Manifesto for a New World Order.* London: Flamingo, 2003: 203.

45. Walden Bello, *Deglobalization: Ideas for a New World Economy.* London: Zed Books, 2002; Oxfam, "Growth with Equity Is Good for the Poor," *Oxfam Policy Papers* 6/00; Oswaldo De Rivera, *The Myth of Development.* London: Zed Books, 2003;

Robin Board, *Global Backlash*. New York: Rowman & Littlefield Publishers, Inc., 2002; and Joseph Stiglitz, "Globalism's Discontents," *The American Prospect* 13(1) (January 1–14, 2002). http://www.prospect.org/cs/articles?article=globalisms_discontents.

46. Anthony Giddens, *Runaway World*. New York: Routledge, 2003; Heather Bourbeau, "Introduction," *Globalization: Challenge and Opportunity*. Foreign Affairs Editors' Choice, 2002; and Stanley Hoffman, "Clash of Globalization," *Foreign Affairs* 81(4) (July/August 2002): 104–115.

47. United Nations Development Programme, *Human Development Report 2002*. New York: Oxford University Press for the United Nations Development Programme, 2002.

48. Ibid.

49. World Bank, *World Development Report*. Washington, DC: World Bank, 2002.

50. Ignacio Ramonet, "A New Totalitarianism," *Foreign Policy* 116 (Autumn 1999): 116–121.

51. Jeff Madrick, "Grim Faces on Global Poverty," *New York Times*, August 7, 2003, electronic version.

52. Giddens, *Runaway World*. 2003: xxvii; and Richard W. Mansbach and Edward Rhodes, eds., *Global Politics in a Changing World*. New York: Houghton Mifflin Company, 2003: 124.

53. John Rapley, *Globalization and Inequality*. Boulder, CO: Lynne Rienner Publishers, 2004: 129.

54. World Bank, *World Development Report*.

55. William F. Fisher and Thomas Ponniah, eds., *Another World is Possible: Popular Alternative to Globalization at the World Social Forum*. London: Zed Books, 2003: 152.

56. Monbiot, *The Age of Consent*, 17.

57. Madrick, August 7, 2003, electronic version.

58. World Bank, *World Development Report*.

59. William F. Fisher and Thomas Ponniah, eds., *Another World is Possible: Popular Alternative to Globalization at the World Social Forum*. London: Zed Books, 2003: 152.

60. Nugroho, "Rethinking Globalization: Nirvana or Armageddon?" *The Jakarta Post*, January 5, 2004, electronic version.

61. Ramonet, "A New Totalitarianism."

62. United Nations Development Programme, *Human Development Report 2004*. New York: Oxford University Press for the United Nations Development Programme, 2004.

63. Stiglitz, "We Have to Make Globalization Work for All."

64. Amsden, *Asia's Next Generation*; World Bank, *The East Asian Miracle*; Evans, *Embedded Autonomy*; and Aoki et al., eds., *The Role of Government*.

65. Thomas L. Friedman, *The World Is Flat: A Brief History of the Twenty-First Century*. New York: Farrar, Straus & Giroux, 2005.

66. Ibid.

67. Ibid.

68. The market-oriented perspective posits that the state's economic role should be limited to (1) maintaining macroeconomic stability, (2) providing incentives for investment and high savings rates, and (3) enhancing human capital.

69. Rapley, *Globalization and Inequality*, 37.

70. World Bank, *The East Asian Miracle*, 5.

71. Stiglitz, *Globalization and its Discontents*, 186.

72. Joseph S. Tulchin and Gary Bland, *Getting Globalization Right: The Dilemmas of Inequality*. Boulder, CO: Lynne Rienner, 2005: 221.

73. Editorials, "Where Does the Money Go?" *Los Angeles Times*, July 18, 2005, electronic version.
74. In particular, Burkina Faso, Cameroon, Central African Republic, Chad, Gabon, Somalia, Togo, and Uganda.
75. In particular, Bolivia, Haiti, and Peru.
76. In particular, Bhutan, Cambodia, Indonesia, Myanmar, and the Philippines.
77. Jean-Claude Shanda Tonme, "All Rock, No Action," *New York Times*, July 15, 2005, electronic version.
78. James M. Cypher, "Is Chile a Neoliberal Success?" *Dollars and Sense* (255) (September/October 2004): 30–35.
79. Bhagwati, *In Defense of Globalization*, 66.
80. Tulchin and Bland, *Getting Globalization Right*, 2.

Democratization

Globalization and other dynamic forces will continue to
rid the world of dictatorships.

*—Robert D. Kaplan, National Correspondent
for the* Atlantic Monthly[1]

Globalization is a logical extension of imperialism, a
victory of empire over republic, international finance
capital over local productivity and nation-state democracy
(such as it is).

—Michael Parenti, Author and Political Scientist[2]

INTRODUCTION: GREAT EXPECTATIONS
OR FALSE HOPES?

For its proponents, globalization brings humankind closer together. It
represents a horizontal broadening of political power across the globe. It also
represents a new awakening of sorts whereby governments can no longer
dominate in a vertical, top-down fashion the lives of their peoples. For
New York Times journalist Thomas L. Friedman, globalization in the form of
the fax, private telephone companies, the digitalization revolution, and the
interconnectivity afforded people across the planet challenges the authoritarian
impulses of states in economics, technology, culture, and politics.[3]

The erosion of borders among countries and the declining salience of
national distinctions throughout the world will likely dampen nationalist
passions, religious zealotry and hatreds, and centuries-old state-to-state
rivalries such as border antagonisms. The geopolitical significance of the state
holds less meaning for most Europeans than the material benefits conferred by

rising economic standards of living. As the boundaries of Europe are dramatically expanded eastward, notwithstanding the parochial impulses, raised by the 2005 rejection of the European Constitution by the people of France among others, Europe has been the archetype of the triumph of globalization. It is robust, inclusive, and by and large nonmartial. The belief that a progressively more inclusive European superstate confers rights and privileges on vastly larger numbers of peoples is the clearest indication of the declining importance of the outworn nineteenth-century concept of a state that enfolds one political community and one coterminous ethnonational people. While advocates for a European superstate may promise that mutual material gain will prevent conflict and inspire cooperation, many Europeans also acknowledge that such a vision still remains very much an aspiration.

REALITY CHECK: MARGINALIZATION, FRAGMENTATION, DISINTEGRATION

Critics charge that if globalization fosters larger and more embracing political and economic networks, it also appears to be stimulating trends to further **fragmentation**. Enhanced communication and transportation networks also may fuel the breakdown of states and the polarization of their peoples, providing fertile ground for nationalist, tribal, ethnic, racial, religious, and/or xenophobic/anti-immigrant movements. Unprecedented opportunities to publicize old grievances form new bases of social and political movements aided and abetted by globalization. As a consequence, borders are increasingly contested, and pockets of disaffected minority groups have given rise to dreams of annexation, secession, and ethnic cleansing. The prospects of terror due to Islamic fundamentalism, an inescapable by-product of a globalized world, have become a central concern of world politics.

As the borders of states become even more permeable, bisecting dispersed ethnic populations in different states, demands for annexation, integration, secession, irredentism, and state formation complicate regional balances of power, interstate relations, and the domestic politics of a host of countries. Since the belief in a unitary nation-state was itself an aspiration of nineteenth-century nationalism and thus never very much of a reality, patterns of immigrations and transportation have aided greater levels of ethnic, religious, and racial pluralism in the multinational states of the world. Issues of political legitimacy and political process complicate issues of political participation, distribution of resources, and effectiveness of government itself. The multinational communities in the Balkans and the Caucasus fell victim to fission and wars due to these unresolved and newly surfaced tensions (in Abkhazia, Bosnia, Kosovo, Moldova, Nagorno-Karabakh, and South Ossetia). The implosion of three federal states in Eastern Europe—Czechoslovakia, the Soviet Union, and Yugoslavia—shows how culture and ethnicity have proven stronger than state institutions and empires created after World War II.

In the Middle East, the Israeli–Palestinian conflict remains unresolved and intensified by the war in Iraq; India and Pakistan are currently engaged in a nuclear arms race; and the September 11, 2001, terrorist attack on the United States, the 2004 Spanish railway bombing, and the July 7, 2005, London bus and tube bombings have unleashed, at least from the perspective of radical Islamists, a "Clash of Civilizations"[4] between the West, specifically the United States and its allies, and the Muslim world. Far from greater understanding, tolerance, and harmony, the era of globalization has, thus far, been marked more by rising **marginalization**, fragmentation, **disintegration**, and state and transnational movements seeking to punish states than by inclusion, unity, and integration.

Marginalization

In the course of bringing together societies and political entities that are administered by disparate organizations and structures such as states, nongovernmental (transnational) organizations, and international governmental organizations, globalization has also helped to create marginalized and alienated groups excluded from the dominant currents of world politics. Markets, it must be remembered, are "contractual rather than communitarian."[5] While they may satisfy material wants and needs, they do not automatically provide for a unified identity or communal fellowship.

Marginalized individuals and groups long for political and socioeconomic protection seemingly guaranteed by the nature of statehood that interposes between them and the global market. Many groups and social movements want to belong to a particular community that is not functionally and economically determined beyond their control. For activists in more affluent societies, globalization becomes a process of domination and exploitation pitting a small rich elite against the world's vulnerable peoples. As protesters at the WTO's Seattle meeting in 1999; the International Monetary Fund–World Bank summit in Prague, Czech Republic, in 2000; the G8 Summits in Genoa, Italy, in 2001, and Scotland in 2005; and the World Social Forum in Brazil in 2005 illustrate, notwithstanding the fact that transnational networks present them with unprecedented abilities to organize, to breakdown geographical barriers, and to reduce political isolation, globalization also underscores who and what entities make decisions and those who do not.

Fragmentation

Contrary to popular perception, the proliferation of intrastate tensions, conflict, and wars that is sweeping across the globe today is not simply a remnant of the unleashing of ancient nationalist aggravations. Rather, the fragmentation and accompanying catastrophic social unrest may be one of the unintended by-products of globalization, and instead of examining these two phenomena as mutually exclusive, they should perhaps be considered as linked—mutually reinforcing. As borders become more open to goods, ideas, people, and above all, communications, globalization also makes it easier for ethnic groups to both segregate and unite. Globalization also increases the need for identity, and the intrinsic desire of human beings to belong to a particular community can no longer be denied. Globalization has made these groups more devoted to their kinsmen and less willing to construct the necessary structures/arrangements that might aid in reconciling their desire for an identity with the need to integrate and assimilate in their current state.

Robert Frost, an American poet, described this longing in terms of what home means: "the place where, when you have to go there, they have to take you in." Samuel Huntington and Robert Kaplan, for example, note the reemergence of cultural forces—in particular, the increasing need to segregate based on one's clan, ethnicity, race, religious group, and/or civilization that shuns and barely tolerates anyone outside of the group—in both intra- as well as international relations.[6]

During the waning decades of the twentieth century, a sizable portion of the globe's nation-states has evolved toward greater respect for human rights. One consequence of this development is more support and legitimacy accorded to the rights of minority groups. In like manner, the estranged peoples who exist within these states are demanding greater rights, asserting their ethnic, religious, linguistic, or regional identities, and questioning the integrity, authority, and legitimacy of their existing national governments. Indeed, as the demand for respect for the rights of minorities throughout the world becomes louder, it is getting harder for national governments to ignore the mounting legal and illegal challenges posed by alienated groups within, across, and beyond their borders.

Disintegration

One of the ironies of the globalization process is that the same forces that integrate people also have the potential to tear them apart. In this regard, globalization is shaping up to be as much about disintegration as it is about integration.

Since the implosion of the Soviet empire, old populist, socialist, and communist institutions and beliefs have been discredited in favor of greater freedoms politically, economically, socially, and culturally within states. An unintended consequence of this newfound sense of independence, however, has been the increasing erosion of common values and similar political, economic, social, and cultural bonds that often formed the basis needed to establish a self-sustaining community with which people can identify—in other words, a nation.

The establishment of some 22 newly minted independent states illustrates in dramatic fashion the negative effects when marginalization, fragmentation, and ultimately disintegration drive groups to turn ethnic, linguistic, racial, and religious grievances into nationalism as well as the powerful call of statehood: In all these instances, the aim of the breakaway groups was not to abolish the nation-state, but rather to establish one of their own.

Indeed, during the second half of the twentieth century, we have witnessed the birth of more states than at any time in history, as evidenced by the jump in membership in the United Nations from 51 to over 190 within a 50-year span. Though the rate of new-country creation has varied, new states seem to be established with greater frequency in lockstep with the globalization process: From 1950 to 1990 (the Cold War period), around two new states were founded per year, up from an average of one state per year from 1900 to 1950. The post–Cold War globalized period (from 1990 to 1998) has been the most active yet, with the rate jumping to about three new countries per year.[7] We can expect this figure to remain steady, if not increase, in the coming years. For in an era of globalization, separatist movements have become increasingly more vocal and demanding and less tolerant and accommodating on all continents. A number of new states may well continue to emerge based on the creation of ethnonational entities in advanced societies (Quebec, Scotland, Wales, and the Basqueland) or in developing societies such as Mindano Island in the Philippines and elsewhere.

On the economic front, small states (e.g., Singapore and Switzerland) are among the most dynamic and fastest-growing members of the globalizing market system. This is not surprising since they have demonstrated their ability to be the most prodigious traders in the globalizing era. According to a World Economic Forum (1999) report on global competitiveness, despite their lack of natural resources, these small economic dynamos are "almost twice as competitive in terms of quality of infrastructure, technology, and business management as Australia, Ireland, New Zealand, the United States, and the United Kingdom, four times more than Asia's manufacturing states, almost six times more than the EU, and seven times more than Latin American states."[8] The ability of these small states to be successfully competitive and efficient has proved a blueprint for other regions and groups within ethnically, religiously, or linguistically divided states for successfully establishing an independent state.

DEBATING GLOBALIZATION

Lui Hebron: Globalization Promotes Democracy

John, since 1988, the number of democratic countries has nearly doubled. With Freedom House reporting that about two-thirds of the nation-states around the world are recognized as having freely elected governments, more countries today boast democratic systems than at any time in history. Moreover, according to the Economist Intelligence Unit's measure of democracy, half of the world's population now lives in a democracy of some sort (The Economist Intelligence Unit's Index of Democracy 2008). Perhaps more telling is that democracy has been established across every continent and has thrived in countries that have lived through a plethora of ethnic, historical, linguistic, and religious experiences. These trends all suggest that democracy is not only increasingly becoming an expectation, but is also steadily establishing itself as a universal norm.

Within this context, a strong case can be made that the dynamic forces of globalization have played a significant role in promoting the diffusion of democratic ideas and basic freedoms. Globalization's ability to reduce information costs, promote transparency in the decision-making process, and press for government accountability together fosters greater democracy.

To be sure, the march toward universal democracy has suffered a setback in recent years. Freedom House reports that for three years running now (2005–2008), citizens have experienced a marked decline in freedom worldwide. A particularly troubling development of this already upsetting trend, according to the organization, is the number of countries where a previously democratic or democratizing state has reverted back to authoritarianism.

Numerous reasons can be provided to explain why a state's march toward democracy might get sidetracked and/or derailed. Political transitions, after all, are frequently turbulent, if not chaotic, phases in a state's development. If pandemonium reaches a heightened level, society may well come to the conclusion that physical and economic security under a less democratic regime outweighs political freedoms and rights. In like manner, unfulfilled democratic promises by elected officials may lead to public disillusionment and distrust for the system and a reversion back to authoritarian rule.

These setbacks are likely to be only temporary, however, since the vast majority of people throughout the world continue to value and seek a democratic form of government. A World Public Opinion poll of 19 countries conducted around the world found overwhelming public support for the democratic principle that "the will of the people should be the basis for the authority of government"—"on average 85 percent agree and 52 percent strongly." (The poll of 17,525 was conducted between November 29, 2007, and March 20, 2008, involving research centers from around the world and with surveys drawn from China, India, the United States, Indonesia, Nigeria, Russia, Argentina, Azerbaijan, Britain, Egypt, France, Iran, Jordan, Mexico, Poland, South Korea, Turkey, Ukraine, and the Palestinian Territories. The countries surveyed represented 59 percent of the world population. See WorldPublicOpinion.org.)—Lui

John Stack: Globalization Diminishes Democratic Governance

Lui, my take is different. Globalization during good times raises standards of living across the planet in some continents and countries more than in others. Africa is a conspicuous example of a continent where many have been left out. But I do not believe that we can easily or lightly equate the upswing in democratic governance with the economic uplift brought about by globalization even in good times. To accept your premise confounds cause with effect and philosophically ties the establishment of democratic societies to the growth of material gains. Affluence does not guarantee protection of basic rights and freedoms, nor does it guarantee transparency in the functioning of governments. My concern with the premise that democracy follows economic growth is that it simply ignores the political and cultural struggles for the protection of individual rights and the establishment of the rule of law that define the establishment of democratic governments since the Enlightenment of the seventeenth century.

Without a careful examination of how social, political, cultural, and economic forces come together to forge democratic norms and values, we are left with *a narrow economic determinism*. As a consequence, cause follows effect, and affluence seemingly opens the door to cooperation, and from cooperation, democratic governments, and societies emerge. Thus the logic suggests that economic growth becomes the most important catalyst out of which democratic societies are born.

Such an assessment ignores the struggles of more than three centuries as democratic movements evolved and the state system spread from Europe to encompass the globe. The case of the post–World War II emergence of the European Union is good example of how politics defined the emergence of democratic societies instead of affluence. Not only did democracy fail to germinate during the wealth creation of nineteenth-century colonialism and empire building, but it set the stage for World War I and its aftermath, the rise of nationalism, fascism, communism, and militarism, leading again to a world war. Indeed, the affluence that followed World War II was based on a political strategy to contain nationalism and militarism in Europe to prevent the flames of nationalism and war from reigniting. The creation of democratic societies in Europe was far more dependent on the reconstruction of societies from the ground up after World War II, including massive amounts of U.S. foreign assistance in the face of the threat posed by the Soviet Union. The establishment of democratic societies in Europe and Japan following the war was the product of military and political reconstruction rather than economic growth.

Finally, the spread of democratic sentiments should not be confused with the establishment of democratic societies. Most of the peoples and countries cited in the World Public Opinion Survey neither have democratic governments in any accepted definition of the term nor do they guarantee the civil and political rights of their citizenry. Globalization's ability to proliferate ideas and values is, indeed, impressive. But the assertion that globalization somehow builds democratic governance is an illustration.—John ■

Even more significant than the proliferation of new states is the sea change driving the process in which this is occurring. Throughout history, the disintegration of states and the redrawing of borders have been predominantly triggered by and have been a consequence of international wars between and among countries. As we embark on the twenty-first century, the dynamic of globalization has resulted in the astounding proposition that today, the greater threat to sovereignty comes from forces within a state than from without in Africa, Central Asia, the Middle East, and even Western Europe.

DEBUNKING THE MYTHS: SELF-EMPOWERMENT AND NGOS

While dramatic, these developments should not be viewed as critical roadblocks to increasing levels of globalization. Rather, processes of marginalization, fragmentation, and disintegration should be seen as the evolutionary next step in the transformation of the state, based on IGOs and NGOs as major components of the twenty-first century's political system.

Empowered Individuals and Groups

One of the most profound political effects of globalization has been the proliferation of empowered special interest citizen groups: Lester Salamon, director of the Center for Civil Society Studies at Johns Hopkins University, reported that "People are forming associations, foundations and similar institutions to deliver human services, promote grass-roots economic development, prevent environmental degradation, protect civil rights and pursue a thousand other objectives formerly unattended or left to the state. The scope and scale of this phenomenon are immense . . . [and] may prove to be as significant to the latter twentieth century as the rise of the nation-state was to the latter nineteenth."[9]

We are currently witnessing the formation of new global/transnational citizen-activist social movements that are increasingly demonstrating an ability to influence and pressurize national governments and international institutions to rewrite the regulations and practices of globalization to take into account cultural, human, and labor rights.[10]

As citizens' groups have increasingly become powerful at the corporate, national, and international level, how they have become so and what this means are questions that urgently need to be addressed. Is the establishment of citizens' groups, as many of their supporters claim, the first step toward an "international civil society"? Do they represent a dangerous shift of power to unelected and unaccountable special-interest groups such as NGOs?

"[A]actors with little economic and traditional political power have become an increasingly strong presence through the new politics of culture and identity, and an emergent transnational politics embedded in the new geography of economic globalization," according to one of the most distinguished scholars of globalization, Saskia Sassen.[11] An unprecedented and revolutionary transformation in state–society relations which effectively assigns a significant and tangible segment of interstate activities beyond the supervision and jurisdiction of the nation-state is underway. The flip side of the coin is that the revolution in globalized communications has given ordinary citizens specialized knowledge, greater access to **nongovernmental organizations** (**NGOs**), and a sense of empowerment ranging from global networking to political protests when dealing with the complex institutional structures and issue areas of world politics. The Internet has shrunk the world and in so doing has propelled powerful, horizontal currents that challenge authority from the ground up as Thomas L. Friedman observes.[12] If there has been any signal development since the official establishment of the state system at the Peace of Westphalia in 1648, it is the opening-up of individual participation among the councils of states and IGOs. This reflects the belief that people can change global-level issues and problems comprising the terrain of contemporary international law and international organizations. The Westphalia model denied people a formal standing in the arena of sovereign states. Globalization and the proliferation of nonstate actors in such areas as human rights, the environment, free trade, and a host of other issues have conferred the belief that individual action matters even in a world of sovereign states. This is a revolutionary assumption.

That this individually driven movement is well informed and fully global is almost certainly a function of the omnipotent spread of communications technology and the powers of the Internet as noted earlier. Rapid advances in microelectronic technology shifting the power relations among states, between states and nonstate actors, and among states and global economic forces is an integral part of the process of global change and empowerment now underway. These technologies in turn are accelerating the movement not only of goods, services, and capital across national boundaries but of ideas and information as well. In particular, the development of the information superhighway such as the Internet and other advances in mass communications offer enormous and unprecedented scope for the dissemination of information. Empowered dissident individuals and groups have a greater say and impact on the decision making and behavior of corporations and a whole spectrum of issues by enabling them to mobilize and coordinate their activities on a global scale.

The horizontal connections of globalization have thus revolutionized the manner in which citizens can come together to express disquietude. Empowerment takes the form of individuals "from terrorists like Osama bin Laden to activists like Jody Williams, who organized a global ban on land mines using e-mail."[13] Activists now routinely use the Internet and/or mobile phones to rally a sundry of groups to coordinate their agenda(s) and build coalitions. Significantly, these advances in mass communications facilitate the construction of new transnational partnerships between socially active groups. For example, armed with strong evidence of substandard or inhumane local labor conditions or environmentally harmful practices from NGOs and IGOs, activists can much more effectively attack deleterious corporate and governmental policies and behavior.

The Internet and/or mobile phones have provided social activists with a potent weapon, and have repeatedly demonstrated the ability to be a crucial and indispensable instrument for energizing, organizing, and managing any supporter-based organization for protest. When large-scale group communications were limited to landline telephones and fax machines or regular mail, the dissemination of information and the coordination of agendas, policies, and activities between different transnational organizations were prohibitively expensive. Through the use of advances in communications technologies, information can now be distributed much more quickly, if not instantaneously, and to great effect. E-mail, text messaging, and blogs have made it much easier and more efficient to disseminate information, rally activists, and besiege a targeted audience with worldwide protests. The economic costs of global communications have effectively been reduced to something approaching zero. As a result, huge barriers to global communications and, in some cases, governmental control have simply collapsed.[14] The advances in telecommunications were evident during events in Yugoslavia and the Philippines at the end of the century.

The Internet played a critical role in the 2000 Yugoslav elections. President Slobodan Milosevic cracked down on Internet journalism on the eve of the elections, including the arrest of Miroslav Filipovic, a journalist working for a London-based Internet news service. At the time of the elections, half a dozen news agencies delivered online news to approximately half a million Yugoslavs.[15] Internet cafes also played an instrumental part in the final assault on Slobodan Milosevic in Belgrade by rounding up military Web surfers as shock troops to storm the customs office. The Web proved to be an essential communications link for protestors who brought down Milosevic.[16]

In the Philippines, hundreds of thousands of demonstrators who took to the streets of Manila used cell phones and the Internet to plan and organize the ouster of the scandal-tainted regime of President Joseph Estrada. Through the use of text messages, the demonstrators were able to call meetings at short notice. Just as significantly, they were also able to rapidly picket a local bank in response to rumors that Estrada's allies were running off with their ill-gotten gains. According to reports: "Within minutes, thousands of protesters received the message: B AT CITIBANK B4 9. ERAP [Estrada's nickname] LAWYRS PLANNING 2 WDRAW $30M. WE HV 2STOP DIS."[17] In 2005, demonstrators used cell phones and the Internet to coordinate rallies protesting against the administration of the current president, Gloria Macapagal-Arroyo.

In addition to assisting opposition/protest movements to arouse and bolster support for their goals and objectives, the Internet is also encouraging greater transparency to the political process, and perhaps prompting the compliant and passive media to become more active. Throughout the world (from South and Southeast Asia to the Middle East), Web sites, cell phones, pagers, and satellite dishes are undermining the ruling elites, or at the very least, putting them under greater scrutiny: In India, a news portal, Tehelka.com, exposed corruption in India's military, which added to the pressure resulting in the ouster of the minister of defense, sending shock waves throughout the state.[18] In Thailand, the royal family, which has never confronted much in the way of criticism from the local press, has been "ferociously lampooned in cyberspace."[19] In Singapore, the most electronically connected country in Asia, literally the only opposition to its authoritarian government can be found on the Internet. Thus far, the formidable Singaporean government has not been able to put a stop to criticisms in Web sites and e-mails.[20] In the Middle East, the Qatar-based Al-Jazeera satellite TV station, with its 24-hour news programming, has become a potent "political phenomenon."[21] Al-Jazeera's no-holds-barred, "free and lively" reporting of timely news, and the scrutiny of Arab officials, rulers and kings, and the war in Iraq has been notable, while in effect "sham[ing] the groveling official Arab media."[22] Indeed, Al-Jazeera has become a major political force in the Muslim world for states, individuals, and terrorist groups, among others.

Nongovernmental Organizations

Over the past decade, the breadth and complexity of a fast-growing network of NGOs have proliferated to fill what is regarded to be a void due to the inability or unwillingness of governments to adequately address major social and political concerns. Operating at the global, regional, and local levels, NGOs champion a variety of concerns from the environment to food safety; from human, worker's, and consumer's rights to education; and from child labor to debt relief. According to the *Yearbook of International Organizations*, the number of NGOs is now reported to be at more than 47,000.[23]

Connected by the World Wide Web and united by a common purpose and goal, NGOs are increasingly playing an indispensable role in global affairs. By assembling a transnational network of specialists as agents/envoys of the global "civil society," NGOs function fundamentally as self-appointed monitors, watchdogs, guardians, and lobby/pressure/advocacy groups.[24] Moreover, in their efforts to publicize their concerns, goals, and objectives, NGOs are able to raise the consciousness on a host of global, regional, corporate, and governmental actors. This development was disparagingly termed the *NGO swarm* in a RAND study by David Ronfeldt and John Arquilla.[25] NGOs can sting, to be sure. They prove to be difficult for corporations and governments to "handle" because NGOs are often relentless in pressing social, economic, and ethical agendas. NGO swarms, say the RAND researchers, have no "central leadership or command structure"; they are "multi-headed, impossible to decapitate." They can sting a victim to death.[26] Yet NGOs are yet another illustration of the horizontal lines that Friedman sees as part of the revolution in globalized communications networks as the world flattens in the twenty-first century, thus challenging the authority of states, IGOs, and other major global actors.[27]

The successes of NGOs in altering the policies and behavior of governments and corporations are also striking. These include the 1992 Earth Summit in Rio de Janeiro, Brazil, when a coalition of environmental NGOs generated enough societal outrage to compel the delegates to pass agreements to control greenhouse gases;[28] in 1998, an ad hoc alliance of consumer-rights activists and environmentalists was instrumental in denying the passage of the Organization for Economic Cooperation and Development's Multilateral Agreement on Investment (MAI), a treaty designed to harmonize the rules for foreign investment.[29] A global coalition of NGOs, Jubilee 2000, victoriously lobbied for a significant abatement in the debts of the poorest countries;[30] in the summer of 2000, more than 50 corporations united with NGOs to sign the United Nations'

Global Compact, aimed at promoting high standards on human rights and environmental and labor practices among transnational corporations;[31] and at the end of 2000, Consumers International, a 263-strong consumer advocacy group, implored the World Trade Organization and international financial institutions to "advocate social justice and consumer protection in the global market."[32] Finally, 10 years after the original live aid concert and following on the heels of the Live 8 concert, a diverse coalition of activists "including evangelists, activists, and celebrities" gathered in Gleneagles, Scotland, "to urge leaders of the Group of Eight industrial nations to 'make poverty history.'"[33] According to John D. Brennan, a Washington-based spokesman for Bread for the World, a central purpose of this gathering was to "press the leaders to double assistance to Africa, relieve African debt and ease trade barriers, as well as take meaningful steps to combat global warming."[34] As P.J. Simmons points out, NGOs are "changing societal norms, challenging national governments, and linking up with counterparts in powerful transnational alliances. And they are muscling their way into high politics, such as arms control, banking, and trade, that were previously dominated by the state."[35]

As the *Economist* reported, "Assaulted by unruly protesters, firms and governments are suddenly eager to do business with the respectable face of dissent."[36] In Ndjamena, Chad's capital, government and oil company officials readily attest to the impact NGOs are having on their policies. "We call NGOs the fifth branch of government here," said one oil company official. "That is how much influence they have gained. I have never seen anything like it."[37]

And significantly, recognizing and accepting the power and influence of NGOs, the World Economic Forum increased the number of NGOs invited to the 2001 meeting. NGOs have become an integral part of the twenty-first century's economic and political system. Indeed, NGOs exemplify how globalization and information technology have revolutionized lobbying industry into a transnational enterprise that assembles activists together from the farthest corners of the globe to plead for their concerns and issues.

The ever-expanding clout of both mainstream and radical NGOs raises an important question: Do NGOs truly help to encourage and facilitate the **democratization** of global governance? This assault on NGOs is emanating from two sources. At one end, critics are increasingly questioning, if not disputing, the stated declaration of NGOs to represent with virtuous certitude the interests of the voiceless masses in both industrialized and developing states. While NGOs may claim to be representing and advancing the interests of the people—it should be noted that so do the targets of their scorn—the U.S. government, multinational corporations, and such intergovernmental organizations as the World Bank, the IMF, the WTO, and the G8. At the other end of the spectrum, some critics see NGOs as commandeering a directive and role that has not been bestowed on them by any democratic or representative mechanism. This involves the absence of both transparency and accountability. For if among democratic states, governments and their bureaucracies are ultimately responsible to voters, then who holds loose coalitions of activists in the form of NGOs accountable?

In the final analysis, the question countries and intergovernmental organizations increasingly confront is how NGOs can be integrated in a framework to overcome the adversarial nature seemingly embedded in their approach to states and IGOs among others. For in the long run, IGOs, states, corporations, and NGOs all have interests in the conduct and functioning of global affairs. The goal, therefore, must be to include diverse viewpoints to bear on common issues and concerns. Only this will open the door to new possibilities in the creation of planetary civil society. NGO activism has demonstrated a key dimension of evolving world politics. The era of international public opinion has arrived and will not likely fade away.

CONCLUSION: "FRAGMENGRATION"

States are under increasing pressure to perform domestically, regionally, and globally. There are pressures that make states dysfunction and likely to break up, even in the West. In like manner, there are also countervailing forces consolidating the power of governments and helping states to govern more effectively. As a result, we take as our point of departure for this concluding section a concept developed by the distinguished political scientist James Rosenau, **"Fragmengration."**[38] According to Rosenau, one of the characteristics of the globalization process is the presence of two powerful and contradictory dynamics in world politics: fragmentation and integration. The "fragmentation" of the nation-state in foreign affairs can be explained by at least two interrelated developments: (1) the emergence of global interdependence, and the accompanying changes in foreign policy agendas leading to (2) the advent of new structural relationships in global affairs. This is an incomplete and contradictory process, but it is important to understand given the enormity of the forces of change. Fragmentation, unfortunately, does not lead to unambiguous conclusions about the nature of the state in contemporary world politics. We are confronting change and that undercuts both certainty and predictability in the middle term. It is frustrating and unsettling.

The evolving global environment driven by greater economic interdependence, advances in technology, and heightened communications means that in the twenty-first century most of the important political, economic, and social issues will not be exclusively national in scope. They will likely share characteristics of both the global and/or local. This development, in turn, introduces the prospect, want, and need for localities to embrace an international orientation; and for national governments to encourage the supervised participation of regional authorities in specific policy areas of foreign relations. These transformations or alterations are particularly important for localities across the globe because the flow of people and goods and above all communication will continue unabated. On the global level, a sundry of transnational issues such as market openness, environmental protection, public health, nuclear proliferation, and human trafficking have become much more pressing matters for both national and regional as well as local governments. There is an obvious practical need for countries to play a more active and greater cooperative role in the containment, if not resolution, of these transnational concerns. Indeed, solutions will not come without collaboration at all levels of community.

Globalization's realignment of world politics has made the power structure as complex as at any other previous era. Ironically, the potency of globalization not only dictates severe restrictions on central governments, but also empowers states in fresh and innovative ways. In this regard, globalization does not necessarily lead to the depreciation of a government's authority and legitimacy and consequently its ability to function effectively, but rather the process alters a state's strategies and readjusts its energies and priorities. The state-system has moved from one that was organized exclusively around the supposedly unitary character of countries to one that can be described as founded around three complex structural relationships that overlap and influence one another.

The first is the growing relationship between governmental subnational actors and the international system. The ever-increasing transnational, interdependent, and connected nature of interstate relations has transformed the character of the world politics. The integration that comes with the globalization process has decentralized authority from the national government to regional ones and other localities. Indeed, a state's entry into world affairs and the global economy and the ensuing increases in autonomy (independence) of its regional and local governments over foreign trade and investment, cultural exchanges, and so on have transformed these subnational groups into leading participants in a country's various external political, social, cultural, as well as economic activities.

A second more recently formed relationship in the globalizing order is the one between private individuals/groups and states. Globalization's ability to remove many of the barriers that had restricted the flow and scope of people's activities, and the process's power to connect the world, has resulted in giving greater and more direct power and influence to private individuals/groups than ever before. To be sure, individuals have always played a prominent and significant role in world affairs throughout history, for example, Julius Cesar, Napoleon, and Jimmy Carter. These individuals, however, were all officially sanctioned by the state. Today we are witnessing the accession of superempowered private individuals playing a larger and more influential role in global affairs that were previously the exclusive domain of states and official world leaders. As Thomas L. Friedman observed, "Some of these super-empowered individuals are quite angry, some of them constructive, but all are now able to act directly on the world stage without the traditional mediation of governments," IGOs, and other major transnational actors.[39]

Finally, the traditional relationship between states remains relevant for it continues to explain much of the events throughout the world. Moreover, international governance remains buttressed on the ability of sovereign states to supply and insure stability, offer their citizens protection, and guarantee access to the political process. As Martin Wolf notes, "The bedrock of international order is the territorial state with its monopoly on coercive power within its jurisdiction. Cyberspace does not change this: economies are ultimately run for and by human beings, who have a physical presence and, therefore, a physical location."[40] In sum, globalization does not render states irrelevant. On the contrary, states are needed now more than ever before to provide individuals and groups a certain degree of identity and the comfort of belonging. But the exclusive role of states and the ability of governments to more or less dictate the global agenda have been challenged and will likely continue to change, resulting in a dispersal of power for state actors.

KEY TERMS

democratization   76
disintegration   67
fragmengration   77

fragmentation   66
marginalization   67

Nongovernmental
   Organizations (NGOs)   72

FIVE QUESTIONS TO CONSIDER

1. What are the central characteristics of all states/countries in the world? What common characteristics do all successful states share in common? What central dimensions do failing states share in common?
2. How does globalization increase marginalization, fragmentation, and disintegration of countries across the world?
3. What are the other participants of the global political system? How do they interact with states?
4. To what extent have states been diminished as major participants in world politics as a result of globalization?
5. What constitutes "fragmentation?"

FURTHER READINGS

Daniele Archibugi, *The Global Commonwealth of Citizens: Toward Cosmopolitan Democracy*. Princeton University Press, 2008.

Critically examines the prospects for democracy as a viable and humane response to the challenges of globalization after the end of the Cold War. It envisions a world politics in which democratic participation by citizens is not constrained by national borders, and where democracy spreads through dialogue and incentives, not coercion and war.

Peter Evans, "Fighting Marginalization with Transnational Networks: Counter-hegemonic Globalization," *Contemporary Sociology: A Review Journal* 29(1) (2000): 230–241.

Evans focuses on the emergence of transnationally organized political, economic, and cultural networks in providing a voice for dispossessed groups and communities in the Third World. Viewing these global campaigns on behalf of the environment, labor, and women's rights as "a kind of globalization from below," the impact of these "counter-hegemonic" networks toward the reconstruction of global governance are examined.

Margaret E. Keck and Kathryn Sikkink, "Environmental Advocacy Networks,"
Activists Beyond Borders: Advocacy Networks in International Politics. Ithaca,
NY: Cornell University Press, 1998.

Examines a new pressure group largely ignored by political analysts: networks
of activists that coalesce and operate across national frontiers. Their targets may be
international organizations or the policies of particular states. Transnational
activism has had a significant impact on human rights, women rights, and the
global environmental.

Klaus Schwab, "Global Corporate Citizenship; Working with Governments and Civil
Society," *Foreign Affairs* 87(1) (January/February 2008).

The phrase "corporate social responsibility" is a confusing oversimplification. It
demands separate definitions for corporate governance, philanthropy, social
responsibility, and corporate social entrepreneurship recognizing that companies
must both be engaged with their stakeholders and become stakeholders alongside
governments and civil society.

NOTES

1. Robert D. Kaplan, "We Can't Force Democracy," *Washington Post*, March 2,
2006: A21.
2. Michael Parenti, "Globalization and Democracy: Some Basics," *Political Affairs*,
May 28, 2007, http://www.politicalaffairs.net/article/articleview/5344/1/264/
3. Thomas L. Friedman, *The World Is Flat: A Brief History of the Twenty-First
Century*, 2005.
4. Samuel Huntington, *The Clash of Civilizations and the Remaking of World
Order*. New York: Simon & Schuster, 1996.
5. Benjamin R. Barber, "Democracy at Risk: American Culture in a Global Culture,"
World Policy Journal 15(2) (1998): 29–41.
6. Samuel Huntington, "Clash of Civilizations?" *Foreign Affairs* 72 (3) (Summer
1993): 22-49; and Robert Kaplan, "The Coming Anarchy" *Atlantic Monthly* 273
(2) (February 1994): 44–76.
7. Juan Enriquez, "Too Many Flags? (Analysis of Nation State)," *Foreign Policy*,
116 (Fall 1999): 29–48.
8. World Economic Forum (1999) report cited from Enriquez, "Too Many Flags?"
9. Lester M. Salamon, "The Rise of the Nonprofit Sector," *Foreign Affairs* 73(4)
(July/August 1994): 109.
10. Ronnie D. Lipschutz, "Reconstructing World Politics: The Emergence of Global
Civil Society," *Millennium* 21(3) (Winter 1992): 389–420; Paul Wapner,
"Politics Beyond the State: Environmental Activism and World Civic Politics,"
World Politics 47 (April 1995): 311–340; M. Keck and K. Sikkink, *Activists
Beyond Borders: Transnational Advocacy Networks in International Politics*.
Ithaca, NY: Cornell University Press, 1998; Jackie Smith and H. Johnston, eds.,
Globalization and Resistance: Transnational Dimensions of Social Movements.
Lanham, MD: Rowman & Littlefield, 2002; and Mary Kaldor, *Global Civil
Society: An Answer to War*. Cambridge: Polity, 2003.
11. Saskia Sassen, *Globalization and Its Discontents*. New York: New Press, 1998:
XXXIV.
12. Friedman, *The World Is Flat*.
13. Thomas L. Friedman, *New York Times*, December 19, 2000, electronic version.
14. Friedman, *The World Is Flat*.

15. Craig Francis, "Internet Brings New Dimension to Yugoslav Election," CNN, September 21, 2000, electronic version.
16. Paul Watson, "Dot-Camaraderie Helped in Milosevic's Ouster," *Los Angeles Times*, October 18, 2000, electronic version.
17. John Thornhill, "Asia's Old Order Falls into the Net," *Financial Times*, March 16, 2001, electronic version.
18. Ibid.
19. Ibid.
20. Ibid.
21. Thomas L. Friedman, "Glasnost in the Gulf," *New York Times*, February 27, 2001, electronic version.
22. Ibid.
23. Union of International Associations. Yearbook of International Organizations. Munich: K.G. Sauer, *Yearbook of International Organizations*, Vol. 3, 2001/2002.
24. H. Anheier, et al., eds., *Global Civil Society 2001*. Oxford: Oxford University Press, 2001; M. Edwards and J. Gaventa, eds., *Global Citizen Action*. Boulder, CO: Rienner, 2001; M. Glasius, et al., eds., *Global Civil Society 2002*. Oxford: Oxford University Press, 2002; J. D. Clark, ed., *Globalizing Civic Engagement: Civil Society and Transnational Action*. London: Earthscan, 2003; R. Taylor, *Creating a Better World: Interpreting Global Civil Society*. Bloomfield, CT: Kumarian, 2004; and R. D. Germain and M. Kenny, eds., *The Idea of Global Civil Society: Politics and Ethics in a Globalizing Era*. London: Routledge, 2005.
25. *Economist*, "The Non-governmental Order," December 9, 1999, electronic version.
26. Ibid.
27. Friedman, *The World Is Flat*.
28. Ibid.
29. Ibid.
30. Ibid.
31. Alan Cowell, "Advocates Gain Ground in a Globalized Era," *New York Times*, December 18, 2000, electronic version, http://select.nytimes.com/search/restricted/article?res=F60614FE3E5DOC7B8DDDAB0994D8404482.
32. Ibid.
33. Susan E. Rice, "We Must Put More on the Plate to Fight Poverty," *Washington Post*, July 5, 2005, electronic version.
34. John Daniszewski, "Activists Plan 'Final Push' to Pressure G-8," *Los Angeles Times*, July 6, 2005, electronic version.
35. P. J. Simmons, "Learning to Live with NGOs," *Foreign Policy* 112 (Fall 1998): 84.
36. *Economist*, "The Beginning of a Great Adventure," September 23, 2000, electronic version.
37. Douglas Farah and David B. Ottaway, "Watchdog Groups Rein in Government in Chad Oil Deal," *Washington Post*, January 4, 2001: A14.
38. James Rosenau, "The Complexities and Contradictions of Globalization," *Current History* 96(613) (November 1997): 360–364.
39. Thomas L. Friedman, "DOSCapital," *Foreign Policy* 116 (Fall 1999a): 110–116.
40. Martin Wolf, "Will the Nation-State Survive Globalization?" *Foreign Affairs* 80(1) (2001): 178–190.

6

Sovereignty

... the leaders of the G-20 have a responsibility to take bold, comprehensive and coordinated action that not only jump-starts recovery but launches a new era of economic engagement to prevent a crisis like this from ever happening again.

—*Barack Obama, President of the United States*[1]

Increasingly, policies that used to be made by national governments are now formulated for developing countries through global processes and institutions, including the IMF, the World Bank and the WTO. . . . As a result, developing countries have found it extremely difficult to steer through the turbulent waters of globalization.

—*Mahathir bin Mohamad, former Prime Minister of Malaysia*[2]

INTRODUCTION: GLOBALIZATION AND STATE SOVEREIGNTY

One of the most heated debates within the globalization literature is the issue of the continued viability of state (economic) sovereignty. For some scholars and analysts, globalization has not been kind to the nation-state.[3] These **"hyperglobalists"**[4] argue that the increasing reach and power of global markets challenge and undermine the geopolitical assumptions of realism. For classical realists like Hans Morgenthau, the physical survival of the state through the use of military power is a central and irreducible dimension of contemporary world politics.[5] Realism's corollary that states are autonomous, unitary actors capable of pursuing independently determined policies while exercising political power has in fact been under attack for more than 25 years.[6]

Globalization has, in essence, effectively "ended the nation-state's monopoly over internal sovereignty, which was formerly guaranteed by territory."[7] For "[i]n this 'borderless' economy, national governments are relegated to little more than transmission belts for global capital."[8] The assumption is that the role and function of states will ultimately diminish to nothing more than serving as "a superconductor for global capitalism."[9]

Without question, globalization presently has a profound effect on the power-relation dynamics between the state on one side and the global market (transnational financial and corporate actors) on the other. Particularly in the key areas of macroeconomic, environmental, and social policy, the ability of national governments to manage their economies within the globalization process has become increasingly more complex and arduous.

In the economic arena, states are undergoing a realignment as the complex and contradictory forces driving globalization such as fiercer competition, capital mobility, and technological changes increase in scope and erode national borders. The result is that the new global system makes it more difficult for governments of both industrialized and emerging economies, let alone third-world states, to exclusively regulate the marketplace. States find it more and more challenging to mandate environmental and worker protection laws (minimum-wage laws, rules on working hours, and health-and-safety standards in the workplace) and to administer social safety nets (unemployment insurance, pensions, and family benefits) as a means of protecting their citizens from the vagaries of globalization.

Governments are less able to afford and to provide for social safety nets because an important part of national tax bases supporting these services has become more difficult to capture due to the increased mobility of capital under conditions of globalization. For as the world's financial markets become more integrated, and as capital gains greater discretion over where to locate, some economists and policy makers fear that globalization "may drain governments' tax revenues either by making [tax] evasion easier or by encouraging economic activity to shift to lower-tax countries."[10]

Conventional wisdom posits, therefore, that the competition between states to attract investments has become so fierce that if governments implement socially and environmentally conscious policies such as stern labor standards or stringent environmental regulations, they will make their home markets uncompetitive (because such requirements supposedly decrease earnings by increasing the costs of doing business) and may even cause firms and financial actors to move on, leaving their workers without jobs and arresting the development and/or growth of their economy. Confronted by such a possibility, governments are under tremendous pressure to relax their rules and laws so as to continue to attract foreign direct investments and/or avert capital flight.

The state has, in effect, been reduced from the primary sovereign organization that decides the rules for economic activity within its territorial borders to an entity whose freedom of action is now dictated by, or is at the mercy of, the global market system embracing both transnational financial actors and corporations. In other words, stripped of any meaningful economic role, purpose, or influence, the state is fast losing its relevance.[11] The sovereignty of states appears to be much weaker at the beginning of the twenty-first century than at the midpoint of the twentieth century—even at the height of the Cold War, when intense global superpower rivalries of the Soviet Union and the United States placed countries under tremendous pressure to align themselves with one or another camp.

REALITY CHECK: ECONOMIC SOVEREIGNTY REDEFINED

To what extent does globalization undermine the ability of national governments to regulate their economies and curtail their freedom of action to further social and political ends? Has the growing international torrent of goods, services, and capital diminished the power of the state by making governments weaker and less relevant than ever before? And if so, Martin Wolf ponders, "Does globalization, by definition, have to be the nemesis of national government?"[12]

The view that the global economy has both seized and drained power from the state, that governments today are shackled by integrated global markets and, therefore, stand helpless before the gale of international forces beyond their control, is a gross exaggeration of what has evolved. According to studies conducted by Mark Hallenberg, Geoffrey Garrett, and Peter Katzenstein, the claim that globalization strips states of their domestic autonomy does not have much empirical support.[13] However, this is not to say that governments do not feel challenged by the pressure exerted by the forces of globalization. The nature of sovereignty transcends the preferences of the global marketplace. The political process in states encompassing elected officials, administrative and regulatory agencies, judicial systems, political cultures, interest groups, and political parties continues to have significant influence on fiscal and monetary policies.[14] States retain substantial autonomy in regulating their economic systems and in designing social policies that limit the openness and vulnerability of their economies, regulatory bureaucracies, and judicial systems. Econometrics studies show that increased capital mobility has not constrained the ability of states to tax capital.[15] So though markets have increasingly taken a larger stake in the governing and policy-making function of states, they have often done so with the acquiesce and increasingly willing participation of governments, political elites, and regulatory agencies because the benefits of integration are so fundamental to state interests. There are, moreover, strong arguments for believing that the restrictions voluntarily accepted and/or imposed[16] on governments by globalization are, for the most part, desirable—especially, the belief that an economic transformation will occur beginning with rising standards of living.

What, then, does globalization mean for states' **economic sovereignty?** Despite the massive flow of investment, the considerable progress made in trade liberalization; the revolution in transportation, communications, and information technology; and an ever-expanding agenda of global issues, for example worker rights and environmental concerns, the ability of states to make independent regulatory decisions has not been significantly usurped by the integrative forces of globalization because national economies continue to remain strongly grounded in a distinctive geopolitical environment while remaining largely independent from each other. As one study reported, there is evidence of "a surprisingly strong association across countries between the degree of exposure to international trade and the importance of the government in the economy."[17]

The significance of continuing economic independence between the globe's national markets can best be illustrated by American–Canadian trade. Trade between Canada and the United States is among the freest in the world. A study conducted by Canadian economist John McCallum reveals that trade between a Canadian province and an American state is on average 20 times smaller than trade between two Canadian provinces,[18] indicating that despite the large volume of trade between the two neighboring countries, the U.S. and Canadian markets remain significantly delinked from each other. If this relationship is true for one of the world's largest and unequal trading partnerships, then it may also be relevant for other similar bilateral trade relationships. That states continue to have at their disposal the option of interventionist policies in a wide array of economic and market policy decisions such as subsidization or taxation policies, monetary policy, and international trade regulation suggests that states continue to wield considerable power. Sovereign democratic states are still able to maintain their freedom of action to comply with whatever economic policies their government prefers, provided, of course, it follows the wishes of its citizens.

At the same time, a country that chooses international economic integration implicitly accepts that surrendering a certain degree of national sovereignty in terms of policy options is a natural and inevitable process in the march toward greater economic interdependence. In this regard, engagement in the global economy encourages governments to follow more market-oriented economic policies sometimes perhaps at the expense of labor and the environment because globalization has raised the costs that must be paid for antimarket policies. With capital more free flowing and mobile than ever, countries that continue to practice antimarket policies may often find themselves being shut out of global competition for investments. In this economic environment, the necessity of sustaining "international competitiveness" looms much larger and dictates an explicit bias to policy making. The repercussions are being felt everywhere. In Asia, large Japanese corporations have begun to reevaluate the practice of providing lifetime employment. In Europe, French and German unions are in the midst of a heated battle over government attempts to cut benefits. And developing countries in Latin America, Southeast Asia, and Central Asia are restructuring their economies by liberalizing trade, deregulating markets, and privatizing public enterprises. In sum, national governments have an enormous incentive to embrace and espouse policies that stimulate foreign investment and market-led growth.

Finally, to reap the full benefits from globalization, governments must remain vigilant by pursuing sound policies. Indeed, an effective state role is a prerequisite for effective participation in the globalized world economy.[19] According to Nicholas van Praag, a spokesman for the World Bank, "It's not enough to say that markets can do it all."[20] The recent economic achievements of the world's most successful states are not due to blind engagement in the global economy alone, but also to more stable fiscal and monetary policies, deregulation, free trade, and sound social-welfare programs to minimize the social impact and possible disruptions of the national economy. A number of studies have revealed that the state continues to retain substantial capacities to govern its global economic activities—that it remains the prime regulatory force in international economic relations.[21] There is an astonishingly robust correlation across countries between a state's international trade integration and the degree of governmental involvement in its economy. The last 60 years have witnessed what at first instance appear to be two paradoxical trends: the growth of both trade and government. The supposition that the global economic system can now function almost solely on the basis of such free-market principles as the law of supply and demand; comparative and competitive advantage; and other invisible, self-regulating market forces is belied by a number of indicators. In the United States, for example, the institutions for regulating the economy, designing social policies, and monitoring labor and environmental standards have all increased at the federal, state, and local levels. Governments are not coming apart at the seams, but becoming increasingly implicated in wider sets of relationships with other nations, transnational entities, and IGOs operating across state political boundaries. In sum, the globalization of markets implies, not the elimination, but rather a redirection of the state's role, forms, and functions in global economic relations and policy making to fit the evolving international environment.[22]

DEBUNKING THE MYTHS: THE AGE OF MICRO- AND MACROGOVERNMENTS[23]

The connection between sovereignty and globalization is a complex and often shifting set of policies and realities. As we have argued throughout, globalization is not a unilinear process. Globalization processes may attenuate and morph into regional institutions. Deglobalization, as Robert Keohane and Joseph Nye argue, is an historically documented process.[24] For while the forces of globalization may impose constraints on the sovereign power of states, these same forces have also strengthened many governments and empowered them in new ways.[25]

Political globalization does not suggest a simplistic erosion of national sovereignty, but more of a redefinition, redirection, and reconfiguration of its

DEBATING GLOBALIZATION

Lui Hebron: Regulation Needs to be Reasonable

John, a major criticism of the globalization process revolves around a state's increasing incapacity to regulate its economy due to the internationalization of finance and trade. With the onset of the global economic crisis, however, we are witnessing a backlash against free trade and financial deregulation in favor of big government. Indeed, a growing consensus among economists, politicians, and academics increasingly endorses more, not less, government involvement in the economy. In terms of policy, this new orientation embraces "Keynes at home and Smith abroad."

On the domestic level, given that the resources to stabilize the economy lies predominately in the hands of the state, greater government involvement in the market has been implemented to stimulate economic recovery and hopefully preserve social stability. In so doing, the state has become more active and assertive, both in becoming shareholders in companies (e.g., Washington had to come to the rescue of banks and the automobile industry) and urging them to do what is needed (i.e., tightening regulation of banks and building more fuel-efficient cars).

On the global stage, the United Nations' 2008 World Economic and Social Survey contends that government needs to play a much larger (interventionist) role in the global economy in order to temper the sometime extreme economic cycles and disparities as well as to shield people from the brutal and unpleasant effects of globalization. The UN report calls for a greater governmental role in the regulation of international capital flows and in addressing income inequality. The UN's critique and recommendations were supported by a separate study conducted by the International Monetary Fund. The IMF study concluded that the most effective means to address the current global financial crisis would be for nation-states to respond to the situation in a multilateral manner. G20 leaders have responded to the call for greater multilateral cooperation by pledging to coordinate their efforts to stimulate the global economy from its current downturn.—Lui

John Stack: Globalization Needs a Regulatory Framework

Lui, unregulated and underregulated financial and trade markets have plunged the global economic system into the worst financial crisis since the Great Depression of 1929. The speed and unpredictability of interconnected financial markets and the proliferation of fraudulent and flawed financial instruments point to a critical vulnerability in the mythology of self-regulating free markets much touted by the disciples of Adam Smith. We are experiencing the downside of globalization—in terms of the speed, interconnectivity, and unpredictability of financial markets worldwide. If we are in the midst of a backlash against "two decades of intense reliance on free trade, open markets and deregulation in favor of big government," I believe that changing course is essential for the economic and political stability of states and the global economic and political system.

Big government is not the problem, but the lack of both international and multilateral regulatory structures is desperately needed to put the global economy back on track. Some countries are less affected by the current global economic meltdown than others because domestic regulations prevented companies, especially in the financial sectors, from diving into flawed financial instruments whose value proved to be illusory. France and Spain are two examples of countries whose regulations have sheltered banks, financial institutions, and investors from the worst effects of the financial sector's collapse. Responsible domestic economic regulations are necessary to stabilize interconnected and globalized markets, but that is just the first step.

The new policy consensus of "Keynes at home and Smith abroad" simply will not work. We need, as you correctly suggest, far greater levels of multinational oversight of globalized markets. The belief that somehow Adam Smith's unrestrained markets will result in the greatest good for the greatest numbers did not work in the nineteenth century and does not work in the twenty-first century. The prolonged economic damage from the Asian financial crash in the 1990s and the economic wreckage of both the Great Depression and the Great Recession within countries and throughout the world should serve as a lesson.

Globalization and sovereignty as we suggest in this chapter coexist. Globalization will not destroy sovereignty, but if left unregulated internationally, it can bring untold economic and political suffering and upheaval to billions around the globe. The consequences of the collapse of the global economic order of the 1930s were an important contributing factor to the rise of authoritarian politics in Europe and Asia and the onset of World War II. Too much regulation can stifle markets and creativity but too little at home and abroad threatens political and socioeconomic stability.—John ■

purpose and influence in the international system "to fit the exigencies of the global market."[26] Specifically, governance (authority and regulation) "has become increasingly 'multi-level' or 'multi-scalar' across substate (municipal and provincial) bodies and suprastate (macroregional and transworld) agencies as well as state organs."[27] Such a "reorganization" of sovereignty, in turn, has led to the shifting of authority either to (1) transnational actors and local governments—eager to play an active role in foreign affairs—or to (2) quasi-supranational actors such as the International Monetary Fund, the European Union (EU), and the Organization of Petroleum Exporting Countries (OPEC) that are able to reject or bypass the power of some states. According to Jan Aarte Scholte (2005), "No single 'level' reigns over the others, as occurred with the primacy of the state over suprastate and substate institutions in territorialist circumstances. Instead, governance tends to be diffuse, emanating from multiple locales at once, with points and lines of authority that are not always clear."[28]

The Rise of Micro- and Macrogovernments

In the twilight of the twentieth century, a most peculiar phenomenon happened to national governments. Large segments of the state's economic system attempted to flee from the confines of the traditional economic regulatory frameworks of the states in which they found themselves to have been "imprisoned." For a number of reasons, ethnic, religious, ideological, and economic policy-making frameworks embraced the movement toward both fission/secession and fusion/integration, in just about every corner of the globe. An increasing segment of national populations seems to feel that political and economic systems were no longer effectively serving their needs in an adequate manner.[29] For many groups, a sense of disquietude took hold, spurring a kind of return "to their roots" whether expressed in terms of linguistic and cultural revivals, secessionist movements, or a variety of other manifestations of heightened feelings of ethnonationalism. The seemingly surprising revitalization of ethnicity was expressed in a large number of states in both developed and developing countries such as the Basques in Spain, the Quebecois in French-speaking Canada, the Achen in Indonesia, as well as such superregional movements as Albanian Kosovars and Macedonians in the Balkans.[30] These ethnonational revivals spanned the globe, finding fertile soil in stable, postindustrial states; rapidly developing societies; and poor, nondeveloping states, as well as heightening suspicions that the impact of globalization was being felt in unexpected ways.[31]

International relations in the age of globalization has become very complex for it involves not only the traditional interactions between states dealing with a variety of economic, military, and diplomatic issues, but also a varied assortment of actors ranging from supranational organizations and international governmental organizations (IGOs), NGOs to transnational corporations (TNCs) to community groups, all pursuing their own, often narrowly defined social, environmental, and economic interests. These developments, in turn, mean that transnational public, political, economic, social, and environmental issues are no longer under the exclusive domain of national governments. The integrative character of globalization means that governmental power in most countries will be exercised in pursuit of domestic and international myths and policies. To be dealt with effectively, a host of issues, conflicts, and policies will likely have to migrate either up to regional entities or within states down to smaller administrative and political organizations in search of the appropriate level.

As the twenty-first century moves forward, the role of the country as the most basic and meaningful source of individual identification may be changing. More than ever, a state's function must be both inward and outward looking if it hopes to be effective in meeting the needs of its citizens and residents. Since the midpoint of the twentieth century, a number of trends have supported transnational attachments between peoples in affluent and developing societies. Technological, communications, and transportation processes bind countries together in expanding networks. The impact of demonstration, events in one country having an impact elsewhere in the world whether in political, financial, cultural, or economic spheres, occurs on a daily basis. Daniel Bell, one of the most perceptive sociologists of his time, wrote, " . . . new and larger networks and ties within and between societies have been woven by communication and transportation, shocks and upheavals are felt more readily and immediately, and reactions and feedbacks come more quickly in response to social changes."[32] The political arena in most advanced industrial societies has expanded since World War II. Economic and social welfare issues are now a key point of conflict in virtually every country rich or poor throughout the world, for example, as evident in the ongoing debates about immigration.[33] Similarly, the power of religious groups to challenge the values of modern secular governments and societies is now a hallmark of world politics.[34] The proliferation of radicalized Islam, as evident in Hamas, other extremist Jihadist movements, or the reach of al-Qaeda in the years both before and after 9/11, is an example of this process.[35] Within this realm, religious groups marshal resources transnationally to accomplish specific ends.[36] The power of individuals to effect change is dependent on their ability to work through transnational networks. What results can be of great importance because " . . . challenges to the present day distribution of place and privilege and the questioning of the normative justifications and legitimations which have sanctioned the status quo . . . "[37] may result.[38] This adds to the difficulty of building consensus politics in the absence of a common enemy or imminent threats to national security. A third dimension of change in both affluent and developing countries is the search for "more inclusive identities."[39] As countries become increasingly urban, bureaucratic, and remote from their citizens, the search for meaningful group identities intensifies. Indeed, the search for ethnic and religious identities highlights the often unexpected importance of transnational groups as global actors.

Microgovernments: Devolution

At one end of the spectrum, one of the least understood though most intriguing political developments has been the proliferation of **microgovernments**— smaller institutional entities that have expanded their autonomy and authority to deal with issues, problems, and/or crises at the subnational level. In many areas of Europe (France, Spain, the United Kingdom, and Russia) and Asia (Japan, Indonesia, and India), national governments have been ceding their administrative and managerial responsibilities to ethnic, racial, religion, and culture-based regional authorities. In the following section are a few examples of national governments voluntarily or involuntarily devolving their powers.

In France, the National Assembly approved a controversial bill to grant more powers to the Mediterranean island of Corsica—where separatists have staged violent protests against Paris for more than 20 years. In addition to allowing the island's schools to teach the Corsican language as part of its curriculum, the bill gives Corsica's regional assembly the right to amend some national legislation to suit the island's needs. This autonomy law follows the same sort of regional **devolution** (powers and autonomy) already being practiced by Spain and Britain.[40]

In Spain, 79 percent of those voting in Catalonia on June 18, 2006, approved the Statute of Autonomy of Catalonia, increasing Catalonia's autonomy and powers of self-government within Spain. It strengthened the political powers of the government of Catalonia vis-à-vis the Spanish state and increased Catalonian control over economic development, taxation, and immigration. As importantly, the Statute of Autonomy of Catalonia reaffirmed the importance of the Catalonian language and culture within Spain and Europe.[41]

In the United Kingdom, devolution proceeded for Scotland and Wales despite the fact that even before the granting of greater formal regional governing authority in the form of legislative bodies, Scotland and Wales already had developed greater autonomy from established structures—cabinet ministers, departments, and committee assignments within Parliament. And while the argument can be made that devolution was initiated in part as a tactical rebuttal to squelch the rising undercurrent of nationalistic identity in Scotland and Wales, the stronger motivational force was that devolution is about good governance—one in which a decentralized system of decision making would lead to more responsive government. This allows local input into regional policy, and provides a mechanism that will bring together the economic, political, social, and cultural forces within a region in order to identify its assets and liabilities. It is also a means for devising strategies for tackling problems and creating the conditions for economic prosperity and sociopolitical stability. Indeed, based on the successes of the Scottish Parliament and the Welsh Assembly, there are increasing calls for the establishment of regional governments for England as well. (Though the Scottish Parliament, like the Welsh Assembly, will have the power to levy some taxes and make laws on issues such as education, the Parliament at Westminster will continue to make foreign, defense, and overall economic policies.[42])

In Russia, after the collapse of the Soviet Union, the country devolved into a loose federation of regions, with governors literally establishing their own little fiefdoms. In some cases, these regional leaders "passed laws in contradiction to the constitution, and used federal military, legal and financial resources for their own ends."[43] Though President Valdamir Putin remains embroiled in a protracted campaign to reign in Russia's rebellious regional governors and restore the Kremlin's authority, it would appear that the era when "Russia was ruled from the Kremlin, from czars who imposed their will on a far-flung empire to the Soviet Communist Party, which attempted to dictate every aspect of political and economic life from Moscow" is now long passed.[44]

In Japan, some of the governors of the country's 47 prefectures have increasingly become more assertive and independent minded due to the country's continuing economic woes and frustration with top-down rule. Japan's governors have traditionally enjoyed intimate and cordial relations with the central government, characterized by "uniform, centrally-determined policies and docile obedience in carrying them out."[45] Once the malleable tools of Tokyo, today, these unruly governors' "[c]alls for referendums are being heard all over Japan, on all manner of issues from rubbish dumps to airports."[46]

In Indonesia, Jakarta, the power center of the country, is becoming increasingly irrelevant to the affairs of the state as the economic and political influence is shifting out of this sprawling capital city and into the far-flung provinces. Since 2001, the central government has been devolving powers, like some tax policies and control of certain industries, to local governments. The country has also been decentralizing economically with more money earned from exports flowing to the provinces. These revolutionary developments were best summed up by Douglas Ramage, head of the Jakarta office of the Asia Foundation, a U.S.-based institution that studies the region's culture and politics, when he commented that "A lot of local governments are ignoring what's going on in Jakarta and getting on with their own business."[47]

India too would appear to be imploding in several areas as the country struggles to administer the vast diversity and intense poverty of its 1.1 billion people. In no less than 10 regions across India, groups are demanding to divide existing states into smaller units better suited to the ethnic and economic demands of their inhabitants.[48] Zoya Hasan, a professor of politics at Jawaharlal Nehru University in New Delhi, interprets these movements in this manner: "Widespread and simmering discontent among people about skewed development and inequity finds expression in different ways. But a deep sense of neglect and economic marginalization is at the heart of it all."[49]

Finally, American[50] and Australian states, Canadian[51] and Chinese[52] provinces, and German[53] Länders have established overseas offices (trade and investment bureau) that operate with considerable autonomy from their authorities.[54] While it remains far from clear whether or not these trends toward greater devolution have undermined or marginalized the function and influence of the state, the fragmentation caused by this reconstitution is the political challenge facing all states (modern and developing) today.

Macrogovernments: Regionalization[55]

On the other end of the spectrum, there is the case of Alpine Diamond: a European alcove of about two million people at the intersection of France, Italy, and Switzerland. This fledgling regional government came about because the denizens who reside in the area "decided that none of their existing governments—national, provincial or local—were capable of managing the region's economic development."[56]

On a much larger scale, there is the success of the North American Free Trade Agreement (NAFTA) and the EU, which created a free trade zone in North America and a common market in Western Europe, respectively. Observing the benefits of NAFTA and the EU, regional groupings of countries are at varying stages of establishing greater economic integration.

In all these cases, the driving action was the same: "Public issues are not respecting traditional boundaries. Something larger is needed to handle them."[57]

CONCLUSION: THE FUTURE OF THE NATION-STATE

The claim by critics that globalization inhibits and/or immobilizes the capacity of government to operate autonomously is a gross exaggeration of the globalizing process's effect on states. First, as the linchpin of order and foundation of governance, states, as Daniel Drezner has pointed out, " . . . are assigned tasks, such as the provision of public goods [i.e., national security, social safety nets, protection of the environment, etc.] and the establishment of the necessary rules and institutions, that cannot be easily replicated by other actors."[58] In light of the 9/11 terrorist attacks on the United States, and given the ever-increasing complexity of this evolving international order, states will matter more, not less, in a globalized world.

Second, states are not the acquiescent victims of the globalization process.[59] What states do does matter, as we have argued throughout the book, from high politics to domestic policies. Like it or not, it is the state that is the primary expression of territorially bounded sovereignty and will continue to exercise fundamental decisions about the workings of the political process and resource allocation decisions in the areas of traditional police powers—health, welfare, morals, education, human rights, and economics among very many areas of governance. Indeed, many of the limitations placed on a government's freedom of action are self-imposed in the hope that it will bring about beneficial results such as greater economic and physical security. And if engagement in globalization is a matter of choice, rather than an unstoppable force, it cannot render states as being weak and powerless, although it may likely complicate decisions at many levels of the political process.

Third, while globalization may not render states irrelevant, let alone obsolete, the process is altering the way government operates. David Held and his team of scholars point out that national governments are "being reconstituted and restructured in response to the growing complexity of processes of governance in a more interconnected world."[60] In certain instances, a more activist state is needed to direct the successful liberalization of markets.[61]

Assertions, therefore, that the state has been fundamentally altered are exaggerated and overblown. The main issue is not whether the state will survive, but rather how and in what manner it will be transformed as globalization becomes more embracing. Is this transformation a threat to state sovereignty and the existing state system? The answer would have to be in the negative. The modern state has repeatedly demonstrated its ability to "reinvent" itself, and to adapt to more than 450 years of upheaval, including the bloodbaths of religious hatred, nationalism, the Cold War, and global terror.

KEY TERMS

devolution 91

economic sovereignty 85

hyperglobalists 82

macrogovernments 86

microgovernments 86

regionalization 92

FIVE QUESTIONS TO CONSIDER

1. Does sovereignty exist for states under conditions of globalization?
2. What does the term "economic sovereignty" mean?
3. How does globalization promote the rise of macro- and microstates? What functions do hybrid states fulfill under conditions of globalization?
4. To what extent does globalization render states irrelevant?
5. What psychological functions do states provide for their citizens?

FURTHER READINGS

John Agnew, *Globalization and Sovereignty.* Lanham MD: Rowman & Littlefield Publishers, Inc., 2009.

Offers a new way of thinking about sovereignty, both past and present while challenging the idea that state sovereignty is in worldwide decline in the face of the overwhelming processes of globalization. It advances the idea of effective sovereignty and the geographical forms in which sovereignty actually operates in the world.

Economist, "Is Government Disappearing?" September 27, 2001.

Refutes the argument by some antiglobalists that economic integration via the globalization process has made companies more powerful than governments. Noting that governments continue to tax at will to provide for social spending, it argues that states are far from being at the mercy of the dictates of the international marketplace.

Thomas Friedman and Robert Kaplan, "States of Discord," *Foreign Policy*, March/April, 2002.

Two influential commentators diverged sharply over the future of the nation-state at a debate in Washington, D.C. One sees technology and markets as a key to the future, while the other sees in attributes of traditional state power the most important lens to view central to understanding globalization, democracies, and transnational terrorism.

Kenichi Ohmae, *The End of the Nation State: Rise of Regional Economies.* New York: Simon and Schuster, 1995.

Argues that not only have nation states lost their ability to control exchange rates and protect their currencies, but they no longer generate real economic activity. States have forfeited their role as critical participants in the global economy becoming inefficient engines of wealth distribution, while crucial economic choices are made elsewhere.

David Wessel and John Harwood, "Market Economy Begins to Reach Further Into Government, Society," *Wall Street Journal*, May 14, 1998.

Examine the clashes that have transpired as profit-making companies continue to penetrate those areas once thought to be the exclusive purview of government. As the various cases studies from the privatization of firefighter service, to the open bidding for health care services, to the outsourcing of a state's welfare system over to private contractors illustrates, the "advance of market forces is being meet with pockets of resistance . . . "

Martin Wolf, "Will the Nation-State Survive Globalization?" *Foreign Affairs* 80(1):178, 2001.
Globalization will not spell the end of the modern nation-state because of the following: the willingness of societies to take advantage of international economic opportunities depend on the quality of public goods as determined by states, states normally define identity, and global governance is shaped by individual states that largely guarantee stability.

Martin Wolf, "Countries Still Rule the World," *Financial Times*, February 5, 2002.
Debunks the antiglobalist argument that states are at the mercy of "unbridled corporate power." Pointing to both the conceptual flaw (measurement of economic size) as well as the misguided analytical framework (comparing corporation with states) upon which the argument is based, the author concludes that "corporations are neither as big nor as powerful as critics claim."

NOTES

1. Quoted from Barack Obama, "Making the World Work Again," *Los Angeles Times*, March 24, 2009, electronic version.
2. Quoted from "Globalization and Developing Countries," in Frank-Jürgen Richter and Pamela Mar, eds., *Recreating Asia: Visions for a New Century.* Singapore: John Wiley and Sons (Asia), 2002.
3. Kenichi Ohmae, *The Borderless World: Power and Strategy in the Interlinked World Economy.* New York: Harper Business, 1990; J. A. Camilleri and J. Falk, *The End of Sovereignty? The Politics of a Shrinking and Fragmenting World.* Aldershot: Elgar, 1992; Susan Strange, *The Retreat of the State: The Diffusion of Power in the World Economy.* Cambridge: Cambridge University Press, 1996; Lester Thurow, *The Future of Capitalism: How Today's Economic Forces Shape Tomorrow's World.* New York: William Morrow, 1996; and Saskia Sassen, *Losing Control? Sovereignty in an Age of Globalization.* New York: Columbia University Press, 1997.
4. David Held and Anthony McGrew, "Globalization," *Entry for Oxford Companion to Politics*, http://www.polity.co.uk/global/globalization-oxford.asp
5. Hans Morgenthau, *Politics Among Nations*, 5th ed. New York: Knoph, 1973.
6. Patrick James, "International Relations: A Perspective Based on Politics, Economics, and Systems," *Journal of International Relations and Development* 6 (2003): 344–357; Kenneth Waltz, *A Theory of International Relations.* Boston: Addison-Wesley, 1979; Lester C. Thurow, "The American Economy in the Next Century," *Harvard International Review* 20 (Winter 1998): 54–59; and Alexander Wendt, *Social Theory of International Politics.* Cambridge: Cambridge University Press, 1999.
7. Wolfgang H. Reinicke, "Global Public Policy," *Foreign Affairs* 76 (November/December 1997): 127–138.
8. David Held, Anthony McGrew, David Goldblatt, and Jonathan Perraton, *Global Transformation: Politics, Economics and Culture.* Stanford, CA: Stanford University Press, 1999: 3.
9. Lowell Bryan and Diana Farrell, *Market Unbound: Unleashing Global Capitalism.* New York: Wiley, 1996: 187.

10. *Economist*, "Disappearing Taxes: The Tap Runs Dry," May 31, 1997, electronic version.

11. M. Horsman and A. Marshall, *After the Nation-State: Citizens, Tribalism and the New World Disorder.* London: Harper Collins, 1994; J. Dunn, ed., *Contemporary Crisis of the Nation State?* Oxford: Blackwell, 1995; L. A. Khan, *The Extinction of Nation-State: A World without Borders.* The Hague: Kluwer Law International, 1996; Y. Hudson, ed., *Globalism and the Obsolescence of the State.* Lewiston, NY: Mellen Press, 1999; and M. Bamyeh, *The Ends of Globalization.* Minneapolis: University of Minnesota Press, 2000.

12. Martin Wolf, "Will the Nation-State Survive Globalization?" *Foreign Affairs* 80(1) (2001): 178.

13. Mark Hallenberg, "Tax Competition in Wilhelmine Germany and Its Implications for the European Union," *World Politics* 48(3) (April 1996): 324–357; Geoffrey Garrett, "Capital Mobility, Trade, and the Domestic Politics of Economic Policy," *International Organization* 49 (Autumn 1995): 657–688; and Peter Katzenstein, *Small States in World Markets.* Ithaca, NY: Cornell University Press, 1985.

14. Geoffrey Garrett, *Partisan Politics in the Global Economy.* Cambridge, UK: Cambridge University Press, 1998; and Charles Boix, *Political Parties, Growth and Equality.* Cambridge, UK: Cambridge University Press, 1998.

15. Duane Swank, "Funding the Welfare State: Globalization and Taxation of Business in Advanced Market Economies," *Political Studies* 46(4) (1998): 671–692; and Dani Rodrik, "Why Do More Open Economies Have Bigger Governments?" *Journal of Political Economy* 106(5) (October 1998): 997–1032.

16. It should be noted that emerging economies are in principle vulnerable to "race to the bottom" effects because since economic growth is more reliant on the attraction of foreign capital, competition to attract investment through lower environmental and labor standards is always a theoretical possibility.

17. Dani Rodrik, "Sense and Nonsense in the Globalization Debate," *Foreign Policy* 107 (Summer 1997): 19–37.

18. John McCallum, "National Borders Matter: Canada-U.S. Regional Trade Patterns," *The American Economic Review* 85(3) (1995): 615–623.

19. Robert Pastor, ed., *A Century's Journey: How the Great Powers Shape the World.* New York: Basic Books, 1999; and Thomas L. Friedman, *The Lexus and the Olive Tree.* New York: Farrar, Straus & Giroux, 1999.

20. Cited from Benjamin J. Cohen, *The Geography of Money.* Ithaca, NY: Cornell University Press, 1998.

21. E. Helleiner, "Electronic Money: A Challenge to the Sovereign State?" *Journal of International Affairs* 51(2) (Spring 1998): 387–410; Linda Weiss, *The Myth of the Powerless State: Governing the Economy in a Global Era.* Ithaca, NY: Cornell University Press, 1998; and Paul Hirst and Graham Thompson, *Globalization in Question: The International Economy and the Possibilities of Governance*, 2nd ed. Cambridge: Polity Press, 1999.

22. Jan Aarte Scholte, "Global Capitalism and the State," *International Affairs* 73(3) (July 1997): 427–452; Robert Keohane and Joseph Nye, *Power and Interdependence*, 3rd ed. Glenville, IL: Scotts Foresman, 2003; and Stephen D. Krasner, ed., *Problematic Sovereignty: Contested Rules and Political Possibilities.* New York: Columbia University Press, 2003.

23. Kenichi Ohmae argues that the authority invested in nation-states is devolving to regional organizations. Ohmae, *The Borderless World: Power and Strategy*; and Kenichi Ohmae, *The End of the Nation State.* New York: Free Press, 1995.

24. Keohane and Nye, *Power and Interdependence*, 107.
25. William Pfaff, "Look Again: The Nation-State Isn't Going Away," *International Herald Tribune*, January 11, 2000, electronic version.
26. Ankie Hoogvelt, *Globalization and the Postcolonial World*. Baltimore: Johns Hopkins University Press, 1997: 67. Other studies supportive of this thesis include the following: James N. Rosenau, *Along the Domestic–Foreign Frontier: Exploring Governance in a Turbulent World*. Cambridge, UK: Cambridge University Press, 1997; A. Herod, et al., eds., *An Unruly World? Globalization, Governance and Geography*. London: Routledge, 1998; and J. Keane, *Global Civil Society?* Cambridge: Cambridge University Press, 2003.
27. Jan Aarte Scholte, *Globalization: A Critical Introduction*, 2nd ed. New York: Palgrave, 2005: 25.
28. Ibid., 186.
29. Benjamin Barber, "Democracy at Risk: American Culture in a Global Culture," *World Policy Journal* 15(2) (1998): 29–41; Barbara Crossette, "Globalization Tops Agenda for World Leaders at U.N. Summit," *New York Times*, September 3, 2000, electronic version; and Alan Ehrenhalt, "Demanding the Right Size Government," *New York Times*, October 4, 1999, electronic version.
30. Anthony D. Smith, *Nationalism and Modernism: A Critical Survey of Recent Theories of Nations and Nationalism*. London: Routledge, 1998; John F. Stack, Jr. and Lui Hebron, "Canada's Ethnic Dilemma: Primordial Ethnonationalism in Quebec," in David Carment, John F. Stack, Jr., and David Harvey, eds., *The International Politics of Quebec Secession: State Making and State Breaking in North America*. Westport, CT: Praeger, 2001; and Walker Connor, *Ethno-Nationalism: The Search for Understanding*. Princeton, NJ: Princeton University Press, 1994.
31. Sheila L. Croucher, *Globalization and Belonging: The Politics of Identity in a Changing World*. Rowman & Littlefield Publishers, 2004: 35–36, 115–121; John F. Stack, Jr., "The Ethnic Challenge to International Relations Theory," in David Carment and Patrick James, eds., *Wars in the Midst of Peace: The International Politics of Ethnic Conflict*. Pittsburgh: University of Pittsburgh Press, 1997: 11–15; John F. Stack, Jr., "Ethnic Groups as Emerging Transnational Actors," in John F. Stack, Jr., ed., *Ethnic Identities in a Transnational World*. Westport, CT: Greenwood Press, 1981: 32–40; and John F. Stack, Jr., "The Ethnic Mobilization in World Politics: The Primordial Perspective," in John F. Stack, Jr., ed., *The Primordial Challenge: Ethnicity in the Contemporary World*. Westport, CT: Greenwood Press, 1986: 1–5.
32. Daniel Bell, "Ethnicity and Social Change," in Nathan Glazer and Daniel P. Moynihan, eds., *Ethnicity: Theory and Experience*. Cambridge: Harvard University Press, 1975: 142.
33. Croucher, *Globalization and Belonging*, 62–70. Croacher demonstrates just how important global immigration is to both rich and poor countries throughout the world.
34. Mark Juergensmeyer, *Terror in the Mind of God: The Global Rise of Religious Violence*. Berkeley: University of California Press, 2002: 219–228.
35. Dale F. Eickelman and James P. Piscatori, *Muslim Politics*. Princeton: Princeton University Press, 1996: 138–155; and Juergensmeyer, *Terror in the Mind of God*, 19–36, 61–80.
36. Mary Habeck, *Knowing the Enemy: Jihadist Ideology and the War on Terror*. New York: Yale University Press, 2007: 161, 164–166.
37. Bell, "Ethnicity and Social Change," 142.
38. Juergensmeyer, *Terror in the Mind of God*, 229.
39. Bell, "Ethnicity and Social Change," 142.

40. Agence France-presse, "French Parliament Approves Limited Autonomy for Corsicans," *New York Times*, December 19, 2001, electronic version.
41. Statute of Autonomy of Catalonia 2006, http://www.gencat.net/generalitat/eng/estatut/preambul.htm, last visited July 18, 2007; and Renwick Mclean, "Spain Grants New Powers of Self-Government to Restive Region," *New York Times*, March 30, 2006, electronic version.
42. Joyce Quin, "Labour's Forgotten Regions," *Financial Times*, June 27, 2001, electronic version.
43. Peter Baker and Susan B. Glasser, "Regions Resist Kremlin Control: Governors Cling to Power in Defiance of President," *Washington Post*, May 31, 2001: A01.
44. Ibid.
45. *Economist*, "The Day of the Governors," June 14, 2001, electronic version.
46. Ibid.
47. Michael Schuman and Timothy Mapes, "Who's in Charge in Jakarta? For Indonesia's Provinces, the Answer Matters Less and Less," *Wall Street Journal*, June 15, 2001, electronic version.
48. Rama Lakshmi, "Unhappy with the State They're In," *Washington Post*, July 8, 2001: A17.
49. Ibid.
50. E. H. Fry, "Substate Governance," in R. Robertson and J. A. Scholte, eds., *The Encyclopedia of Globalization*. London: Routledge, 2006.
51. Ibid.
52. S. Breslin, "Decentralisation, Globalisation and China's Partial Re-engagement with the Global Economy," *New Political Economy* 5 (July 2000): 205–226.
53. R. Kaiser, "Sub-State Governments in International Arenas: Paradiplomacy and Multi-level Governance in Europe and North America," in G. Lachapelle and S. Paquin, eds., *Mastering Globalization: New Sub-States' Governance and Strategies*. London: Routledge, 2005: 90–113.
54. Scholte, *Globalization: A Critical Introduction*.
55. Edward D. Mansfield and Helen V. Milner, eds., *The Political Economy of Regionalism*. New York: Columbia University Press, 1997; M. Schulz, et al., eds., *Regionalization in a Globalizing World: A Comparative Perspective on Forms, Actors and Processes*. London: Zed, 2001; and S. Breslin, et al., eds., *New Regionalisms in the Global Political Economy: Theories and Cases*. London: Routledge, 2002.
56. Ehrenhalt, "Demanding the Right Size Government."
57. Ibid.
58. Daniel Drezner, "Globalizers of the World, Unite!" *The Washington Quarterly* 21(1) (Winter 1998): 209–225.
59. G. Sorensen, *The Transformation of the State: Beyond the Myth of Retreat*. New York: Palgrave Macmillan, 2004.
60. Held, et al., *Global Transformation*, 8–9.
61. Taking this activist state model to heart, Manfred Steger states, "In order to advance their enterprise, globalists must be prepared to utilize the powers of government to weaken and eliminate those social policies and institutions that curtail the market. Since only strong governments are up to this ambitious task of transforming existing social arrangements, the successful liberalization of markets depends upon the intervention and interference by centralized state power." Manfred B. Steger, *Globalism: The New Market Ideology*. New York: Rowman & Littlefield Publishers, Inc., 2002: 52.

7

Culture

Culture is not a zero-sum game, so the greater reach of one culture does not necessarily mean diminished stature for others. In the broad sweep of history, many different traditions have grown together and flourished. American popular culture will continue to make money, but the 21st century will bring a broad mélange of influences, with no clear world cultural leader.

—*Tyler Cowen, Profeesor of Economics, George Mason University*[1]

Globalism has less to do today with multinationals, World Trade Organization agreements and e-mail connections than with the way each one of us chooses to define community, home and ourselves. How much will we take in the neighbors, how much expand our narrow orbit?

—*Pico Iyer, Essayist and Novelist*[2]

INTRODUCTION: THE BACKLASH AGAINST CULTURAL GLOBALIZATION

Critics have charged that globalization has become the vehicle for destroying the rich diversity of regional, national, and/or local cultures; traditions; and myths due to the powerful **homogenization** effects—pressure to conform to Western capitalism, lifestyle choices, and values—which accompany the progressive transformation of these societies. While Professor Francis Fukuyama of the John Hopkins School of Advanced International Studies views these developments in a positive light—the establishment of a global order guided by the worldwide acceptance of economic and political liberalism *a la* the proliferation of market democracies—others are not so sanguine.[3] As early as 1996, Harvard political scientist Samuel Huntington foresaw the possibility of a clash of cultural values so deep and so pernicious between the West and Islam as well as other cultural systems that he described these conflicts in terms of a **"clash of civilizations."**[4] In like manner, University of Maryland professor Benjamin Barber anticipated increasing cycles of conflict between the unifying values of **"McWorld"** on one side, as opposed to forces of ethnonational and cultural fragmentation on the other side.[5] This raises the concern of many that globalization driven by rampaging world capitalism will result in the further development of a culture of consumerism oriented toward materialism, indulgent personal values, and ultimately the destruction of once vibrant and irreplaceable local cultures. Globalization's ability to impose commercial culture (its ways of thinking and behaving) has resulted in, for the first time, globally directed consumerism. A.O. Scott, movie critic for the *New York Times*, describes this state of affairs in the following manner, "the multinational North becomes the supplier, pushing its product on the rest of the world. Or, more benignly, inventing new ways to give people what they want."[6] The result unfortunately is a prescription for cultural genocide based on the power of globalization to eradicate cultural distinctiveness in vibrant communities throughout the world.[7]

For militant critics, globalization is regarded as a frontal assault on cultural diversity, blurring distinctions in food, fashions, music, and the arts, as well as undercutting deep-seated customs and practices. Lifestyle-driven changes in food production, consumption patterns, and even in shopping habits bring about changes in family, religious practices, sexual mores, and occupational preferences. This integration of emerging economies into the global marketplace accompanied by the proliferation of mass media in major cities throughout the developing world certainly stimulated massive flows of isolated indigenous peoples into ever-increasing urban shantytowns encircling every major city of the developing world. Moreover, the upending of traditional hierarchies within families, the loss of respect for elders, and the increasingly delicate balance between men and women are reflected in the evolving attitudes about gender equality, family hierarchies, and democratic values. The International Forum on Globalization, a San Francisco–based alliance of scholars, has complained that U.S. advertising has glorified "Western taste, dress, food and lifestyle as being a sign of progress, while non-Western traditional values and cultures are viewed as backward and out of date."[8] Since the integration of developing countries producing agricultural products is imposed from outside the country, and often the region, the impact of globalization appears to be even greater in magnifying the local community's sense of loss of control over the changes that occur in family practices, gender, and social values.

Globalization and Authenticity: What Price Harmony and Homogenization?

All of these issues and anxieties come to form the emotional heart of concerns about globalization. In essence, there is the fear that not only is one's economic sovereignty at risk but that one's cultural identity is also at stake. The loss from the destruction of the latter is simply incalculable for many because it foreshadows the destruction of both individual and collective authenticity.

In the end, the backlash against globalization raises nothing less than the battle for the preservation of a people's national cultural inheritance against the onslaught of Western capitalism. The globalization process, therefore, bespeaks a **"cultural imperialism"** far more threatening and transforming than the nineteenth-century European political/military version. The danger is more than just the indiscriminate infusion (imposition) of Western **popular culture** and material goods (consumer brands).

How authenticity is defined is a crucial but often underestimated dimension in the battle over globalization. It follows that a near-constant concern is the assimilation both subtle and overt of Western (American) ideas, beliefs, and values. The way one views such issues as human rights, gender equality, democratic processes, and social justice has the potential to fundamentally rock the foundation of a country's political, religious, and cultural makeup. As one informed observer, the sociologist Peter Berger of Boston University, commented, "Take the case of rock music. Its attraction is not just due to a particular preference for loud, rhythmic sound and dangerously athletic dancing. Rock music also symbolizes a whole cluster of cultural values— concerning self-expression, spontaneity, released sexuality, and, perhaps most importantly, defiance of the alleged stodginess of tradition."[9]

Both emerging market countries in Latin America, Southeast Asia, and Eastern Europe and such advanced industrial states as Japan, Canada, and France have expressed profound reservations about the continuing degradation of the cultural content of their respective societies based on America-dominated globalization. A sense, therefore, of a cultural state of siege afflicts many countries. For these states, there is a genuine, widespread concern about the dilution of nationhood in the form of the erosion of national authority and identity through the intrusion and integration of globalization. Benjamin Barber underscored the magnitude of globalization as a worldwide process leading to greater anxieties for many elites in the developing world when he observed that too many people in developing countries "spend far too much of their time each day in one of the commercial habitations of the new world being 'imagineered' in Hollywood."[10] Echoing this sentiment, Samuel Huntington noted that "[w]hat Westerners see as benign global integration, such as the proliferation of worldwide media, non-Westerners see as nefarious Western imperialism. . . . To the extent that non-Westerners see the world as one, they see it as a threat."[11]

The fear of not being able to preserve one's distinctive cultural traditions under conditions of globalization is perhaps best illustrated by the case of

Japan. Having reached the tenth year of its recession, Japanese businesses and the government were under tremendous pressure to abandon their system of life-time employment and to end the protection of their fragile agricultural industry as a way to jump-start the economy. One of the central dimensions of neoliberal economic adjustments, especially in the area of agriculture, will result in the displacement of thousands of families from their ancestral lands, the destruction of local communities, and the likely demise of local festivals and cultural activities. In contrast to the top-down direction of the global economy, the Japanese government has resisted these economic reforms, in part, based on the primacy of cultural factors. "Because the Japanese operate their economy to sustain their society and not the other way around, they correctly think that it is idiotic to destroy what they value most for the sake of a minor increase in efficiency."[12] The dilemma facing states as they try to decide if joining the globalization caravan is the correct approach for the growth and development of their economy was expressed by former Singaporean senior minister, Lee Kuan Yew, when he lamented, "The problem is how to change but changing cultures and values is not easy."[13]

As we shall see in the next section, the United States, as the leading proponent and practitioner of globalization, not surprisingly, is the object of much of this criticism. It is, as the philosopher Martin Heidegger puts it in reference to Americanism, "the emerging monstrousness of modern times."[14] The extent of American power and influence, however, in defining and driving globalization may not be as potent as critics claim.

The Politics of Resistance and Discord

The prevailing view of contemporary global culture contends that American commercial and popular culture occupies an almost hegemonic presence on the world, as exemplified by its prominence in the world marketplace and the glamorization of the American lifestyle: The United States can boast of being the world's most powerful economy. Perhaps most irritating of all for its competitors, as well as its trading partners, is that the United States remains at the forefront in the research and development of the most promising new technologies. For many around the world, globalization calls to mind negative images because the word has become both a synonym and a euphemism for the pervasiveness of American popular culture based on the attractiveness of its consumer goods, the magic of its technology, the power of its entertainment industry, and the ascendance of English as the new global language. According to Clyde Prestowitz, president of the Economic Strategy Institute, a Washington-based think tank, "There is a widespread view abroad that globalization is being forced on the world by American corporations, that globalization is **Americanization**."[15]

The United States, at the beginning of the twenty-first century, can lay claim to possessing over half of the globe's most popular and recognizable consumer brand names—in 2009, of the world's top 100 brand names, 52 were American, according to Interbrand, a marketing research firm specializing in brand names.[16]

America's entertainment industry, including movies, music, software, and television broadcasting, is one of its largest export sector. In the film universe, a strong case can be made that the movies coming out of Hollywood dominate world cinema and perhaps without much of a stretch an emerging world culture. Though it does not produce the most feature films (that designation belongs to India's Bollywood, the nickname for the Bombay-based film community centered around Mumbai [Bombay], which releases upwards of 800 films a year).[17] American cinematic efforts are the only ones that have penetrated every market in the world. "The highly successful films of India [the Philippines, Britain] and Hong Kong hardly travel outside their regions."[18] In contrast, films such as the *Star Wars* series are hits on every continent. Because "sound and pictures are how what passes as 'knowledge' gets 'communicated' to most people around the globe,"[19] the domination of American popular culture on the world via films, music, and technology is perhaps more significant than the hegemony of the high-tech U.S. armed forces. The *Economist* reported in 1998 that "In major markets around the world, lists of the biggest-grossing films are essentially lists of Hollywood blockbusters in slightly differing orders with one or two local films for variety."[20] Twelve years later, the current state of affairs remains the same.

In the small screen too, the story is the same. A quick glance of the top-rated television programs in almost any country will show that they are produced locally. Closer examination, however, reveals that these "home-grown programs" curiously resemble popular American shows reconfigured for local tastes. Thus, we see a French or Thai version of *Wheel of Fortune*; a Polish version of *The Price is Right* rechristened as *Guess the Price*; an Indonesian incarnation of *The Honeymooners*; and popular telenovelas in the Spanish-speaking world that have been clearly inspired by American soap operas.[21]

The spectacular rise of America's popular culture can also be attributed to the globalization of the English language. According to English-language specialist and author David Crystal,[22] "The English language snowball has got so big now that it's virtually unstoppable."[23] As a result of the *Pax Britania*[24] and *Pax Americana*,[25] English has become the *lingua franca* for politics and diplomacy, technology, science, business,[26] academia, and cyberspace[27] and of international meetings.[28] As Benjamin Barber notes, " . . . although they produce neither common interests nor common law, common markets do demand, along with a common currency, a common language. . . . "[29] And with globalization, the establishment of a common language has been a fundamental need to conduct world affairs. This might explain why English has become the principal language for oral and written communications throughout the world and shows no signs of diminishing. Indeed, the extensiveness of the language has become so ingrained in the world's consciousness that it is problematic for one to become globally successful without a fluent command of English.

Further evidence of English's global stature is its ascension as the first or second language of choice for much of the developed and the developing worlds. All over Asia and the Pacific, no education is complete today without the study of English because proficiency in the language has become a must-have skill: Indeed, in schools across the Pacific Rim, an ever increasing number of students are starting their study of English in grade school, rather than in middle school, in order to hone their fluency because companies are grooming and promoting their English-speaking employees to better paying and more exciting jobs. Governments, as well, eager to entice American transnational corporations to open offices or plants, are making a concerted effort to encourage and in some cases demand that their citizens achieve a greater command of English. The leaders of a number of countries, including Chinese president Hu Jintao, Indonesian president Susilo Bambang Yudhoyono, Philippines president Gloria Macapagal-Arroyo, and South Korean president Roh Moo Hyun, speak English fluently.

Throughout most of Europe, the story is the same, with English being spoken as fluently and nearly as commonly as the native languages. In the Scandinavian countries and the Netherlands, for example, spoken English has become so pervasive that it is now accepted as an everyday language.[30] With the expansion of the European Union to encompass the whole of Europe, an English-speaking continent is projected to be in place by the end of the twenty-first century.[31] That English is driving the Europeans toward a universal language for the first time in about 500 years[32] is a monumental development that cannot be overstated. More important even than monetary union, the establishment of a new *lingua franca* would be one of the most significant milestones to date in this endeavor to construct a unified Europe. For not only would the continental adoption of English allow Europeans to become a stronger competitor in the marketplace, but just as importantly, it would also serve as a neutralizing common denominator among the multilingual nations of Europe.

As is frequently the case, with success comes a palpable sense of unease, if not downright resentment. The overwhelming success of America as one of the world's major economic powers, certainly its most recent military engagements, and it being the largest exporter of popular culture have contributed to a noticeable increase in anti-American rhetoric, and with it, a backlash against globalization because of a growing consensus around the world that the process has disproportionately benefited the United States' interests and values. Reports David Sanger of the *New York Times*, "Almost any place one lands these days—Tokyo or Bombay or Brussels—the complaint is the same: the United States is trying to rig the global trading system to benefit its own, and its own want to own the world."[33]

One of the most vociferous criticisms by globalization's detractors is that the process leads inexorably to the triumph of American popular culture. To many, even some inside the United States, the spectacular diffusion of American popular culture is viewed as an unwelcome intrusion that seems uncontrollable. Abroad, people see these developments as a dangerous invasion by American commercial culture because it reflects, among other things, a feeling that national identities are being undermined by the market-based American model of capitalism. Specifically, the United States has been accused of suppressing genuine, indigenous culture: "It is regarded as homogenization, one-dimensional life, the effacement of difference. For some cultural nationalists, like Alexandre Kojeve, it will be the end of history."[34]

According to Latin American novelist and author Mario Vargas Llosa, "This delirium of persecution—spurred by hatred and rancor toward the North American giant—is also apparent in developed countries and nations of high culture and is shared among political sectors of the left, center, and right."[35] Increasing opponents of the Americanization/Westernization of the world have urged that the pace of globalization should be slowed if not halted. This American-led process is increasingly viewed as an extension of vulgar capitalism. The political and economic dimensions of liberalization threaten to spread the American habits of excessive inequality and rampant individualism that undermine indigenous communities. Rudy Koursbroek, a well-known Danish essayist, perhaps best captured the opposition to this American-led globalization process when he wrote, "The Ayatollah was right . . . America is the Great Satan, American culture is vulgar rubbish, the free market is killing literature, tasteless youth culture rules all and civilization as we know it must be protected against the barbaric businessman."[36]

In this hostile environment, even the benefits of English as a global tongue enabling people around the world to more easily communicate and conduct business with more efficiency have come under attack. Since languages are both a medium of communication and repositories of culture and identity, for many countries the all-engulfing advance of English threatens to damage, if not destroy, authentic local culture. This concern is being voiced even in England itself. For while the language now encircling the world may have English roots and heritage, the culture being conveyed with it is American.

REALITY CHECK: THE AMERICANIZATION OF THE GLOBE?

While the nature of American cultural domination forms a central and cohesive dimension of the antiglobalization movement, many of these concerns are not only extreme, but misinformed. The reasons for American cultural predominance stem more from its unique historical development, ideological orientation characterized by equality and adaptability, as well as its economic prowess rather than just a grand scheme to dominate the world: "U.S. popular culture sells abroad, observers say, because it reflects many of the appealing themes and myths of the United States itself: individuality, wealth, progress, tolerance, optimism."[37] This equality and flexibility is best reflected by an American culture that is a sophisticated and eclectic conglomeration of influences from around the globe. It is deliberately melded (sometime turbulently) into a social, economic, and political milieu that not only allows but encourages and exalts individual freedoms and a mishmash of cultures to thrive.

Moreover, the American lifestyle is "marketed" with a mass-market orientation. It is not the traditional elites who are its main target, but what Naomi Klein calls "the global teen." Klein sees it thus: "It's the young people living in developed and semi-developed countries who are the great global hope. More than anything or anyone else, logo-decorated middle-class teenagers, intent on pouring themselves into a media-fabricated mold, have become globalization's most powerful symbol."[38]

What then is the United States' role and influence in the globalization process? Clearly, America's imprint can be seen on globalization. The United States' economic, political, social, and cultural power has given it a leading role in the establishment of a global culture. But given the fact that American culture is able to direct the habits and practices, and furnish the imageries and aspirations, of a worldwide audience, does this transnational popularity indicate a condition of hegemony in a pejorative sense? The answer would have to be in the negative. Indeed, far from looking at the "Americanization" of the world in a pejorative light, it should be viewed as a vehicle for an increasingly integrated world. This means that countries and peoples are provided with ways of overcoming isolation. Emerging as well as developed states should understand that technology-driven changes are inevitable. The power of America is the synergy that its culture, economics, politics, and technology create transnationally.

DEBATING GLOBALIZATION

Lui Hebron: Cultural Annihilation Is a Myth

John, the globalization of culture, has been described by its detractors, as a seamless process resulting in homogenizing the world's diverse cultures. Consumers from St. Petersburg to St. Louis to San Paulo now download the same music, attend the same movies, wear the same clothes, and eat the same foods. In the mind of many people, this homogeneity in taste and consumption is mostly American dominated, and for this reason, globalization has become synonymous with the "Americanization" of the world. The proliferation of these increasingly interchangeable consumerist societies has resulted in turn, with the establishment of a global culture held hostage to culturally specific American trends and quirks, according to globalization's most vocal critics.

The belief that the globalization process is erasing distinctive national identities and producing a common "Americanized" culture around the world has become so prevalent that it has become a universally accepted fact. This perspective, however, is not an accurate portrayal of the effects of globalization on culture. On the surface, the people of the world may look, sound, and act even more homogeneous today than they did just 20 years ago. But underneath the surface, they remain unique and diverse. As evident by Disney's experience in Europe, transplanting a popular American concept to foreign soil can be tricky. The near failure of Euro Disney was as much about the company's cross-cultural gaffes (e.g., blunder in not adapting to the local culture, such as maintaining an alcohol-free policy in a society where wine is an integral component of the cultural scene) as taking on too heavy a debt load.

Recognizing the need to accommodate national differences and cultural sensitivities, for its Hong Kong Disneyland the Walt Disney Company made sure to include local food and music as well as provide services in both Mandarin and Cantonese (in addition to English). Observed Robert Thompson, professor of popular culture at Syracuse University: "It used to be Disney was exported on its own terms. But in the late 20th and early 21st century, America's cultural imperialism was tested. Now, instead of being the ugly Americans, which some foreigners used to find charming, we have to take off our shoes or belch after a meal." (Quoted from Laura M. Holson "The Feng Shui Kingdom," *New York Times*, April 25, 2005)

The deeper one examines the interaction between globalization and culture, the easier it becomes to refute the complaint by antiglobalists of the onset of an impending "cultural imperialism." For while it is true that globalization does have a homogenizing effect, whereby cultures do lose their distinctiveness to some extent, substantial cultural differences continue to exist between societies. Indeed, the peculiarities of a country's historical experiences, local traditions, and indigenous values and attitudes are far more influential sources of a society's cultural character than those that have been imported via globalization or "Americanization."—Lui

John Stack: Cultural Matters Impact Globalization

Lui, the history of globalization is the battle for the minds and hearts of peoples across the globe. Culture matters, of course, as it is influenced and shaped by the power of the media in the form of mass marketing campaigns, the selling of consumerism, and the false consciousness that arises as a consequence of the creation of values supportive of American materialist society. For more than a century, social activists have seen in the preoccupation of market-driven consumerism in the United States the slow unraveling of civic consciousness because the thirst for buying things overshadows the need to build civic values supportive of responsible democratic governance. The creation of the appetite to consume, therefore, trumps the need to create a civic culture based on meeting the needs of all. The creation of a viable civic culture, however, demands citizens who see government as making difficult choices—not simply as a vehicle to facilitate the acquisition of products that have no intrinsic value except to satisfy the need to consume more.

One need not be an antiglobalist, as you call it, to understand the devastating effects of wanton consumerism on the creation of responsible citizens who believe in values that transcend the narrow self-interest of the marketplace as defined by corporations designed to sell products that will better their bottom line. The European resistance to American culture is not based, by and large, on the proliferation of English as the world's *lingua franca* but on the values of consumerism that are embedded in many of the most appealing delivery vehicles of globalization—the Internet, movies, video games, and music. The problem is that the creation of consumer societies dominated by unneeded products and unquenchable thirts affects directly how societies will evolve and what policy choices will be made under conditions of increasing globalization— which is to say larger markets and heftier bottom lines to meet. Let me note just one of these important areas considered in the text.

One of the central battles of globalization will be the ability to secure and sustain basic resources in the global economy. The requirement to provide basic resources in the form of food, water, transportation, housing employment, and education will ultimately confront every country and every society across the planet with difficult choices. The creation of artificial needs and wants, the stock and trade of consumerism, will make the question of who receives what even more difficult. The problem with the creation of a global consumer society devoted to the selling of good irrelevant to state building and nation building substantively damages prospects for the creation of sustainable societies worldwide necessary to meet the needs of diverse peoples.

Consumerism in the form of American- and Western-dominated culture directly poses a challenge to how the process of globalization will play out in the years to come. History suggests that when expectations rise and are unmet, revolution, conflict, and wars may follow. The process of the creation of sustainable societies in the rich North, the emerging economies of Latin America and Asia, and the impoverished South suggests that culture hugely matters.—John ■

DEBUNKING THE MYTHS: THE GLOBALIZATION OF AMERICA

While it has become universally acknowledged that American popular culture exerts a powerful influence across the globe in shaping attitudes, trends, and styles, the assimilative effects of Americanization have been dramatically overstated and exaggerated. It is likely that the globalization process will only superficially "Americanize" non-American/Western cultures throughout the globe. For while much of this new global culture is being modeled in the image of America and/or the West, it is unlikely that language, religion, geography, and history will be easily transformed by Big Macs, music videos, and even rampant patterns of consumption. We examine two issue areas that place the supposed cultural supremacy and hegemony of the United States in doubt: **"world" English** and **"global" entertainment** (films and television programs).

"World" English

There is no question that with globalization, English has become an essential agent for the execution of international transactions and communication. Has the ascension of English as a "global tongue," however, come at the expense of the other great languages? The short answer is probably not, while the exact opposite may be true.[39]

While English is now widely spoken throughout the globe, the language's identification as the exclusive tongue of Britain or the United States no longer holds true. According to Wang Gungwu, a professor at the National University of Singapore, "Today, fewer and fewer people think of English in terms of either England or America."[40] This lack of globalization of American and British English is most evident from the fact that those people for whom English is their native tongue are now outnumbered by those who speak English as a second language.

As English becomes more widespread, the power of new speakers to transform and modify it both orally and literally likewise increases. Today, an enormous number of people are not only learning English in so many places, but are also modifying, "localizing," the language in ways barely recognizable to an American or a Briton. As a result, umpteen variations to standard English grammar—what linguists have dubbed "Englishes"—have evolved throughout the world.[41] These speakers converse in a locally distinctive form of English. For example, many Singaporeans speak Singlish—a mixture of English and Chinese. In the Philippines, Tanglish, a mixture of Tagalog and English, has become the normal form of oral and written communication. And in India, Hinglish, a mixture of Hindi and English, is becoming increasingly common. Indeed, in many major cities within the United States and throughout the states of the Southwestern United States, Spanglish, a mixture of Spanish and English, has become part of the natural landscape, as Samuel Huntington notes.[42] As Huntington argues passionately, the political destiny of the United States is under siege from the growing Hispanization of the United States. Far from confirming the cultural hegemony of American political culture and language, Huntington envisages a cultural conflict so deep and pervasive that fundamental Anglo-Saxon political culture is at risk.[43]

A key aspect about "world" English is that the language is being appropriated and remade in the image of this adopted setting. Instead of being viewed as a tool of economic hegemony, it is an instrumental means of reflecting the hopes, fears, and aspirations of non-Westerners because it has become the vessel for the expression of local culture, history, and politics. In this regard, the rise of English is by no means a signal that indigenous linguistic worlds (national languages, regional dialects, and even entire cultures) are going to disappear.

Besides, these permutations of Englishes are not replacing the mother tongue. Rather, the reformulated Englishes cropping up globally should be viewed as reflecting the milieu, character, and linguistic needs of their adopted country. The implications of this English-language phenomenon perhaps were best summed up by the Filipino poet Gemino Abad, who declared, "The English language is now ours. We have colonized it."[44] As a younger generation—in Europe, Latin America, Africa, and Asia—grows up surrounded by English, they will enter this second-language group too, in which English will become part of their everyday lives.

On the World Wide Web, the unassailable dominance of English can no longer be taken at face value. While at the start of the twenty-first century, Americans comprised by far the largest group of all Internet users, the projections are that as Internet access expands globally and more companies and institutions conduct their businesses online, the privileged position of English on the Internet is anticipated to dramatically decline. Data collected by Forrester, an IT market research group, confirm that a substantial majority of surfers would like to have Web sites in their native tongue. Even more telling for businesses is the revelation that shoppers are more likely to purchase items online if they can use their own language.[45] These projections and trends would indicate that as the Internet becomes more and more a part of our daily lives, companies wanting to take full advantage of the power of the Internet to reach global markets will need to provide numerous versions of their Web sites.

"Global" Entertainment

No more is the globalization of America evident than in its selection and worldwide output of movies, videos, music, television programming, and pop culture where the go-ahead for projects is increasingly being determined by its ability to sell tickets overseas. Since 1998, overseas ticket sales account for over 50 percent of Hollywood's box office receipts according to the Motion Picture Association of America. With experts estimating that growth will continue to climb at a rate of about 6 percent to 7 percent annually—about three times as fast as the national benchmark of gross domestic product— studios have targeted disparate corners of the world with movies made to please. Studio executives, well aware that 45 of the top 50 (90 percent) and 84 of the top 100 movies of all time have made more profit abroad than in the United States, many by a significant margin (e.g., over 60 percent of gross for *The Da Vinci Code*, the *Matrix* trilogy, the three *Mission Impossible* movies, and *Titanic* were made overseas[46]), have increasingly come to the conclusion that courting audiences abroad makes sound business sense. The fact is American money is no longer worth as much to Tinseltown as it used to be. There soon will be so many moviegoers around the world that the revenue generated in North America may be practically irrelevant. *New York Times* reporter Laura M. Holson reports that "Industry analysts predict an increase in worldwide movie attendance over the next five years, with Asia and Central and Eastern Europe the fastest-growing regions."[47] Holson further cites a study by PricewaterhouseCoopers, which stated that "global spending on film entertainment from 2006 to 2010, including movie tickets and DVDs, is projected to grow at an annual rate of 5.3 percent."[48]

Due to the increasingly unavoidable reality that exportable movies are estimated to bring in one and a half times the revenues of the domestic box office,[49] the decision-making process of Hollywood's studio executives and moguls[50] (everything from financing and distribution[51] to the actors and director[52] themselves), as well as the content of its products (i.e., story line and dialog), is frequently determined by cinematic tastes around the globe. *The Da Vinci Code*, which has grossed over $745 million[53] ($528 from foreign box office receipts), provides a textbook case study of how movies have become an increasingly global endeavor. Brian Grazer, the film's executive producer, and executives at Sony Pictures Entertainment made a concerted effort to hire "culturally relevant" actors from Britain and France in order to give the film a truly global feel.[54] Says Glenn Rigberg, who represents several international film stars at the talent management firm of Rigberg, Roberts, Rugalo: "Movies these days have to be made for their worldwide potential."[55] Echoing these sentiments is Ken Lemberger, copresident of Sony Pictures, when he stated, "In a sense, we're making films for export."[56] And the global market has determined that generic, short-on-dialog, high-on-special-effects, plot-challenged movies which eschew fine-grained cultural observation are its best sellers because such films can be understood by audiences with minimal grasp of English and/or Western culture. No more is the power of the international cinematic market on display than with the casting, release, and huge overseas box-office receipt of *Pirates of the Caribbean: At World's End*. The second sequel of Disney's blockbuster series featured an international cast from the United States (Johnny Depp), Europe (Orlando Bloom and Geoffrey Rush), and Asia (Chow Yun-Fat), as well as a simultaneous global opening in 104 countries that has brought in $245 million (of the $401 million total) outside of the North American market in just its first six days of release.[57]

American television viewers also have an outrageously huge collection in their entertainment choices thanks to greater and more affordable cable access and/or satellite dishes. For some of America's neoconservatives (and liberals), however, this expansion of foreign-language programming is viewed with horror. They see this emerging trend as a menacing and unwelcomed intrusion on the country's melting-pot ethos. The United States, they fear, is "dissolving into a babble of discordant ethnic voices without a common cultural identity or a shared national purpose. And they put much of the blame on the proliferation of foreign-language media outlets. One of the most popular television channels in Los Angeles is KMFX 34, which broadcasts in Spanish; there are also channels which broadcast exclusively in Korean, Cantonese and Japanese, and others that rent air-time for Yiddish and Russian broadcasts."[58] From this perspective, it would appear that the effect of globalization on entertainment is not of America "corrupting" the world, but rather of the world corrupting America.

CONCLUSION: THE EVOLUTION OF GLOBAL CULTURE, THE "GLOCAL"

What can we say then about the relationship between globalization and culture? According to the 1999 United Nations Human Development Report, "The debate on whether there is cultural homogenisation remains open. There are no surveys showing that people are becoming alike."[59] At the very minimum, this examination of culture within the matrix of globalization should tell us that since the process is not merely the convergence of a diversity of cultures toward a single global culture, we are far from the fanciful conception of a culturally homogeneous global village.

From one perspective, projections, theories, and idyllic visions of the inevitable establishment of a unified, homogenized "global culture" driven by globalization underestimate the resiliency of indigenous identities, customs, habits, values, attitudes, and belief systems in the developing and developed worlds. Increasingly, the nation defined in terms of a cultural entity has repeatedly demonstrated an ability not to be wholly engulfed by the plethora of exogenous cultural influences it is being exposed to via globalization. Nevertheless, the dynamic power struggle between international representations and national/local ones is now an integral part of national identity construction within a globalizing world. With this fact in mind, globalists must learn to coexist with people for whom the nation-state can still mobilize passions more effectively than the international bureaucratic structures that try to manage globalization. As Jean-Marie Guhenno (1999) observed, "History teaches us that contrary to the conventional wisdom, human beings are much more willing to die for their ideas than for their interests; interests can be bargained for, but ideas are the foundations of identities, and nobody wants to compromise his identity."[60]

At the same time, it is obvious that due to the emergence of new global infrastructures, advances in transnational communications, and the information revolution, denizens are experiencing a broader array of influences from around the world and that their scope, therefore, is no longer restricted to their parochial habitats but has undertaken a worldwide milieu. In this sense, globalization is a welcomed and positive development to expand the horizons of each individual's experiences. One of the effects of the globalization process is its ability to generate an enormous capacity for cross-border interaction since people are constantly bombarded with a variety of cultural habits, values, and norms. This development, in turn, is re-enforcing the tacitly understood notion that within our evermore mobile and highly integrated world, individuals increasingly harbor not just one but a multitude of identities (emanating from their racial profile, national origin, ethnic background, religious affiliation, etc.). These multilayered individuals of the world generally do not feel the need to relinquish one or more of these identities in favor of another.

Our examination of the relationship between globalization and culture strongly suggests that national/local identity, ethnicity, and culture cannot and will not be easily replaced by, or engulfed into, a converging, all-encompassing global cultural. Now, if a global culture is to be established, this global society must somehow coexist with their local identity and culture. And in order for this cohabitation to be successful, the culture of a nation can no longer be regarded as something that must remain unadulterated or genuine, but as something that has always been touched and altered by disparate cultural influences.[61] History has repeatedly shown that the most successful cultures are those that have always demonstrated a capacity to embrace the values, goals, and practices they want and need, while rejecting the ones that they do not find to be beneficial or useful. Since every culture must be viewed as a living organism that is evolving, "[t]he critical prerequisite for gaining the optimum benefits of global integration is to understand which cultural attributes can and should be tolerated—and, indeed, promoted—and which are the fissures that will become fault lines," according to David Rothkopf.[62]

According to Samuel Huntington, the "search for commonalities between the contending civilizations, [can begin by opening] a dialogue of cultures."[63] In this regard, the Japanese idea of the "**glocal**," whereby the global becomes local and vice versa,[64] provides an excellent point of departure for establishing a global culture. A more nuanced and textured understanding of cultural globalization will have to take into account that the central dynamic in the fabrication of a "glocal culture" involves the twofold process of the localization of the global and the "Westernization" or "Americanization" of the local in a nonthreatening, mutually affirming manner. The ultimate realization of a "glocal culture," therefore, will depend on how successfully the components of globalization (cosmopolitan, individualized, democratized, and secularized) are "grafted" into preexisting local cultural values, traditions, and practices that are communal, hierarchical, and sacred.

KEY TERMS

Americanization 102	"global" entertainment 108	Mcworld 100
clash of civilizations 100	glocal 113	popular culture 101
cultural imperialism 101	homogenization 99	"world" English 108

FIVE QUESTIONS TO CONSIDER

1. What is culture? Why is it an important dimension of globalization?
2. How malleable are cultural values?
3. Does globalization result in the triumph of American culture and the imposition of Western materialism for the remainder of the world?
4. Does the proliferation of American and Western cultural values constitute a new form of cultural imperialism.
5. What do the authors mean by the term "glocal"?

FURTHER READINGS

Tyler Cowen, *Creative Destruction: How Globalization Is Changing the World's Cultures*. Princeton, NJ: Princeton University Press, 2004.

The great myth is that globalization subverts indigenous culture. Cultural "destruction" breeds not artistic demise but diversity when cultures collide through trade. Manifestations such as the Trinidad's steel bands, Indian hand weaving, and Zairian music result in vibrant cultural expressions driven by markets and cultural exchange.

Lane Crothers, *Globalization and American Popular Culture*, 2nd ed. Lanham, MD: Rowman & Littlefield Publishers, Inc., 2009.

Examines how American movies, music, and television—as goods marketed and consumed around the world—are key elements of contemporary globalization. America's popular culture promotes both a desire for integration into the broader world community while also generating disgust and outright rejection revealing the complexity of globalization.

Philippe Legrain, "In Defense of Globalization," *The International Economy* (Summer 2003).

Examines views on the fear that globalization is imposing a deadening cultural uniformity rather than an explosion of cultural exchange ranging from the belief that polyethnic imagery, market-driven globalization does not want diversity to the assertion. On the other hand, Thomas Friedman, columnist for the New York Times and author of The Lexus and the Olive Tree, believes that globalization is globalizing American culture and American cultural icons.

Omar Lizardo, "Globalization and Culture: A Sociological Perspective," Working Paper CSGP 07/8 Trent University, Peterborough, Ontario, Canada.

Various ethnographic studies of culture consumption produce evidence that the destruction of local culture resulting from media imperialism is overstated. Instead of homogeneity of consumption, diversity of interpretation results; instead of a decline in domestic local culture, increasing "creolization" and revitalization of folk cultures occurs.

James N. Rosenau, *Distant Proximities: Dynamics beyond Globalization*. Princeton, NJ: Princeton University Press, 2003.

Treating people-in-the-street as well as activists and elites as central players in what we call "globalization," Rosenau traces the links and interactions between people at the individual level and institutions such as states, nongovernmental organizations, and transnational corporations conveying a deeper understanding of globalization.

NOTES

1. Tyler Cown, "Some Countries Remain Resistant to American Cultural Exports," *New York Times*, February 22, 2007, electronic version.
2. Pico Iyer, "Changing the Ways We Connect," *Los Angeles Times*, April 7, 2008, electronic version.
3. Francis Fukuyama, *The End of History and the Last Man*. New York: Free Press, 1992.
4. Samuel Huntington, *The Clash of Civilizations and the Remaking of World Order*. New York: Simon & Schuster, 1996.
5. Benjamin R. Barber, *Jihad vs. McWorld*. New York: New York Times Books, 1995; and Benjamin R. Barber, "Democracy at Risk: American Culture in a Global Culture," *World Policy Journal* 15(2) (1998): 29–41.
6. A. O. Scott, "Globalization on Film: Message in a Coca-Cola Can," *New York Times*, March 23, 2001, electronic version.
7. Jeremy Rifkin, "World Culture Resists Bowing to Commerce," *Los Angeles Times*, July 2, 2001, electronic version.
8. Jonathan Peterson, "A World of Difference in Trade Views," *Los Angeles Times*, November 28, 1999, electronic version.

9. Peter L. Berger, "Four Faces of Global Culture," *The National Interest* 49 (1997): 23–29.
10. Barber, *Jihad vs. McWorld*, 97.
11. Huntington, *The Clash of Civilizations*.
12. Cited from Edward N. Luttwak, "Globalizers Are the Bolsheviks of Their Day," *Los Angeles Times*, December 10, 1999, electronic version.
13. Cited from David Ignatius, "The Greenspan Effect in Asia," *Washington Post*, January 14, 2001: B07.
14. Cited from Maryse Conde, "O Brave New World (Positive Impact of Globalization on Less Developed Nations)," *Research in African Literatures* 29(3) (1998): 1–7.
15. Cited from John Burgess, "WTO to Meet as Protesters Rally Forces; Trade Talks to Open Without an Agenda," *Washington Post*, November 29, 1999: A01.
16. http://www.interbrand.com/best_global_brands.aspx?langid=1000.
17. *Economist*, "A Passage from India," October 21, 2000, electronic version.
18. *Economist*, "Culture Wars: Is American Culture, Like a Horror-monster's Foot, about to Crush the World? Only in Film does America Really Rule, and Cultural Protection is no Answer," September 12, 1998, electronic version.
19. Barber, *Jihad vs. McWorld*, 88.
20. *Economist*, "Culture Wars: Is American Culture, Like a Horror-monster's Foot, about to Crush the World? Only in Film does America Really Rule, and Cultural Protection is no Answer," September 12, 1998, electronic version.
21. Paul Farhi and Megan Rosenfeld, "American Pop Penetrates Worldwide," *Washington Post*, October 25, 1998, electronic version.
22. Mr. Crystal is the author of the Cambridge Encyclopedia of the English Language.
23. Cited from Michael Skapinker, "The Tongue Twisters," *Financial Times*, December 28, 2000, electronic version.
24. Thanks to or because of Britain's imperial reach, English speakers are firmly encamped in the Americas, Africa, the Middle East, and Asia. Roughly a quarter of the planet's population—1.6 billion people—now uses the language. Sophie Meunier, "The French Exception (A Growing Movement Against Globalization in France)," *Foreign Affairs* 79(4) (July/August 2000): 104–116.
25. The ascendance of the United States to superpower status during the Cold War and the accompanying predominance of its transnational corporations have propelled English to ever-greater widespread uses. It is predicted that by 2050, half the world will be more or less proficient in it (*Economist*, "The Triumph of English," December 20, 2001, electronic version).
26. According to the *Financial Times* MBA 2001 rankings, English is the language of instruction for 49 of world's top 50 business schools (Linda Anderson, "English: The Mother Tongue of Business-Speak," *Financial Times*, June 4, 2001, electronic version).
27. Despite variations in statistical data, the estimates suggest that between 67 and 80 percent of the Web sites are in English (Julie Schmit, "Asian Countries Experiencing English Boom," *USA Today*, July 21, 2000, electronic version; and Julian Perkin, "Multilingual Websites Widen the Way to a New Online World," *Financial Times*, February 5, 2001, electronic version).
28. Presently, the vast majority of international conferences are conducted in English. (Perkin, "Multilingual Websites Widen"; and Barber, "Democracy at Risk").
29. Barber, "Democracy at Risk."
30. It should be noted that while German continues to be the most widely spoken second language among the masses in Eastern Europe, English is increasingly becoming the

language of choice among the political and economic elite (Natalia Churikova, "Up Against a Language Barrier," *Financial Times*, April 3, 2001, electronic version).

31. According to the *Economist*, English is already used as one of the official languages of 85 percent of all international organizations (*Economist*, "The Triumph of English," December 20, 2001, electronic version).

32. The last universal tongue in Europe was Latin during the Middle Ages, with the exception of French as the language of seventeenth- , eighteenth- , and nineteenth-century Euro-centered diplomacy.

33. David E. Sanger, "Global Economy Dances to Political Tune," *New York Times*, December 20, 1999, electronic version.

34. Cited in Conde, "O Brave New World," 1.

35. Mario Vargas Llosa, "The Culture of Liberty (Liberating Influence of Globalization)," *Foreign Policy* 122 (January 2001): 66–71.

36. Cited from Ian Buruma, "Europe's Mercantile Spirit Rediscovered," *Financial Times*, January 10, 2000: 13.

37. Farhi and Rosenfeld, "American Pop Penetrates Worldwide."

38. Naomi Klein, *No Logos: Taking Aim at the Brand Bullies*. New York: Picador, 1999: 118.

39. According to IDC, a Boston-based information technology market researcher firm, only 5.4 percent of the world's population have English as their native tongue (Perkin, "Multilingual Websites Widen."). But though the number of Spanish and Chinese speakers dwarfs English as a mother language, English is, unquestionably, the world's dominant second language.

40. Cited from Seth Mydans, "Nations in Asia Give English Their Own Flavorful Quirks," *New York Times*, July 1, 2001, electronic version.

41. History has shown that languages evolve and often "fragment into dialects, then into new languages, as Latin did into French, Italian, Spanish and others. Unless the growing interconnection of the world disrupts the pattern, this could be the future of English," according to Larry E. Smith, an expert on international English at the East–West Center in Honolulu (Mydans, "Nations in Asia Give").

42. Samuel P. Huntington, *Who Are We: The Challenges to America's National Identity*. New York: Simon & Schuster, 2004.

43. Ibid.

44. Mydans, "Nations in Asia Give," July 1, 2001.

45. Perkin, "Multilingual Websites Widen."

46. http://www.boxofficemojo.com/alltime/world/

47. Laura M. Holson, "More Than Ever, Hollywood Studios Are Relying on the Foreign Box Office," *New York Times*, August 7, 2006, electronic version.

48. Ibid.

49. Sharon Waxman, "Hollywood Tailors Its Movies to Sell In Foreign Markets," *Washington Post*, October 26, 1998, electronic version.

50. The days when Hollywood was run by a small clique of American moguls has long ago passed.

51. The monetary constraints of financing motion pictures is such that it is now common practice for studios to look overseas for financing, and/or the selling of international distribution rights to cover much, or all, of a movie's production budget.

52. Variety editor Peter Bart noted the substantial inflow of European investments into Hollywood already affected the kinds of movies being produced (Cited in Rick Lyman, "**Error! Main Document Only.** A New Entertainment Giant: the Studio; No Trace of Anti-hollywood Bias in French Purchase of Universal," *New York*

Times June 20, 2000). This observation can easily be extended to foreign money in general. Increasingly, actors and directors are selected by virtue of their potential for success at the international box office—that is, for their ability to dazzle in Tokyo, Frankfurt, and Rio—as much as for their talents.

53. http://www.boxofficemojo.com/alltime/world/
54. Holson, "More Than Ever."
55. Cited from Martin Reed, "Studios Bank on Overseas Box Office," *USA Today*, December 13, 2000, electronic version.
56. Cited from Martin Reed, "Asian Audience is Hollywood's Hidden Dragon," *USA Today*, December 13, 2000, electronic version.
57. http://www.boxofficemojo.com/alltime/world/
58. *Economist*, **"Error! Main Document Only.** Culture Wars: Is American Culture, like a Horror-monster's Foot, about to Crush the World? Only in Film Does America Really Rule, and Cultural Protection Is No Answer" September 12, 1998, electronic version.
59. Cited from *Economist*, "A Semi-integrated World," September 9, 1999, electronic version.
60. Jean-Marie Guhenno, "Globalization and the International System," *Journal of Democracy* 10(1) (1999): 22–35.
61. Eric Hobsbawn, *Age of Extremes*. New York: Vintage, 1994; Earnest Gellner, *Nations and Nationalism*. Oxford: Basil Blackwell, 1983.
62. David Rothkopf, "In Praise of Cultural Imperialism? (Effects of globalization on culture)," *Foreign Policy* 107 (1997): 38–53.
63. Huntington, *The Clash of Civilizations*.
64. Martin Albrow, "Globalization: Social Theory and Global Culture," *Sociology* 27(4) (1993): 732–733.

The Environment

The real cost of carbon emissions is far from zero. Each new scientific report brings proof of a changing climate that promises to disrupt agricultural patterns, set off a scramble for dwindling resources, raise sea levels, propel population shifts and require massive emergency spending as we try to react to the growing crises. These are the costs of inaction.

—*Kristen Sheeran, Executive Director of the Economics for Equity and the Environment Network and Mindy Lubber, President of Ceres*[1]

The IEA [International Energy Agency in Paris] report assumes that existing technologies are rapidly improved and deployed. Vehicle fuel efficiency increases by 40 percent. In electricity generation, the share for coal (the fuel with the most greenhouse gases) shrinks from about 40 percent to about 25 percent—and much carbon dioxide is captured before going into the atmosphere.

—*Robert J. Samuelson,* Washington Post *Columnist*[2]

INTRODUCTION: RACE TO THE BOTTOM

Ever since the 1972 United Nations Conference on the Human Environment in Stockholm launched the modern environmental movement, 35 years ago, ecologists and some economists have been locked in battle over long-held clashing views on the effects of development and economic growth on the environment. Placed within the debate over the environmental consequences of globalization, ecologists and "green" activists, such as Friends of the Earth, the World Wildlife Fund, the Sierra Club, and Greenpeace, contend that globalization itself is defiling the earth by threatening the air, the waters, and the forests of the world. Global development brings with it factors that necessarily contribute to pollution, including urbanization; higher energy consumption—especially, oil, natural gas, and coal; massive population shifts from the countryside to cities; urban sprawl; and industrialization. The sheer magnitude of ecological change resulting directly from just the past half century's economic activity has already resulted in serious and devastating planetary problems such as global warming, the continuing accelerating depletion of the earth's ozone layer, the shocking shrinkage of the polar ice caps and rising levels of the world's oceans, and intensifying storms and hurricanes. The sobering assessment of the United Nations' Department for Economic and Social Affairs' 2002 report on the health of the planet dramatically underscores the fact that the environmental movement's worst-case scenario is coming true. The report paints a dismal picture of the world's overall ecological state, with fresh water and forests disappearing at an alarming rate, accompanied by unacceptable levels of air and water pollution, amid rising global sea levels.

For globalization's critics, the pace and context of transnational economic development leads to a "**race to the bottom**" in environmental standard[3] as ferocious economic competition unleashes market forces upending existing regulatory schemes, while encouraging, if not mandating, rapidly developing economies to eschew more costly safeguards regulating pollution. Specifically, the relaxation of restrictions on trade and cross-border investment has liberated transnational corporations to "shop" for the country where they can earn the highest return. This has resulted in the ability of corporations to dictate to governments what they can and cannot do in mitigating the destruction of the environment. Governments defying the dictates of market forces are "disciplined" by the ability of corporations to scale back investments or establish factories and plants in countries more conducive to less rigorous **environmental standards**.[4] National governments fearing the loss of foreign investment are faced with a stark choice; either conform to the dictates of the global market or suffer the devastating consequences of capital flight. Globalization, from this perspective, is directly responsible for helping to destroy the planet. Thus, powerful global economic elites and their transnational corporate operations, driven by the search for the cheapest and easiest way to maximize profits, pit states against each other, thereby lowering pollution standards worldwide. Globalization *as a transnational process* is in fact undermining more than 40 years of international agreements aimed at reducing planetary **environmental degradation**.[5]

The peoples of the world are the big loser here for John Gray: "The countries that require businesses to be environmentally accountable will be at a systematic disadvantage. . . . Over time, either enterprises operating in environmentally accountable regimes will be driven out of business, or the regulatory frameworks of such regimes will drift down a common denominator in which their competitive advantage is reduced."[6]

The globalizing process, in turn, puts pressure on states to reduce (if not eliminate) their environmental restrictions that increase the costs of doing business, since in this globalized economy, the most successful states will be those that impose the least stringent **environmental regulations**. For historian Jeremy Brecher and union activist Tim Costello, this means that "Corporations can now outflank the controls governments and organized citizens once placed on them by relocating . . . so each [government] tries to reduce labor, social, and environmental costs below the others. The result is a 'downward leveling'—a disastrous 'race to the bottom' in which conditions for all tend to fall toward those of the poorest and most desperate."[7]

Daniel Drezner, a political scientist at the Fletcher School of Law and Diplomacy at Tufts University, clearly and concisely summarizes the propositions of the race to the bottom thesis:

> First, the more exposed a state is to global markets, such as reduced barriers to trade and controls on capital, the more likely its tax and regulatory policies will converge to other states with international exposure. Second, there should be a strong negative correlation between inward capital flows and a country's regulatory standards. Third, this policy convergence will be at the lowest common denominator; in any given regulatory arena, states will gravitate toward the policies of the most laissez-faire country.[8]

REALITY CHECK: OVER EXAGGERATION

While there have been examples of countries, such as Ireland, who have enacted a deliberate strategy of lowering (or ignoring) their environmental standards (or retaining poor ones) in a contest to attract greater foreign direct investments (and/or keep domestic capital at home), there is no definitive indication that other states are racing to follow suit, leading to a generalized worldwide downgrading in environmental conditions.[9] Rather, a 1998 study by World Bank environmental economists Muthukumara Mani and David Wheeler found that developing countries have not increased their share of **pollution-intensive industries**.[10] Moreover, as a six-year study completed by the World Bank in 2000 concluded, pollution havens—developing countries that purposely and actively recruit those transnational corporations that engage in highly polluting activities—have failed to materialize. "Indeed, many developing countries appear to have found that the benefits of pollution control outweigh the costs and are adopting innovative, low-cost strategies to limit pollution while also expanding economic growth."[11]

As appealing and logical as the "race to the bottom" thesis may appear to many antiglobalists, environmentalists, and ecologists, the "litany" of environmental fears is simply not backed up by evidence. Quite the contrary, much empirical work reveals that the evidence for this supposed "race to the bottom" scenario is practically nonexistent.[12] A comprehensive and extensive study conducted by Drezner revealed that not only is the "race to the bottom" thesis incorrect, but that "the lack of supporting evidence is startling."[13] Indeed, two separate research studies conducted by David Wheeler of the World Bank and Hakan Nordstrom and Scott Vaughan of the World Trade Organization revealed that not only have environmental regulations tended to become more stringent as developing countries grow and develop, but that higher environmental standards may actually be a competitive advantage.[14] Furthermore, a study of 24 OECD (Organization of Economic Cooperation and Development) and non-OECD[15] countries by John Wilson, Tsunehiro Otsuki, and Mirvat Sewadeh of the World Bank's Development Research Group found that in some cases a significant negative link existed between dirty exports and environmental regulation.[16]

If globalization actually does foster a "race to the bottom" in environmental regulatory standards, one would expect to find a degeneration in environmental levels relevant to economic development in countries that have opened themselves up to trade and foreign investment as well as an inverse relationship between foreign direct investment and regulatory levels. Countries with relatively high environmental standards and costly regulations should attract little, or at least a declining share of global capital, whereas countries with low environmental standards and few regulations should attract the lion's share of investment. Finally, since as a general rule, environmental regulations are very stringent among the most economically advanced countries in comparison with developing states, transnational corporations should be involved in a massive redeployment to the developing countries in order to lower their production costs.

A World Bank study concluded that "there is no evidence that the cost of **environmental protection** has ever been the determining factor in foreign investment decisions. Factors such as labor and raw material costs, transparent regulation and protection of property rights are likely to be much more important, even for polluting industries. Indeed, foreign-owned plants in developing countries, precisely the ones that according to the theory would be most attracted by low standards, tend to be less polluting than indigenous plants in the same industry. Most multinational companies adopt near-uniform standard globally, often well above the local government-set standards."[17] Furthermore, Gunnar Eskeland of the World Bank and Ann Harrison of the University of California found that "foreign plants and factories are significantly more energy efficient and use cleaner types of energy."[18]

An examination of the destination of transnational corporations' investments found that the relationship between foreign direct investment and stringent environmental standards to be strongly positive. Drezner found that an overwhelming majority between two-thirds and three-quarters of global foreign direct investment went to the wealthy industrialized economies tending to have higher environmental standards, despite the option of being poured into developing countries with lax environmental regulations.[19] The results of this study confirm an earlier study by social theorist Paul Hirst and political economist Graham Thompson, which concluded that "Capital mobility is not producing a massive shift of investment and employment to the developing countries. Rather, foreign direct investment (FDI) is highly concentrated among the advanced industrial economies."[20]

Moreover, Drezner found that openness to trade and investment has not led to a decline, much less the destruction of environmental conditions or regulations of the receiving countries. The very states (e.g., Malaysia, the Philippines, Thailand, Argentina, and Brazil) that have been the most open to outside investments are the very ones that have also imposed the most stringent environmental regulations.[21] As a study by Georgetown University economist Arik Levinson concluded, "environmental regulations do not deter investment to any statistically or economically significant degree."[22] Research conducted by Eskland and Harrison in Mexico, Venezuela, Morocco, and the Ivory Coast found that abatement costs are not a significant determinant of foreign investment.[23] Beata Smarzynska Javorcik of the World Bank and Shang-Jin Wei of the International Monetary Fund found little support for the hypothesis that lower environmental standards attract investments in their study of transnational corporations' foreign direct investment in the former Soviet Union and Eastern Europe.[24] Finally, Judith Dean of the U.S. International Trade Commission, Mary Lovely of the Department of Economics at Syracuse University, and Hua Wang of the World Bank in their study of foreign direct investments and pollution havens in China found that transnational corporations from industrial countries, for example, the United States, the United Kingdom, and Japan, "are actually attracted by stringent environmental levies."[25]

In terms of trade, studies by van Beers and van de Bergh, Xu and Song, Grether and de Melo, and Kahn all found very little or no evidence that environmental regulations play a meaningful role in the determination of trade flows.[26] Indeed, a 2001 study by Jeffrey Frankel and Andrew Rose found a positive correlation between trade openness and environmental quality.[27] "So in reality we do not have a race to the bottom in environmental standards, because while some exceptions will certainly arise, multinationals are, generally speaking, not playing the game of actively looking for locations without environmental regulations or seeking out technologies that are environmentally unfriendly. A race cannot get started unless the competitors sign up to run."[28]

Developing countries continue to display deplorable environmental standards and conditions. As Vijay Vaitheeswaran, the Environment and Energy Correspondent for the *Economist*, acknowledged, the grim reality of environmental degradation and its human costs in developing countries cannot be ignored. These include a million deaths from air pollution and nearly two million fatalities from the inhalation of smoke as a result of cooking appliances in improperly vented dwellings. At least another million deaths resulted from water-borne pathogens. Vaitheeswaran estimated that about 20 percent of all the deaths occurring in poor nations are caused by environmental degradation—a far larger factor "than any other preventable factor, including malnutrition."[29]

The failure of developing countries and the global community to adequately address unacceptable levels of poverty and degradation since the end of World

War II, however, does not in and of itself indicate that globalization itself is either the primary cause or aggravating condition for the continuing plight of the world's poor. As we have argued throughout, the willingness of countries to embrace openness to trade and investments has resulted in both environmental and economic advancements. For as Bhagwati observed, "In fact, as development occurs, economies typically shift from primary production, which is often pollution-intensive, to manufacturers, which are often less so, and then to traded services, which are currently even less pollution-intensive. This natural evolution itself could then reduce the pollution-intensity of income as development proceeds."[30]

The process of trade liberalization also attracts foreign direct investments and the likelihood of the transfer of cleaner environmental technologies as new manufacturing venues are established in developing countries. For example, the World Bank reports that "Average air quality in China has stabilized or improved since the mid-1980s in monitored cities, especially large ones—the same period during which China has experienced both rapid economic growth and increased openness to trade and investment."[31] A study by Wheeler of the three rapidly industrializing countries of China, Mexico, and Brazil (the top three recipients of FDI among developing states) concluded that they experienced significant improvements in air quality.[32]

In marked contrast, many protectionist states traditionally attract some of the worst pollution-intensive industries. For example, Nancy Birdsall and David Wheeler of the World Bank in their study of Latin America found a positive relationship between low trade openness and high environmental pollution in a number of industrial sectors, such as iron and steel, pulp and paper, cement, and chemicals.[33] Further, "A World Bank study of steel production in 50 countries found that open economies led closed economies in the adoption of cleaner technologies by wide margins, resulting in the open economies being 17 percent less pollution-intensive in this sector than closed economies."[34]

Critics of globalization have seemingly taken environmental degradation as a cost of doing business just as it is equated with the existence and continuation of massive human poverty and suffering in the world's poorest countries. What is often left out of the finger-pointing is the context of nineteenth- and twentieth-century industrialization, uncontrollable increases in population in nonglobalizing developing countries, the continued rampaging consumption of fossil fuels, and a poor research and development record in the creation of green technologies.

As trade spurs economic growth, and as countries become more affluent, however, societies begin to demand a cleaner environment.[35] An established body of literature documents how pollution diminishes as societies become more affluent and concerns begin to focus on a number of quality of life issues including family planning, environmental health, and safety and education.[36] "One World Bank study of 145 countries identified a strong positive correlation between income levels and the strictness of environmental regulation."[37]

Economists and environmentalists alike praise the remarkable improvement in air and water quality in the developed world in recent decades. As Stephen Moore, senior fellow at the Cato Institute and the president of the Club for Growth, and Julian Simon, professor of Business Administration at the University of Maryland, declared, "One of the greatest trends of the past 100 years has been the astonishing rate of progress in reducing almost every form of pollution."[38] While some increased pollution may indeed be a side effect of industrialization in many developing countries, there is plenty of blame to go around. Newly developing economies did not in and of themselves create the major conditions of global environmental risk. As the director of the Environmental Assessment Institute in Denmark, Bjorn Lomborg,[39] reminds us, newly industrializing countries "are merely replicating the development of the industrialised countries. When they grow sufficiently rich they, too, will start to reduce their pollution."[40] It is worth noting that energy consumption in the United States, for example, is itself a product of long-term economic development, in part, underwritten by globalization, illustrating just how difficult it is to find a balance that substantively works to reduce ozone-depleting gasses in the face of consumer demands for energy.

DEBATING GLOBALIZATION

Lui Hebron: Climate Change and the Green Economy

John, the issue of global warming singularly captures both the negative consequences and the positive (innovative) aspects of the globalization process. On the negative side, the economic component (drive for growth and development) of globalization has clearly had a detrimental effect on the earth's environment. Mounting scientific evidence of global warming, however, should not automatically be cause for gloom and doom. Finally acknowledging the need to address the issue of a warming world, countries, corporations, and interest groups around the globe have embarked on a "go green campaign."

Since 2006, numerous states have enacted legislation and/or policies aimed at either increasing energy efficiency or changing over to energy sources with lower zero greenhouse gas discharges: China enacted higher fuel economy standards for its newer vehicles. In Brazil, ethanol now powers half its cars and trucks. Sweden is well on its way to becoming the world's first oil-free economy. In Barcelona, Spain, solar power is the primary heating source for hot water for 40 percent of new buildings (Laurie David, "Alone on the Shrinking Ice," *Los Angeles Times*, April 21, 2006). Moreover, negotiation of a new treaty—to be signed in December 2009—is currently underway in Copenhagen, Denmark. According to reports coming from the negotiations, the treaty includes provisions for financial as well as technical assistance to help emerging economies undertake a more environmentally sustainable form of economic development.

On the corporate front, the army of green companies is growing fast. "Carbon Down, Profits Up," a report by the Climate Group, an organization founded in 2004 by various firms and governments, listed 74 companies from 18 industries in 11 countries that are committed to cutting greenhouse-gas emissions (*Economist*, "Can Business Be Cool?" June 8, 2006). Since this movement to "go-green" is being driven by an opportunity to make money rather than by some ambiguous cognition to be more socially responsible, the commitment of these so-called "corporate converts" seems genuine. As an added bonus, going carbon neutral has not only been advantageous from a public relations standpoint, but it has also been financially beneficial for these corporations in terms of the billions of dollars in savings they have garnered through energy conservation. In fact, green energy is projected to be bigger than IT and biotech combined.

Finally, nongovernmental organizations ranging from environmental groups to human rights organizations to socially conscious youths in the developing world have all pledged to keep climate change an integral component of the globalization process. According to a report by *New York Times* columnist Thomas Friedman, "Hal Harvey is the C.E.O. of a new $1 billion foundation, ClimateWorks, set up to accelerate the policy changes that can avoid climate catastrophe by taking climate policies from where they are working the best to the places where they are needed the most" ("Mother Nature's Dow," *New York Times*, March 29, 2009).—Lui

John Stack: Environmental Crisis and Global Governance

Lui, global warming constitutes a looming environmental catastrophe. As such, it places fundamental issues of global governance squarely on the table. It demands a comprehensive response from every major economy in the world. It requires leadership, and it will require sacrifice. Left to the vicissitudes of global markets and without the leadership of the United States, Japan, Europe, and such major emerging economies as China, India, Mexico, and Brazil, to name only a few, the planet confronts unimaginable peril. But the commitment of states to finding solutions to global warming is only part of the solution.

If there is one central lesson to be learned from the current collapse of the global financial system, it is that we need to be skeptical of the belief that globalization works best in an unregulated context. Without robust multilateral participation by states, international governmental organizations, transnational organizations, and nonstate actors including transnational corporations, advocacy groups, and individuals, the battle to reduce global warming will fail. Technology may well offer us ways of combating carbon emissions, but those solutions demand an integrated partnership based on business, government, intergovernmental organizations, and nonstate organizations.

While the concept of a green economy may have captured the imagination of publics, corporations, and countries in the northern hemisphere, the heavy lifting that must be employed to work to a timely solution must be undertaken in a comprehensive framework. If global governance is to succeed in the context of the twenty-first century, it must be accompanied by a transformative revolution that is rooted in a change of values, outlooks, and perspectives. These changes in political orientation are already at work in advanced industrialized societies. But it must be reflected in the determination of political leaders and socioeconomic elites across the globe. This will mean that individual citizens in the northern and southern hemispheres come to accept the necessity of new visions of global politics supportive of both national and global initiatives that will provide political and socioeconomic solutions to the ecological peril now confronting the planet.

Transformative moments can happen. A revolution in sovereignty occurred in 1648 from the carnage of nearly a century of religious warfare in Europe and out of which the modern state system was born. These states served as the incubators of democracies, creating in turn societies based on civil rights, human rights, and the rule of law. The Westphalian revolution resulted in the establishment of states as the building blocks of the global political and economic system. A more recent revolution in statecraft also emerged after the devastation of two twentieth-century world wars out of which a transformed European community of states has emerged.

The perils posed by global warming demand multilateral participation by the world's stakeholders. Ad hoc approaches threaten a global environmental catastrophe.—John ■

DEBUNKING THE MYTHS: GLOBAL PARTNER

Shocking as it may seem to most antiglobalists, economic development and growth need not always come with the degradation of the environment. As Bjorn Lomborg points out, "[e]cology and economics should push in the same direction. After all, the 'eco' part of each word derives from the Greek word for 'home,' and the protagonists of both claim to have humanity's welfare as their goal."[41] Since it is now widely acknowledged (if not yet accepted) that growth and development need not be the enemy of the ecosystem, the key question is how to make the two more compatible whereby domestic and transnational corporations, advanced industrial states and developing countries, and intergovernmental organizations and the multitude of nonstate advocacy organizations find it in their best interests to begin to enact more environmentally responsible policies and practices.

Today, 35 years after the environmental movement first began, economists and environmentalists are increasingly joining forces in a new spirit of understanding and cooperation, with each side more likely to be collaborators rather than antagonists for they now view environmental protection and economic growth not as contradictory forces, but rather as an opportunity for the development of innovative new products that could harness the power of the market without compromising the environmental health of the planet. Indeed, according to one report, "Hundreds of businesses, though still a minority, have added sustainability managers to their executive roster."[42] This trend, no doubt, is being driven by what *New York Times* columnist Matthew L. Wald characterizes as the "conviction that there is profit in greenness."[43]

As Michael Porter of Harvard Business School wrote in a 2000 report published by the WBCSD, the World Resources Institute, and the UN Environment Programme (UNEP): "Products that address environmental scarcities will have enormous market potential."[44] A case in point is the Starbucks Corporation. Responding to criticisms that growing coffee caused rain-forest degradation, Starbucks invested hundreds of thousands of dollars to help Mexican farmers become shade-grown coffee bean producers. The unexpectedly high demand for the premium-priced coffee beans produced by the Mexicans resulted in Starbucks increasing its order for shade-grown beans tenfold since the program began in late 1998. Said Orin C. Smith, the company's chief executive, "We risked this for the environmental benefits, but it now has potential to be a really profitable product."[45] More importantly, this success story indicates that "going green" does not only have beneficial effects for the environment (and developing countries) but also for a corporation's bottom line—profits. "The notion that environment is just an expensive cost is way out of date," said Glenn T. Prickett, executive director of the Center for Environmental Leadership in Business, a unit of Conservation International.[46]

On the international level, the United Nations launched its **global compact** program on July 26, 2000. Drawing from the Declaration of Human Rights, the Social Summit held in Geneva in 1995, and the Earth Summit of Rio de Janeiro in 1992, the compact is a code of good conduct for transnational corporations. The corporations who signed on to the compact promised to prevent environmental degradation; to promote environmental responsibility; and to encourage the development and diffusion of environmentally friendly technologies—in short, to demonstrate responsible global leadership.

Corporations that have committed to the compact come from a wide range of sectors, including petroleum (Royal Dutch Shell), engineering, the media (Pearson), auto production (DaimlerChrysler), financial services (Deutsche Bank), telecommunications, steel, mining, and microelectronics (Ericsson). Additionally, 12 NGOs including the International Confederation of Free Trade Unions, Amnesty International, Human Rights Watch, and the World Conservation Union have pledged to monitor these companies so as to make sure they remain true to their commitments to honor globally recognized minimum environmental (and labor) standards.

It should be noted that the global compact is only a declaration of these principles with a voluntary code for corporate conduct rather than a binding code of conduct with formal legal sanctions for noncompliance. Nevertheless, the UN Development and Environment programs are committed to the compact's success so that rising environmental standards are realized. Finally, the World Bank and the World Trade Organization now have an extensive set of environmental and social policies as a permanent feature on their respective agendas.

On the domestic level, governments are now playing a more active role in regulating what transnational corporations are doing to their environment. Spurred by both community pressure and an awareness of high health care costs caused by pollution, regulators throughout the developing world are now demanding developed world standards and mandating new, cleaner technologies, resulting in rapid cuts in urban air and water pollution. A case in point is Indonesia's "Proper" program. With the aid of the World Bank, the Indonesian government designed a five-tiered ranking system of a company's environmental behavior, from gold for going beyond compliance to black for flagrant violations. The top-ranking companies are publicly applauded, while the worst offenders are given six months to correct themselves before their names are made public. The "Proper" scheme has been so successful that it is now being adopted by the Philippines, as well as by several Latin American countries.[47] So contrary to popular belief, globalization has not undermined the ability of states to regulate corporate environmental behavior within their territories.

On the societal level, transnational corporations, well aware of the growing correlation between public opinion and profits, have adjusted their business practices to take into account their environmental effects as well as to avoid shareholder wrath and consumer boycotts. The *Economist* reports that the ranks of "corporate greens" are expanding. In late 2005, banking giant HSBC joined other financial institutions declaring themselves to be carbon neutral. The *Economist* also noted that Swiss Re, a reinsurer, and the investment bank Goldman Sachs expressed concerns about the effects of carbon dioxide as a central cause of global warming. General Electric (GE) unveiled its "Ecoimagination" initiative intended to reduce output of climate-warming gasses, while investing in clean technologies. Wal-Mart also launched a series of programs intended to reduce fuel consumption of its truck fleet even before gasoline prices soared in 2006. In Great Britain, two huge retailers, Tesco and Sainsbury, are working to become the "greenest." And in June 2006, several leading union bosses lobbied the then prime minister Tony Blair for stricter policies to reduce climate change notwithstanding the necessities of harsher regulation.[48]

Alison Maitland of the *Financial Times* reports that "External surveys show that 75–80 percent of consumers are likely to reward companies for being 'good corporate citizens' and that 20 percent will punish those that are not."[49] Furthermore, the steady growth in socially responsible investment funds indicates that an increasing number of investors take into account environmental performance as a factor in picking stocks.

On the transnational level, NGOs have had a tremendous impact on the policies and behaviors of states and transnational corporations with regard to environmental issues.[50] According to Professor Paul Wapner of American University, "There is a widespread sense that non-governmental organizations greatly influence the way the international system addresses environmental issues."[51] For example, it would appear that NGOs through the use of the

Internet are sensitizing corporations to be more mindful of environmental issues: "Environmental groups have become truly sophisticated in using the Web to move information to millions of people literally overnight, and to attack companies on a global scale," said Carol M. Browner, who headed the Environmental Protection Agency under President Bill Clinton.[52] In so doing, these pressure group networks have made a tremendous and influential impact upon international environmental politics by "educat[ing] millions of people about environmental issues, and then effectively harness[ing] the power of knowledgeable citizenry to pierce the veil of secrecy that all too often surrounds both international negotiations and corporate decision-making."[53]

Evolving partnerships between and among governments, corporations, and transnational groups are working toward the goal of **sustainable development** projects in a number of ways. First, the concept of sustainable development has developed real "traction" as a means of addressing the need for the development of viable local communities working to protect vital environmental needs. Thus, the prospect of implementing environmentally friendly policies on the march toward economic development and growth becomes very attractive. To work effectively, however, there must be a balance between environmental and economic benefits for local development projects. As Bjorn Lomborg points out, "With its focus on sustainability, the developed world ends up prioritizing the future at the expense of the present. This is backward. In contrast, a focus on development helps people today while creating the foundation for an even better tomorrow."[54]

In concrete terms, human-induced climate change via the increases in production of greenhouse gases from the burning of fossil fuels is being blamed for the rise in global sea levels, the increase in the number and fury of storms, and the spread of such diseases as West Nile virus, malaria, cholera, and dengue fever. As these dangers and threats become more acute, states and their policy makers must stop grandstanding. As economist Robert J. Samuelson observed, the main effect of the Kyoto Protocol thus far is that "It [has] allowed countries that joined to castigate those that didn't. But it hasn't reduced carbon dioxide emissions (up about 25 percent since 1990), and many signatories didn't adopt tough enough policies to hit their 2008–2012 targets."[55] In this regard, the world's two leading contributors to climate change, the United States and China, must take the lead in reducing their greenhouse gas emissions. If both China and the United States can demonstrate a willingness to substantively tackle the problem of global warming, then progress will likely be made. Global warming needs to be conceptualized in terms of state policies and objectives rather than simply as the result of transnational economic markets especially in the South. Indeed, the refusal of the United States to adhere to the Kyoto Agreement and its inability to conserve fossil fuels are huge contributing factors to global warming.

Despite these positive developments regarding the precarious relationship between economic growth and the environment, the earth's ecological well-being is still very much under siege from human influences. Within the last three years, there has been a steady stream of scientific research and data to support the global warming thesis:

> Three important scientific associations, the American Meteorological Society, the American Geophysical Union, and the American Association for the Advancement of Science (AAAS) have found that global warming and climate change results from human activites. The scientific evidence supporting these findings is considered to be "compelling."[56]

In December 2003, the American Geophysical Union stated, "Human activities are increasingly altering the Earth's climate . . . scientific evidence strongly indicates that natural influences cannot explain the rapid increase in global near-surface temperatures observed during the second half of the 20th century."[57]

In 2005, the U.S. National Academy of Science joined the national science academies of Brazil, China, Germany, India, Japan, Russia, and other nations in a joint statement declaring, "There is now strong evidence that significant global warming is occurring."[58] In February 2007, the American Meteorological Society confirmed that "there is adequate evidence from observations and interpretations of climate simulations to conclude that the atmosphere, ocean, and land surface are warming [and] that humans have significantly contributed to this change."[59]

CONCLUSION: SUSTAINABLE DEVELOPMENT VIA THE ENVIRONMENT MEETS GLOBALIZATION

The preceding examination of globalization and the environment indicates that not only does the globalization process not bring forth greater environmental degradation, but that economy and ecology are far from being mortal enemies. As a matter of fact, it is in the best interest of the environment if economists and environmentalists work together to bring about greater development throughout the world.

First, the open trade and investment orientation of the globalizing process enables "developing countries to bypass dirtier phases of development"[60] for it allows "access to new, cleaner technologies . . . which may provide a cleaner or greener way of producing goods."[61] In other words, globalization promotes the utilization of environmentally friendly policies and behavior at ever-faster rates.

Second, Allen Hammond of the World Economic Forum reports that "there is significant consensus, even among low-income respondents, that complying with environmental standards improves long-term competitiveness, that lack of clean water hinders business expansion, and that clean production and waste reduction are important to company success."[62] Citing the Executive Opinion Survey for 2005, Hammond further notes that "in the opinion of business leaders, economic development and performance in environmental and social responsibility are reasonably well correlated."[63]

Finally, and perhaps most importantly in the South, it is poverty, and not globalization, which is responsible for environmental degradation for it is in poor societies where people must rely heavily on high-polluting fuels such as wood and coal for cooking and heating. Moreover, poor and hungry people do not have the luxury of worrying about the environmental effects of their actions, let alone doing something about it. In this regard, not only will continued economic growth via globalization enable the estimated 1.2 billion people to reduce the effects of poverty, but just as importantly, "rising incomes increase the ability and willingness of countries to protect their environment."[64] As Pete Geddes, executive vice president of FREE (Foundation for Research and Economics and the Environment) predicts, "Once per-capita incomes cover the basics (e.g., food and shelter), the demand for environmental quality grows."[65]

The most important question, however, is one of global governance. Without the active support of the United States in taking substantive steps to limit greenhouse gas emissions, the devastating effects of global warming will likely continue. Globalization is a multidimensional process requiring economic sacrifices to make ecologically sound decisions. It requires leadership in private and public sectors to be sure. But without the support of the United States and its willingness to find common ground with other public and private stakeholders, the threat posed by global warming to all inhabitants of the planet will result in a race to the bottom. It was perhaps due to this realization that the United States, by the conclusion of the 2007 G8 meeting, finally agreed to negotiate a new climate agreement by 2009 and "seriously consider" a European plan to cut greenhouse gas emissions in half by 2050.

KEY TERMS

environmental
  degradation   119
environmental
  protection   121
environmental
  regulations   120

environmental
  standards   119
global compact   127
pollution-intensive
  industries   120

race to the bottom   119
sustainable
  development   129

FIVE QUESTIONS TO CONSIDER

1. What constitutes the environmental "race to the bottom"?
2. To what extent does global warming and environmental degradation threaten globalization? To what extent will globalization further damage the world's environment?
3. Is sustainable ecological development possible under conditions of globalization?
4. To what extent does the environment demand new forms of global governance?
5. Can the threat of global warming result in the emergence of a new global environmental consensus?

FURTHER READINGS

Lester R. Brown, "Deflating the World's Bubble Economy," *USA Today Magazine*, November 2003.

Brown argues that due to the reckless and overconsumption of the Earth's natural resources, the planet is on the verge of a worldwide bubble economy that if left unchecked will have severe environmental, political, and social consequences. In response, Brown calls for the need for unprecedented global cooperation that "stabilizes population, eradicates poverty, and alleviates climate change."

Bjorn Lomborg, *Cool It: The Skeptical Environmentalist's Guide to Global Warming*. Knopf, 2007.

Argues that many of the elaborate and expensive actions now being considered to stop global warming will cost hundreds of billions of dollars, are often based on emotional rather than strictly scientific assumptions, and may very well have little impact on the world's temperature for hundreds of years.

Jeffrey D. Sachs, *Common Wealth: Economics for a Crowded Planet*. Penguin Press, 2008.

Offers an urgent assessment of the environmental degradation, rapid population growth, and extreme poverty that threaten global peace and prosperity. Sachs predicts the cascade of crises that awaits this crowded planet—and presents a program of sustainable development and international cooperation that will correct this dangerous course.

World Economic and Social Survey 2008: Overcoming Economic Insecurity.

An approach to climate change and sustainable development is urgently needed. The key is a low-carbon, high-growth transformation of the global economy capable of keeping temperature increases consistent with environmental stability while fostering strong growth and economic diversification in developing countries allowing for a convergence of incomes worldwide.

Ernesto Zedillo, ed., *Global Warming: Looking Beyond Kyoto*. Brookings Institution Press, 2008.

This volume of readings from a group of leading experts and policy makers from various parts of the world addresses the issue of climate change mitigation as a public good. The overall conclusion is that tackling the issue of climate change could well be the most complex international undertaking the world has faced.

NOTES

1. Kristen Sheeran and Mindy Lubber, "The Cost of Climate Inaction," *Washington Post*, May 6, 2009, electronic version.
2. Robert J. Samuelson, "Global Warming's Real Inconvenient Truth," *Washington Post*, July 5, 2006: A13.
3. The "race to the bottom" thesis refers to the proposition that globalization is exerting downward pressure on a state's labor and environmental regulations as corporations search for and relocate to countries with fewer or the lowest regulations. For this study, we will be focusing exclusively on the environmental aspect of the "race to the bottom" thesis. Richard McKenzie and Dwight Lee, *Quicksilver Capital: How the Rapid Movement of Wealth Has Changed the World*. New York: Free Press, 1991; Dani Rodrik, *Has Globalization Gone Too Far?* Washington, DC: Institute for International Economics, 1997; Daniel

W. Drezner, "Bottom Feeders," *Foreign Policy* 121 (November/December 2000): 64–70; Daniel W. Drezner, "Globalization and Policy Convergence," *International Studies Review* 3(1) (Spring 2001): 53–78; and Martin Wolf, *Why Globalization Works*. New Haven: Yale Nota Bene, 2005: 191.

4. R. Jenkins, J. Barton, A. Bartzokas, J. Hesselberg, and J. M. Knutsen, *Environmental Regulation in the New Global Economy*. Cheltenham, UK: Edward Elgar Publishing Limited, 2002.

5. *Major Environmental Treaties*—1959 Antarctic Treaty, 1973 International Convention for the Prevention of Pollution from Ships, 1973 Convention on Long-Range Trans-boundary Air Pollution (LRTAP), 1985 Vienna Convention for the Protection of the Ozone Layer, 1987 Montreal Protocol on Substances that Deplete the Ozone Layer, 1992 United National Framework Convention on Climate Change (FCCC), 1992 United Nations Convention on Biological Diversity (CBD), and 1997 Kyoto Protocol.

6. John Gray, *False Dawn: The Delusions of Global Capitalism*. London: Granta Books, 1998: 80.

7. Jeremy Brecher and Tim Costello, *Global Village or Global Pillage: Economic Reconstruction from the Bottom Up*. Boston: South End Press, 1994: 20, 4. The Sierra Club also reports that "in our global economy, corporations move operations freely around the world, escaping tough pollution control laws, labor standards, and even taxes that pay for social and environmental needs." Sierra Club, "A Fair Trade Bill of Rights," http://www.sierraclub.org/trade/ftaa.rights.asp.

8. Drezner, "Globalization and Policy Convergence."

9. H. Jeffrey Leonard, *Pollution and the Struggle for the World Product: Multinational Corporations, Environment and International Comparative Advantage*. Cambridge, UK: Cambridge University Press, 1988; Raman Letuchamanan, "Testing the Pollution Haven Hypothesis," in P. Konz, et al., eds., *Trade, Environment and Sustainable Development: Views from Sub-Saharan Africa and Latin America*. Geneva: ICTSD, Tokyo: UNU/IAS, 2000; and R. Jenkins, J. Barton, A. Bartzokas, J. Hesselberg, and J. M. Knutsen, *Environmental Regulation in the New Global Economy*. Cheltenham, UK: Edward Elgar Publishing Limited, 2002.

10. Muthukumara Mani and David Wheeler, "In Search of Pollution Havens? Dirty Industry in the World Economy 1960–1995," *Journal of Environment and Development* 7(3) (1998): 215–247.

11. World Bank, "Is Globalization Causing a 'Race to the Bottom' in Environmental Standard?" World Bank Briefing Papers Part 4, 2000.

12. Raman Letchumanan and Fumio Kodama, "Reconciling the Conflict between the 'Pollution-Haven' Hypothesis and an Emerging Trajectory of International Technology Transfer," *Research Policy* 29 (2000): 59–79, Judith M. Dean, "Does Trade Liberalization Harm the Environment? A New Test," *Canadian Journal of Economics* 35 (2002): 819–842; Jeffrey Frankel, "The Environment and Globalization," NBER Working Paper Series 10090 (November 2003); Gunnar Eskeland and Ann Harrison, "Moving to Greener Pasture? Multinationals and the Pollution-Haven Hypothesis," *Journal of Development Economics* 70 (2003): 1–23; Pete Geddes, "Trade and the Environment: A Race to the Bottom?" Foundation for Research on Economics and the Environment, 2003, www.free-eco.org; and Matthias Busse, "Trade, Environmental Regulations and the World Trade Organization New Empirical Evidence," World Bank Policy Research Working Paper 3361 (July 2004).

13. Drezner, "Bottom Feeders," 64.

14. David Wheeler, "Racing to the Bottom? Foreign Investment and Air Pollution in Developing Countries," Policy Research Working Paper No. 2524, Development Research Group, World Bank, Washington, DC, 2001; and Hakan Nordstrom and Scott Vaughan, *Trade and Environment*. Geneva: World Trade Organization, 1999.

15. The Organization for Economic Cooperation and Development (OECD) "is a group of like-minded countries. Essentially, membership is limited only by a country's commitment to a market economy and a pluralistic democracy. It is rich, in that its 30 members produce almost 60 percent of the world's goods and services, but it is by no means exclusive. Non-members are invited to subscribe to OECD agreements and treaties, and the Organisation shares expertise and exchanges views on topics of mutual concern with more than 70 countries worldwide, from Brazil, China and Russia to least developed countries in Africa," http://www. oecd.org/document/18/0,2340,en_2649_201185_2068050_1_1_1_1,00.html. The OECD countries included in this study include Finland, Germany, Ireland, Korea, Netherlands, and Switzerland. The non-OECD countries are Bangladesh, Brazil, Bulgaria, China, Egypt, India, Jamaica, Jordan, Kenya, Malawi, Mozambique, Paraguay, Philippines, South Africa, Thailand, Trinidad and Tobago, Tunisia, and Zambia.

16. John Wilson, Tsunehiro Otsuki, and Mirvat Sewadeh, "Dirty Exports and Environmental Regulation: Do Standards Matter to Trade?" Development Research Group (DECRG) of the World Bank (March 2002).

17. World Bank, "Is Globalization Causing" World Bank Briefing Papers Part 4, 2000, cited from G. Dowell, S. Hart, and B. Yeung, "Do Corporate Global Environmental Standards Create or Destroy Market Value?" *Management Science* 46(8) (August 2000): 1059–1074.

18. Eskeland and Harrison, "Moving to Greener Pasture?" 1–23.

19. Drezner, "Bottom Feeders," 66.

20. Paul Hirst and Graham Thompson, *Globalization in Question*. Cambridge: Polity, 1999: 2; Maurice Obstfeld and Alan M. Taylor, "Globalization and Capital Markets," National Bureau of Economic Research Working Paper 8846 (March 2002): 59; and Keith L. Shimko, *International Relations Boston: Houghton Mifflin Company*, 2005: 208.

21. Drezner, "Bottom Feeders," 66.

22. Arik Levinson, "Environmental Regulations and Industry Location: International and Domestic Evidence." In Jagdish Bhagwati and Robert Hudec, eds., *Fair Trade and Harmonization: Prerequisites for Free Trade?* Cambridge, MA: MIT Press, 1996.

23. Eskeland and Harrison, "Moving to Greener Pasture? 1–23.

24. Beata Smmarzynska, Javorcik, and Shang-Jin Wei, "Pollution Havens and Foreign Direct Investment: Dirty Secret or Popular Myth?" *Contributions to Economic Analysis and Policy* 3(2) Article 8 (2004): 1–32.

25. Judith M. Dean, Mary E. Lovely, and Hua Wang, "Foreign Direct Investment and Pollution Havens: Evaluating the Evidence from China," Office of Economics Working Paper U.S. International Trade Commission Trade No, 2004–01-B, 2004.

26. C. van Beers and J. C. J. M. van de Bergh, "Impact of Environmental Policy on Foreign Trade," Timbergen Institute Discussion Paper 069–3, Amsterdam (2000); X. Xu and L. Song, "Regional Cooperation and the Environment: Do 'Dirty' Industries Migrate?" *Weltwirtschaftliches Archiv* 136 (2000): 137–157; J.-M. Grether and J. de Melo "Globalization and Dirty Industries: Do Pollution Havens Matter?" NBER Working Paper No. 9776 (June 2003); and M. E. Kahn, "The Geography of U.S.

Pollution Intensive Trade: Evidence from 1958–1994," *Regional Science and Urban Economics* 33 (2003): 483–500.

27. Jeffrey Frankel and Andrew Rose, "Is Trade Good or Bad for the Environment? Sorting Out the Causality," NBER Working Paper Series 9201 (September, 2001).

28. Bhagwati, *In Defense of Globalization*, 150.

29. Vijay Vaitheeswaran, "Local Difficulties," *Economist*, July 4, 2002, electronic version.

30. Bhagwati, *In Defense of Globalization*, 144.

31. World Bank, "Is Globalization Causing" World Bank Briefing Papers Part 4, 2000.

32. David Wheeler, "Racing to the Bottom? Foreign Investment and Air Quality in Developing Countries," World Bank Development Group unpublished paper (November 2000).

33. Nancy Birdsall and David Wheeler, "Trade Policy and Industrial Pollution in Latin America: Where Are the Pollution Havens?" *Journal of Environment and Development* 2(1) (Winter 1993): 137–149.

34. World Bank, "Is Globalization Causing" World Bank Briefing Papers Part 4, 2000, cited from D. Wheeler, M. Huq, and P. Martin, "Process Change, Economic Policy and Industrial Pollution: Cross Country Evidence from the Wood Pulp and Steel Industries," Paper presented at the annual meeting of the American Economic Association, Anaheim, California, January 1993.

35. Countries regulate pollution more strictly as they get wealthier for three main reasons. First, pollution damage gets higher priority after rising wealth has financed basic investments in health and education. Second, higher-income societies have stronger regulatory institutions because technical personnel are plentiful and budgets for monitoring and enforcement activities are more generous. Third, higher income and education empower local communities to enforce higher environmental standards, whatever stance is taken by the national government. See S. Dasgupta and D. Wheeler, "Citizens' Complaints as Environmental Indicators: Evidence from China," *World Bank Policy Research Department*, Working Paper 1704 (November 1996); and S. Pargal and D. Wheeler, "Informal Regulation of Industrial Pollution in Developing Countries: Evidence from Indonesia," *Journal of Political Economy* 104(6) (1996): 1314+ quoted from David Wheeler, "Racing to the Bottom? Foreign Investment and Air Quality in Developing Countries," World Bank Development Group unpublished paper (November 2000).

36. Economists Gene Grossman and Alan Krueger have found a bell-shaped curve in which pollution levels first rise with income but then eventually fall—the so-called environmental Kuznets curve. Gene Grossman and Alan Krueger, "Economic Growth and the Environment," *Quarterly Journal of Economics* 110 (1995): 353–377.

37. World Bank, "Is Globalization Causing" World Bank Briefing Papers Part 4, 2000, cited from S. Dasgupta, A. Mody, S. Roy, and D. Wheeler, "Environmental Regulations and Development: A Cross-Country Empirical Analysis," *World Bank Policy Research Department*, Working Paper 1448 (March 1995).

38. Stephen Moore and Julian Simon, "It's Getting Better All the Time: 100 Greatest Trends of the Last 100 Years," *Cato Institute*, 2000; and cited in Vijay Vaitheeswaran, "Flying Blind," *Economist*, July 4, 2002, electronic version.

39. Bjorn Lomborg is a statistician at the University of Aarhus and the author of *The Skeptical Environmentalist* by Cambridge University Press, 2001.

40. Bjorn Lomborg, "The Truth about the Environment," *Economist*, August 2, 2001, electronic version.

41. Ibid.

42. Andrew C. Revkin, "Forget Nature. Even Eden Is Engineered," *New York Times*, August 20, 2002, electronic version.
43. Matthew L. Wald, "What's Kind to Nature can be Kind to Profits," *New York Times*, May 17, 2006, electronic version.
44. Quoted from Vanessa Houlder and Alan Beattie, "Shades of Green," *Financial Times*, August 18, 2002, electronic version.
45. Claudia H. Deutsch, "Together at Last: Cutting Pollution and Making Money," *New York Times*, September 9, 2001, electronic version.
46. Ibid.
47. *Economist*, "Economic Man, Cleaner Planet," September 27, 2001, electronic version.
48. *Economist*, "Can Business Be Cool?" June 8, 2006, electronic version.
49. Alison Maitland, "Bitter Taste of Starbucks' Success," *Financial Times*, March 10, 2002, electronic version.
50. Ken Conca, *Governing Water: Contentious Transnational Politics and Global Institution Building*. Cambridge: MIT Press, 2006; Ronnie D. Lipschutz, ed., *Civil Society and Social Movements*. Aldershot, Hampshire: Ashgate Publishing, 2006; and Paul Wapner, "Politics Beyond the State: Environmental Activism and World Civic Politics," *World Politics* 47 (April 1995): 311–340.
51. Paul Wapner, "The Transnational Politics of Environmental NGOs," Paper presented before the United Nations University Symposium on the United Nations and Global Environment, November 14–15, 1997, New York City.
52. Deutsch, "Together at Last."
53. Hilary French, "Coping with Ecological Globalization." In C. Roe Goddard, Patrick Cronin, and Kishore C. Dash, eds., *International Political Economy*, 2nd ed. Boulder: Lynne Rienner, 2003: 482.
54. Bjorn Lomborg, "The Environmentalists Are Wrong," *New York Times*, August 26, 2002, electronic version. For greater elaboration on this point, please refer to Bjorn Lomborg, *The Skeptical Environmentalist: Measuring the Real State of the World*. Cambridge: Cambridge University Press, 2001.
55. Samuelson, "Global Warming's," A13.
56. Naomi Oreskes, "Beyond the Ivory Tower: The Scientific Consensus on Climate Change," *Science* 306/5702: 1686, http://www.sciencemag.org/cgi/content/full/306/5702/1686
57. American Geophysical Union, "Human Impacts on Climate Change," December 2003, http://www.agu.org/sci_soc/policy/climate_change_position.html
58. National Academy of Science, "Joint Science Academies' Statement: Global Response to Climate Change," http://nationalacademies.org/onpi/06072005.pdf
59. American Meteorological Society, "Climate Change," February 1, 2007, http://ametsoc.org/POLICY/2007climatechange.pdf
60. Geddes, "Trade and the Environment."
61. World Bank, "Is Globalization Causing" World Bank Briefing Papers Part 4, 2000.
62. Allen L. Hammond, "The Environment as a Source of Competitive Advantage," in Michael E. Porter, Klaus Schwab, and Augusto Lopez-Claros, eds., *The Global Competitiveness Report 2005–2006*. Geneva: World Economic Forum, 2005.
63. Ibid.
64. World Bank, "Is Globalization Causing" World Bank Briefing Papers Part 4, 2000.
65. Geddes, "Trade and the Environment."

Globalization for All?

> . . . globalization put in balance, is a welcomed development for the contemporary world (a world which due to improved information and communications technology facilities is often described as a planetary village), but a lot still has to be done, especially in the sphere of the IMF and the World Bank's lending policies to help rather than hamper economic prosperity particularly to Third world nations.
>
> —*Henry Ekwuruke, Contributing Editor at the Connect Africa Magazine*[1]

> The world expects that we will speed up the reform of the international financial system and rebuild, together, a better-regulated form of capitalism with a greater sense of morality and solidarity. This is a precondition for mobilizing the global economy and achieving sustainable growth. This crisis is not a crisis of capitalism but the breakdown of a system that drifted away from capitalism's most fundamental values.
>
> —*Nicolas Sarkozy, President of France*[2]

THE PROS AND CONS OF GLOBALIZATION

As the quotations above suggest, globalization is frequently approached as a process, as an objective description of reality, and as a springboard for the assertion of normative aspirations for many proponents and opponents. What results is the emergence of sharply different assessments of reality. Our goal has been to use an approach generally supportive of globalization as a way to take another look at a phenomenon now defining so much scholarship, interest, and debate. Those approaches supportive of globalization, as we have suggested, make the case that an integrated global economy is a positive, logical, and, perhaps even, an inevitable stage in the evolution of global politics, economics, business, finance, and culture. Many hold out the promise for a better, if not brighter future, for most of the inhabitants of the planet, although not all.

GLOBALIZATION'S BLEAK FUTURE PROSPECTS

Perspectives critical of globalization, however, point to a process placing material interests and values above sustainable human values and look with grave concern at a process threatening long-term political stability and democratic governance. Many approaches warn that the world's most distinctive cultural inheritances are at risk as the power of transnational forces relentlessly promotes seductive Western, and, in particular, American forms of mass-marketed culture. The perspective is bleak. A more integrated world means that individuality, diversity, and distinct cultural inheritances are all threatened by rising currents of globalization. From this angle, the world of the twenty-first century will likely confront even more far-reaching changes than those of the nineteenth and twentieth centuries. **Political disempowerment** and uneven economic development, therefore, are looming negative consequences of globalization.

Political Disempowerment

The sense of dissatisfaction and unease about the destructive consequences of globalization forms a core concern of those perspectives critical of globalization as a process forcing change throughout the globe in three respects. First, globalization like all potentially transforming processes alters the fabric of states and societies. The resulting changes and dislocations appear both overwhelming and difficult to channel in positive ways. This perspective points to huge problems absent solutions. Globalization becomes the principal cause for a kind of deracination from above. It constitutes a kind of potential upheaval so vast over many decades of the twenty-first century that long-standing cultural, political, and social ideas and values may be further unhinged. Only a tiny elite will be able to direct its course, and even then, many consequences will be unexpected and unpredicted. While there are benefits associated with globalization, it will also likely generate greater levels of conflict by increasing economic stratification and marginalization across regions and continents. The force of globalization will erode democratic accountability within countries and increase the power of elites beyond the borders of states. **Cultural desolation** will also accompany globalization through assimilation and homogenization to materialistic norms and values. Economic disparities will widen within societies, resulting in vastly increasing levels of inequality everywhere but especially between rich elites and the enormous numbers of the poor worldwide. Military conflicts will also likely accompany the new age of global affluence. Armies will be needed to protect globalization on the ground across the globe.

The process of globalization in the developing world will continue to spawn patterns of destabilization as market forces reinforce uneven patterns of economic distribution without conferring major benefits or increasing desperately needed social welfare networks. Thus, the failure to provide sustainable human development for the most marginalized sectors of the developing world will be a major consequence of a globally integrated economy.

Fear of globalization has already been met with resistance by consumers, some businesses, and tens of thousands of nongovernmental actors and advocates, and in many cases, government officials concerned with the loss of sovereignty and long-term economic, cultural, and political accountability. As the political economist Benjamin Cohen has noted, "Increasingly, globalization is seen by many as not benevolent but malign—not a friend to be welcomed but an enemy to be resisted."[3] Conservative pundit William Benett, the former U.S. secretary of education, observed, "What I'm concerned about is the idolatry of the market. . . . Unbridled capitalism . . . may not be a problem for production and for expansion of the economic pie, but it's a problem for human beings. It's a problem for . . . the realm of values and human relationships because it distorts things."[4]

For many, globalization is increasingly being viewed as an omnipotent force flinging all of humanity—wealthy and poor alike—into an unpredictable future. This apprehension stems from concerns about the top-down nature of the process and perceptions of its rapid and uneven proliferation. This raises the concern that globalization has become perilously unstable and its effects, therefore, become wildly unpredictable.

Economic Uncertainties

For those approaches critical of globalization, economic disruption and the prospects of economic failure constitute a second major area of concern. The mixture of the transformative nature of the process with the apparently unstoppable force of economic integration makes globalization appear inevitable. But globalization's uneven impacts on countries, particularly the poorer ones in Africa, Asia, and Latin America, would seem to suggest that globalization is far from being the inevitable beneficial economic process that many proponents foresee. While some developing countries have been able to exploit globalization to dramatically reduce poverty, the rewards of a globalizing economy still remain beyond the reach of a large portion of the world's poor. According to the World Bank, while living standards have greatly improved over the course of the past 20 years for the 3 billion people residing in developing countries, another 2 billion are trapped in countries falling further and further behind, and with very little real hope of escape. Indeed, Mike Moore, the former director-general of the World Trade Organization, estimated that globalization has bypassed the world's 49 least-developed countries, depriving them of the benefits of increasing market shares and economic integration, thus, further deepening economic and political marginalization.[5] History has already shown that the forces of globalization can be turned back. The initial wave of globalization, from 1870 to 1914, came to an abrupt end, despite the benefits of the process—open markets and free trade, escalating productivity and rising consumption, and worldwide faith and confidence in the international financial systems. In the end, mounting geopolitical tensions and instability were triggered by widening global income disparities, albeit among the industrialized states.[6] Increasingly, the current wave of globalization, from 1990 to the present, shows conditions of political instability due to the uneven distribution of benefits and such forces akin to the rise of antiglobalization protesters fanning the antiliberal fervor that seem eerily similar to what helped to hinder the late-nineteenth-century period of expanding globalization. Many socioeconomic and political conflicts inherent in periods of expanding globalization beginning with the end of World War II took a backseat to the geopolitical battles fought between the United States and the Soviet Union throughout the Cold War.

The demonstrations and acts of protest against the World Trade Organization, the World Bank, the IMF, and G8 provide evidence in stark and harsh terms for the industrialized states' continued failure to include all of humanity in the globalization process.[7] Still as important are the rising aspirations of billions of people yet to be satisfied with the quality of life characterizing the elites that live in their midst throughout the cities of the developing world. The resulting crises of rising expectations and the sense of relative deprivation may well be a hallmark of globalization's path throughout the developing world from China to Haiti. The continuing protest movements unmasked a number of neoliberalism's continuing and nagging problems: the combined stresses of surging population growth, massive unemployment, continued political malfeasances, social dissolution, and environmental degradation among both the world's developing countries and its poorest states and societies.

Capitalism has long acknowledged the existence of these resentments. It now must admit and address the fact that rising levels of discontent among huge numbers of peoples throughout the world can destabilize the foundations of globalizing integrated economies due to a rising tide of heightened expectations and unfulfilled needs throughout the world's poorest countries. Globalization's inability to meet the aspirations of the world's poor becomes yet another justification for rogue states, and would-be states, to unleash barbarous violence. Surely, the national security departments of the United States, Europe, and other affluent countries must begin to address the instability caused by uneven patterns of development facilitated by globalization across the globe.

As the process of globalization continues to foster indifference, it will become increasingly more difficult to ignore or become isolated from the turmoil of impoverished societies and failing states. As a pragmatic and moral imperative, therefore, the beneficiaries of the process must take greater responsibility to make the world a more equitable and humane place by fostering development and growth in the world's poorest countries, bolstering a dynamic global economy and overseeing the movements of people in a more equitable manner so that the billions of people still in poverty may enjoy some of the benefits of globalization.

The sometimes violent clashes at these international meetings on the global economy not only expose the dark underbelly of globalization, but highlight just how steep the climb is to realize substantively greater levels of economic growth and prosperity. Whatever they may wish, these industrial states can no longer turn a blind eye from the plight of the world's poor. The globalizing elites cannot elude the wretchedness and hopelessness of the poor. One of the lessons of the mounting conflicts between the haves and the have-nots is that international politics and economics are inseparable. It also suggests that the power and privilege enjoyed by the developed countries may be more fragile and harder to maintain than previously assumed.

DEBATING GLOBALIZATION

Lui Hebron: The Glass Is Half Full—Globalization's Challenges

John, paradoxically, as the world becomes more integrated economically, more engaged politically, and more interconnected culturally, the call and need for greater global cooperation and systemwide policy intervention have become louder and greater. Twenty years into the "laissez faire, more globalized world order" but faced once again with the possible breakdown—and deleterious consequences—of this third era of globalization, nation-states, intergovernmental organizations, and nongovernmental organizations have come together to jointly address the worldwide financial crisis.

The significance of this coming together by industrialized and emerging states is twofold: First, it is an acknowledgment in starkest terms of the interdependent structure of the global economic system. Second, it represents an admission that globalization still needs further refinement so that it benefits a larger segment of the earth's population.

Front and center tackling the 2009 global economic crisis is the G20. That it is the G20 and not the G8 which has taken the lead in addressing the worldwide financial meltdown indicates the extent to which the economic system has become globalized. Heralding a major development of global economic integration, the rise of the G20 means that industrialized (G8) states must now increasingly work in cooperation with emerging economies in governing the international economic order.

Pledging to build a more inclusive global economy as they combat the worldwide economic crisis, the Group of 20 major economies agreed to implement the necessary policies aimed at repairing the financial system, stimulating the world economy, promoting world trade, and helping the world's poorest countries toward sustainable recovery, growth, and development. G20 leaders also agreed to transform the IMF into an agency that not only aids countries in dire financial straits, but also assumes a more prominent and active role in the monitoring and reporting of states' financial activities and conditions around the world.—Lui

John Stack: The Glass Is Half Empty—Globalization's Leadership Crisis

Lui, the current global economic crisis highlights a number of dimensions that we have discussed and debated throughout the book. Like you, I see globalization as a fact of life. Greater interconnectivity, interdependence, and transnational flows of goods, services, peoples, ideas, and technology characterize the world in which we live. The process of globalization may be uncomfortable because it is both unpredictable and technologically driven. The ability of national leaders, transnational groups, international organizations, and public and private stakeholders to shape and control globalization is difficult and often appears to be illusory. Thus we face a number of challenges. But the most basic and unresolved issue is leadership.

Since the establishment of the modern international system following the Peace of Westphalia in 1648, states have become the central building blocs of the global system exported from Europe in the first modern emanations of globalization beginning with the Age of Discovery in the fifteenth century. Over centuries, levels of interdependence have compromised the ability of sovereign states to act independently. Economics, pandemics, the movement of peoples, ideas, conflicts and wars, and technology, among many other manifestations of globalization, have demanded ways of settling disputes. And visionary thinkers from Immanuel Kant (1795) to Woodrow Wilson (The League of Nations, 1920), Franklin D. Roosevelt (The United Nations, 1945) to the founders of the European Union, Jean Monet, Robert Schuman, and Alcide de Gasperi, have all searched for ways to limit war, promote human rights, and assure economic prosperity.

Globalization more than any other force of our time underscores the desperate need for leadership to confront the issues we have examined throughout the book. And while the expansion of the G8 to the G20 suggests a level of inclusiveness necessary to confront the faltering global economy, the crisis of leadership demands more than trying to stabilize and then grow the world economy. The crisis of leadership that I have in mind is one that must address a range of global issues covering the environment, democratic participation, genocide, conflict resolution, disaster prevention and mitigation, hunger, and poverty. Leadership in the context of globalization means hard choices and priorities that go beyond regulated markets. Global leadership must embrace more than economics. The future of humanity hangs in the balance.—John ■

GLOBALIZATION'S HOPE: CONFRONTING POVERTY AND POLITICAL INDIFFERENCE

Overcoming poverty and political indifference is a central challenge that must be confronted. A number of European countries have adopted policies that constitute substantial breakthroughs on such issues as debt relief, trade initiatives, the reduction of poverty, and programs to build sustainable economies and to battle pandemics such as AIDS. Said Nasser Benjelloun, Morocco's chief trade representative, "This is not just about rich countries living up to their principles, but also recognizing what is in their own self-interest. We represent the markets of the future. The best way to solve problems like poverty and immigration is not to marginalize developing nations, but to give them a substantial stake in the global trading process."[8]

As many of the failed and failing states in Africa, Asia, and Latin America can attest, the maladies now plaguing the globe's poorest peoples result not from too much globalization, but not enough. They are failing not because they are being overwhelmed by globalization, but precisely the opposite. They are becoming even more marginalized because they are being neglected and passed over by the globalization process.[9]

The determination of globalization's positive and negative impacts remains in the balance for states, geographical regions, and the global system. The task for proponents of globalization is to develop avenues whereby the benefits of globalization can be more widely shared. An emerging consensus among many advanced industrialized states and international organizations seemed to be building to extend globalization's reach to include progressively larger segments of humanity.[10]

Increasing the Pie (Three Dimensions Crucial to Reform)

While the processes and forces of globalization are global, the effects are far from uniform. Thus a key objective must be to make its benefits more equitable among and within states. Globalization cannot be left to its own devices. If it is to have the greatest impact on the largest numbers of people, it must be "managed" so as to constructively counter its harmful dehumanizing effects. Finally, if globalization is to be on balance, its practitioners must ensure that it is embedded in broadly shared values and practices that reflect not only socioeconomic needs, but also sensitivity to different cultural milieus. Let us take each of these issues in turn.

First, we have argued that there is still room to expand the benefits of globalization to wider circles of humanity, while attempting to minimize many of its detrimental effects. This is a difficult and uncertain trajectory begun among the G8 countries. Specifically, during the 2005 G8 Summit in Gleneagles, Scotland, the advanced industrial giants moved forward to operationalize their plan of action to meet the **millennium goals**.[11] As set forth in the Gleneagles Communique, the G8 countries have pledged to increase aid to developing states to $50 billion a year by 2010, to eliminate the outstanding debts of the poorest countries, as well as "tackling climate change, promoting clean energy and achieving sustainable development."[12] This is a good start. However, if globalization is to become accountable and its benefits distributed more fairly, then it will be up to the advanced industrialized states to do more to assist those committed to the process by making available the resources and export markets needed to succeed.

Second, the problems facing developing countries are so vast and difficult that many do not have the institutional and technological capacities to implement suitable macroeconomic policies while providing effective governance policies. Realistically speaking, states that lack legitimate political authority, the rule of law, and solid economic infrastructures will not benefit much from globalization. What are needed, therefore, are policies and institutions that will make globalization work for progressively larger members of a country. Specifically, political and economic elites need to promote greater cooperation among governments, intergovernmental organizations, nongovernmental organizations, and transnational corporations if they are to successfully tackle and share the responsibilities for managing economic development and growth in a socially responsible and inclusive manner.

According to Clyde V. Prestowitz Jr., President of the Economic Strategy Institute, a research group in Washington, "What is happening now, is a recognition that the global marketplace, left to itself, is not going to automatically produce wealth and prosperity in less-developed countries unless there is rule-making and new structures that reduce the potential for destructiveness."[13] Placed in this context, the overwhelming objective should be to engage in a world trade round that will genuinely lay the basis for globalwide economic growth. Above all, it must strive to promote political as well as economic liberalization.

Finally, globalization is not occurring in a vacuum: It is part of a broader integrative dynamic in the social, cultural, and political, as well as the economic realms that requires common customs, understandings, procedures, and rules to govern ordinary relations and transactions and handle inevitable crises. Globalization could not have advanced this far without these complementary forces at work. The steamroller of economic globalism, however, has not been matched by the development of a wider global understanding in the other areas of the process that can respond to it. The present phase of globalization of markets unmatched by some elements of wider global governance is becoming an increasingly untenable situation as the "trade and environment" and "development and human rights" debates cannot be swept aside as many proponents had hoped.

Far too frequently, the globalized states, via their control of the World Trade Organization, the International Monetary Fund, and the World Bank, and transnational corporations such as Union Carbide and Nike have tried to superimpose their views on the developing countries. The march toward a world market economy, however, is not a one-size-fits-all program. Globalization, as we have argued, does not mean the imposition of any single model.

Indeed, the presence of distinct West European, North American, and East Asian interpretations of the free market system would indicate that some countries have been able to improvise and, in fact, influence both the form and content of globalization, shaped by its history, culture, and destiny. To a certain degree, the continued viability of globalization as a process and model for economic development and growth will depend on its ability to replicate the successful cases in Western Europe, North America, and East Asia elsewhere—globally.

To be sure, in too many instances, the rewards from engaging in the globalizing economy have fallen far short of its advocates' projected promises. To abandon globalization for its shortcomings, however, is neither rational nor desirable. As already noted throughout the text, globalization has proven itself to bring enormous benefits to millions throughout the world. The challenge, therefore, is how to increase the benefits of globalization to a greater segment of the globe. To this end, it is clear that the globalization process needs further refinement, not abandonment. And with regard to desirability, a 2003 Pew Global Attitude Survey found that "Majorities in 35 [out of 44] countries take a favorable view of four separate aspects of globalization—growing trade and business ties, faster communication and travel, the growing availability of foreign culture, and the wide variety of products available from different parts of the world."[14] This is perhaps the strongest affirmation yet of globalization's ability to bring about greater good to a larger segment of the world's population.

KEY TERMS

cultural desolation   138

millennium goals   143

political disempowerment   138

FIVE QUESTIONS TO CONSIDER

1. How has your understanding of globalization been transformed? What are the most important challenges posed by globalization?
2. How would you characterize globalization in terms of your political values? Is it a conservative or a liberal phenomenon? How would you locate globalization on your own political spectrum? Does globalization veer to the conservative, middle of the road, or liberal (left) side of your political compass?
3. What are the five most important challenges confronting globalization? Can they be successfully resolved?
4. What moral and ethical considerations should be brought into any discussion of globalization?
5. To what extent should the alleviation of poverty and human suffering be explicitly addressed under conditions of globalization? Is globalization more or less a positive or a negative force in world politics? To what extent is it a positive or a negative force in your life?

FURTHER READINGS

Eric Beinhocker and Elizabeth Stephenson, "Globalization under Fire," *Harvard Business*, July 22, 2009.
> Examines the underlying forces that shape the business environment and its discontinuities while focusing on how the global economic crisis may affect business trajectories in such areas as resources, trust in business, a larger role for government, and management of financial entities.

Francesco Guerrera, "A Need to Reconnect," *Financial Times*, March 12, 2009.
> Focuses on the root cause of the world's economic predicament in which corporate restructuring is a dominant theme, with millions of jobs to be cut as profits slide. The question is how radical that restructuring will be. Although the automotive industry may be prime among those needing a shakeout, government support could backfire.

Moisés Naím, "Globalization," *Foreign Policy*, March/April 2009, Issue 171.
> Argues that efforts to minimize the costs of globalization, steer international integration, solve international crises, and better manage the global commons will fall short. The gap between the need for effective collective action at the global level and the ability of the international community to satisfy that need is the most dangerous deficit facing humanity.

Jeffrey D. Sachs, *The End of Poverty: Economic Possibilities of Our Time*. New York: Penguin, 2005.
> Argues that the interwoven economic, political, environmental, and social problems challenge the poorest countries. Provides case studies and policy recommendations designed to reduce the grip of poverty and structures that will uplift the inhabitants of planet Earth.

Joseph E. Stiglitz, *Making Globalization Work*. New York: W.W. Norton, 2006.
> Stiglitz addresses solutions to a host of problems, including the indebtedness of developing countries, international fiscal instability, and worldwide pollution as well as the reform of global financial institutions, trade agreements, and intellectual property laws in order to respond to the growing disparity between the richest and poorest countries.

NOTES

1. Quoted from "Globalization and the developing World!" *African News Network*, February 2, 2008, http://www.africafront.com/news/136/globalization_and_the_developing_world.html.
2. Quoted from Nicolas Sarkozy, "Priority 1: World Growth," *Washington Post*, April 1, 2009, electronic version.
3. Benjamin J. Cohen, "Containing Backlash: Foreign Economic Policy in an Age of Globalization," in Robert J. Lieber, ed., *Eagle Rules? Foreign Policy and American Primacy in the Twenty-First Century*. New York: Prentice-Hall, 2001.
4. Quoted from David Wessel and John Harwood, "Market Economy Begins to Reach Further Into Government, Society," *Wall Street Journal*, May 14, 1998, electronic version.
5. Mike Moore, "How to Lift the Barriers to Growth," *Financial Times*, May 13, 2001, electronic version.
6. Yet another wave of globalization occurred between 1945 and 1980. Though confined largely to the rich, Western, industrial countries, this profound period of global integration was fortunate enough to be free of conflict. A major reason

for this is that this period was more a quasi wave and not truly global because the world was divided into capitalist and communist camps. And each side was able to defuse or mitigate any potentially explosive conflicts.

7. Since the 1999 WTO meeting in Seattle, every international meeting that focuses on the global economy, that is, involving the World Bank, International Monetary Fund, G8, and World Economic Forum, has been met with antiglobalist protests.

8. William Drozdiak, "Poor Nations May Not Buy Trade Talks," *Washington Post*, May 15, 2001: E01.

9. It should be noted that the common denominator of many failed states is that they have often been ravaged by malfeasance, corruption, and incompetence on the part of socioeconomic and political elites. Much of the responsibility and accountability for transforming failing territories into economically viable states lie ultimately with the countries themselves.

10. Steven Pearlstein, "A New Politics Born of Globalization," *Washington Post*, October 1, 2000: H01; and Alan Pike, "An Unrelenting Pressure," *Financial Times*, November 14, 2000, electronic version.

11. "The Millennium Development Goals (MDGs) are the world's time-bound and quantified targets for addressing extreme poverty in its many dimensions— income poverty, hunger, disease, lack of adequate shelter, and exclusion— while promoting gender equality, education, and environmental sustainability," http://www.unmillenniumproject.org/.

12. http://www.number-10.gov.uk/output/Page7883.asp

13. Quoted from Louis Uchitelle, "Globalization Marches On, as U.S. Eases Up on the Reins," *New York Times*, December 17, 2001, electronic version.

14. The project surveyed 38,000 people in 44 countries. Pew Research Center for the People and the Press, "Views of a Changing World," June 2003, 71, http://people-press.org/reports/display.php3?ReportID=185

INDEX